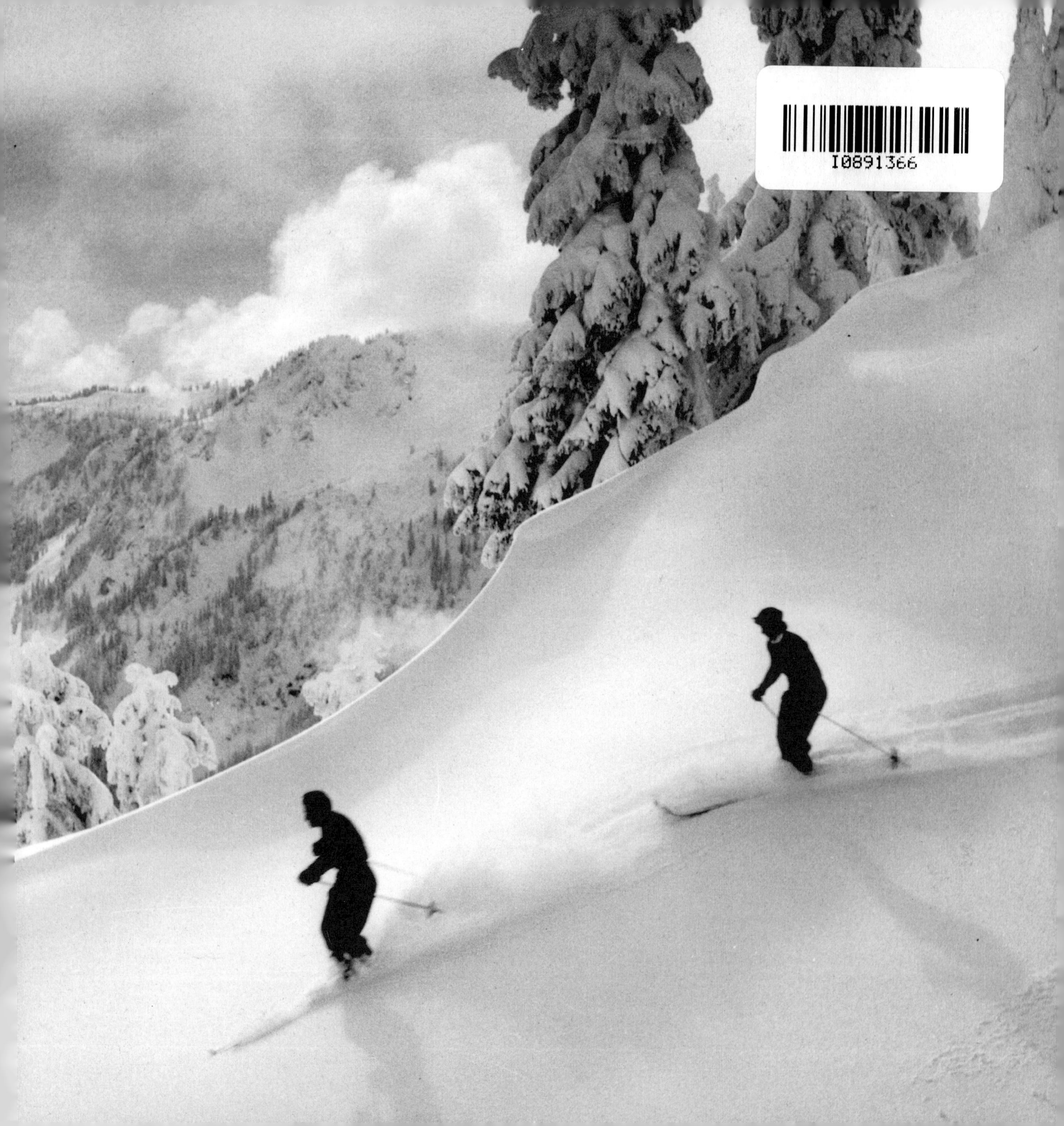

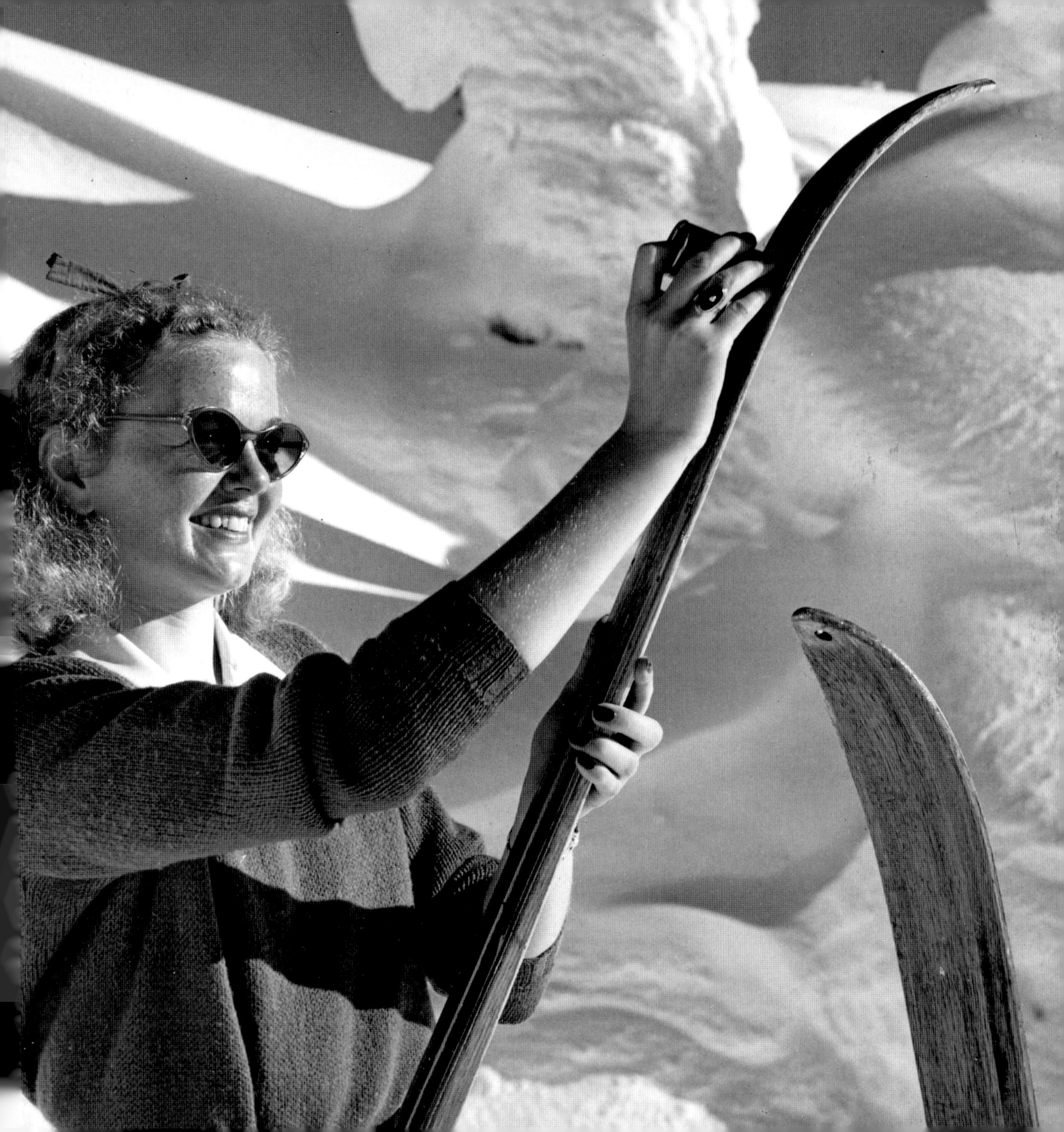

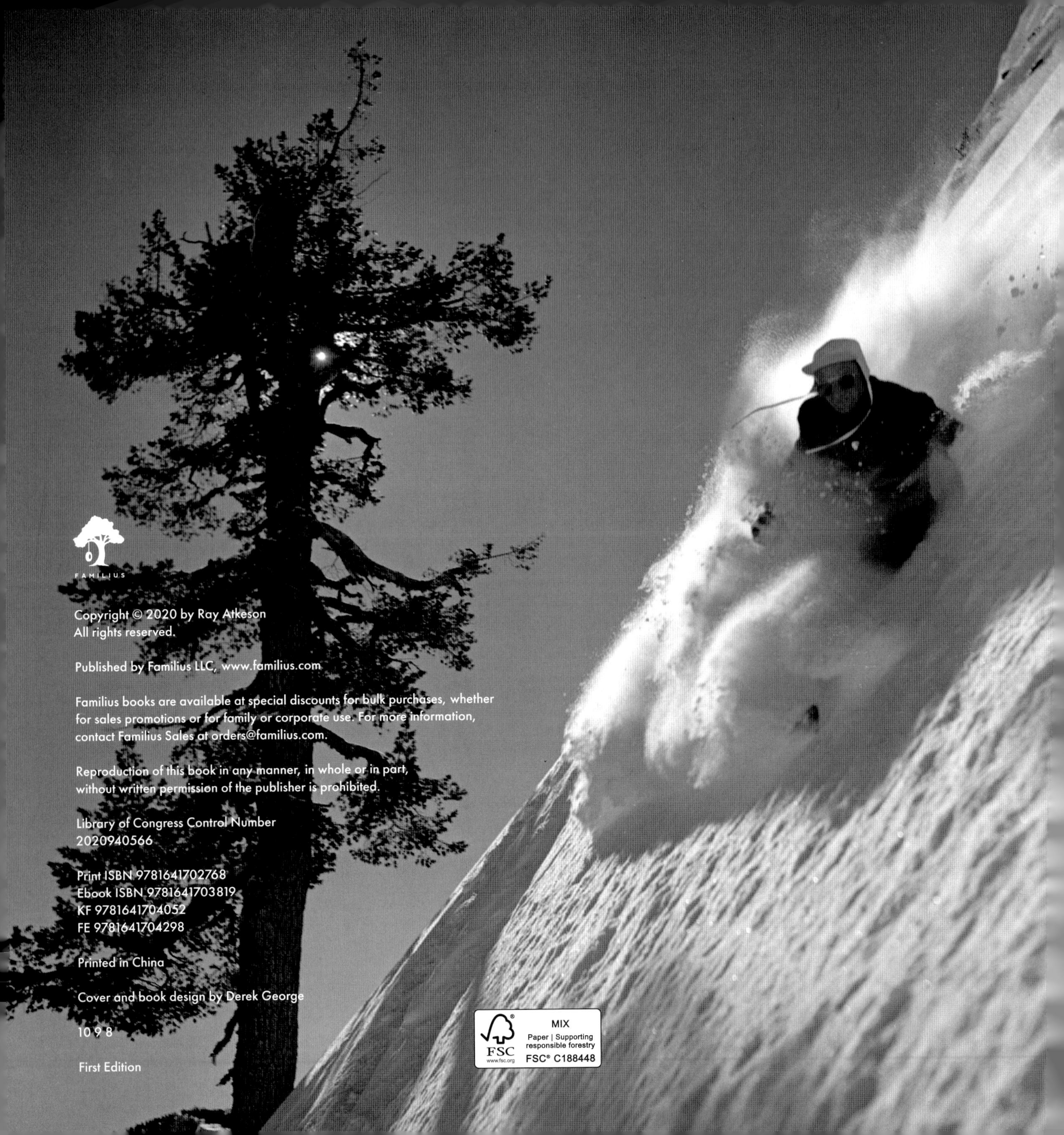

FAMILIUS

Published by Familius LLC, www.familius.com

Familius books are available at special discounts for bulk purchases, whether for sales promotions or for family or corporate use. For more information, contact Familius Sales at orders@familius.com.

Library of Congress Control Number
2020940566

Print ISBN 9781641702768
Ebook ISBN 9781641703819
KF 9781641704052
FE 9781641704298

Printed in China

Cover and book design by Derek George

10 9 8

First Edition

FSC
www.fsc.org
MIX
Paper | Supporting responsible forestry
FSC® C188448

RAY ATKESON

Vintage SKIING

NOSTALGIC IMAGES FROM THE GOLDEN AGE OF SKIING

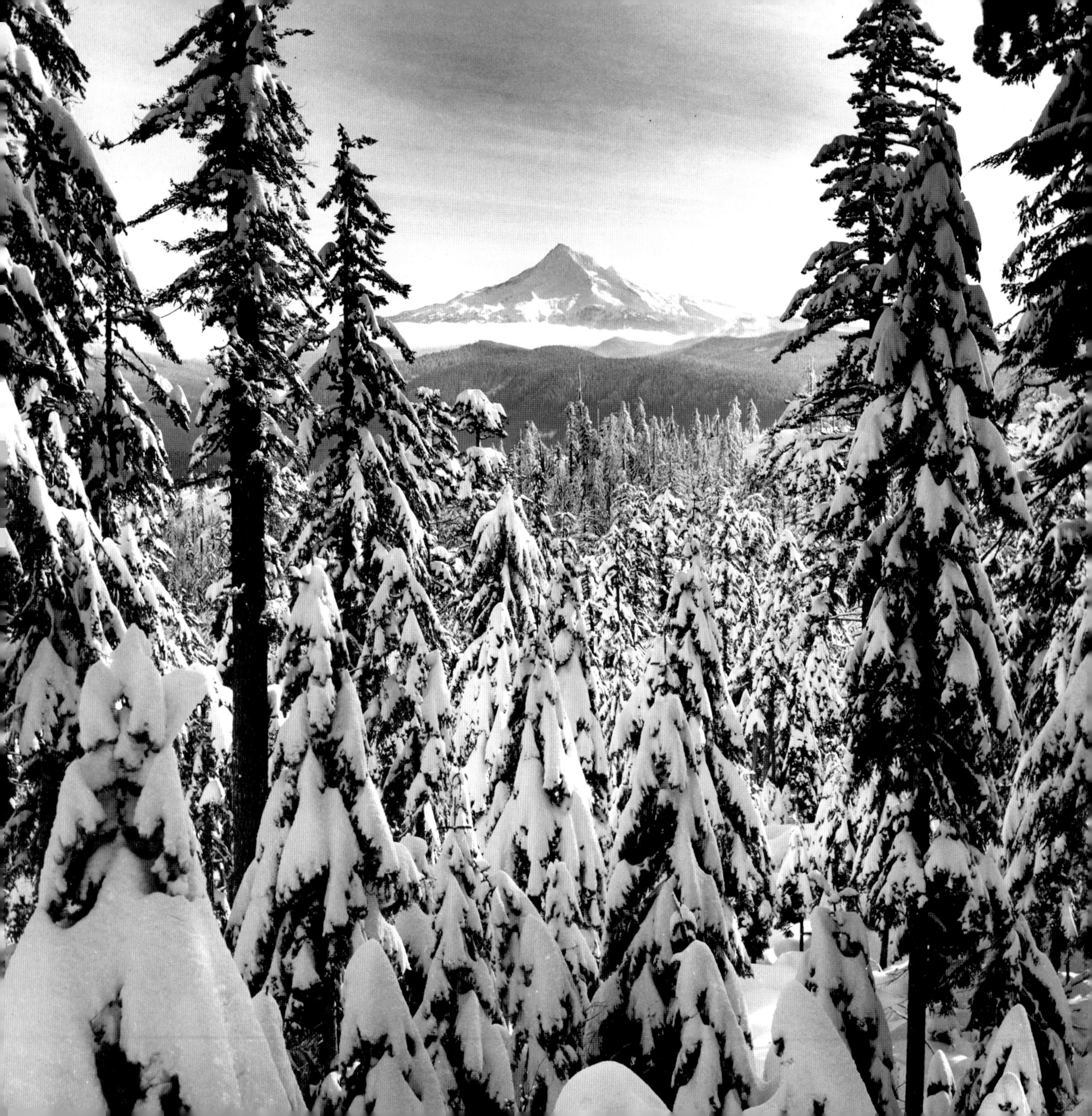

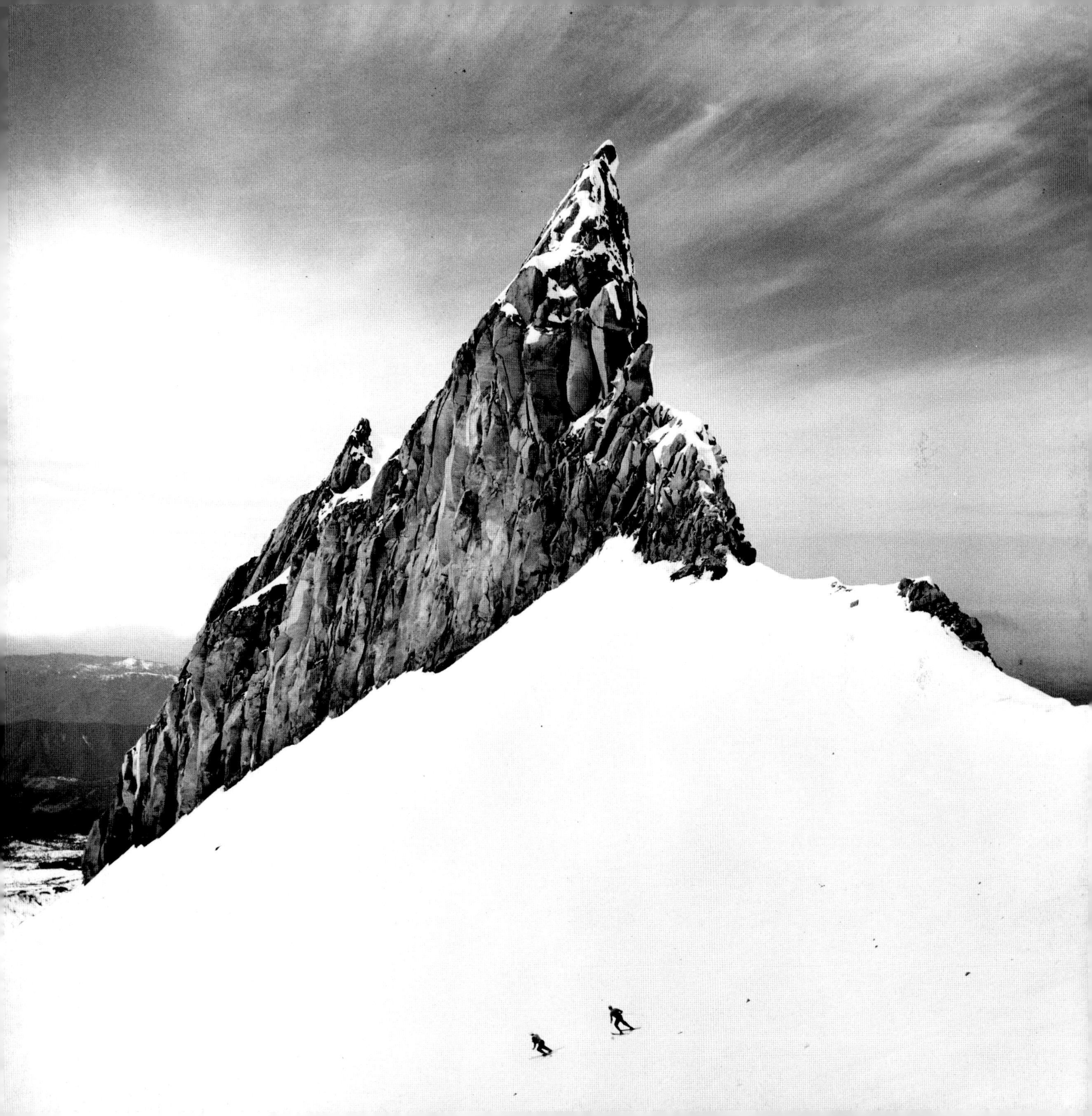

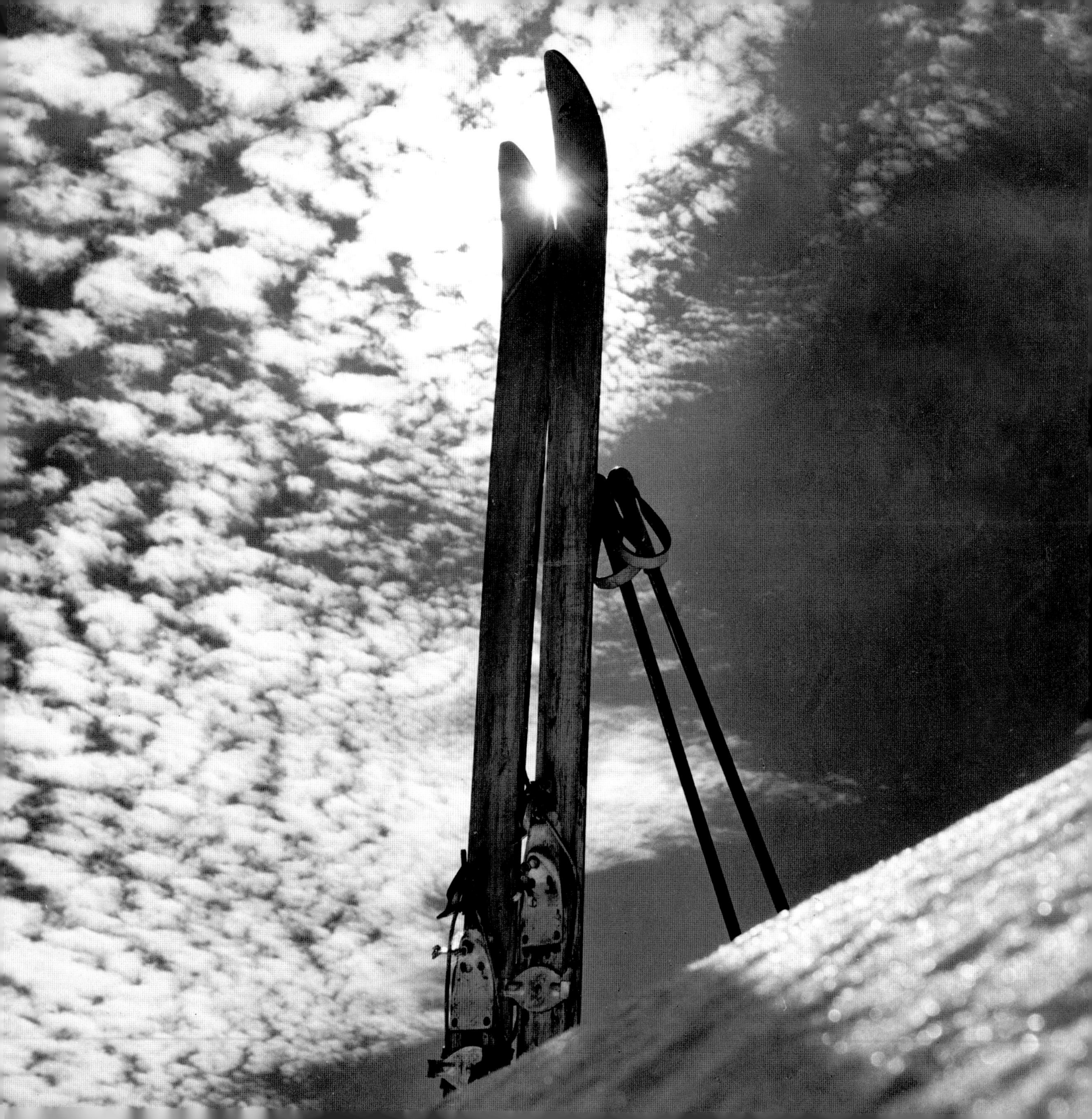

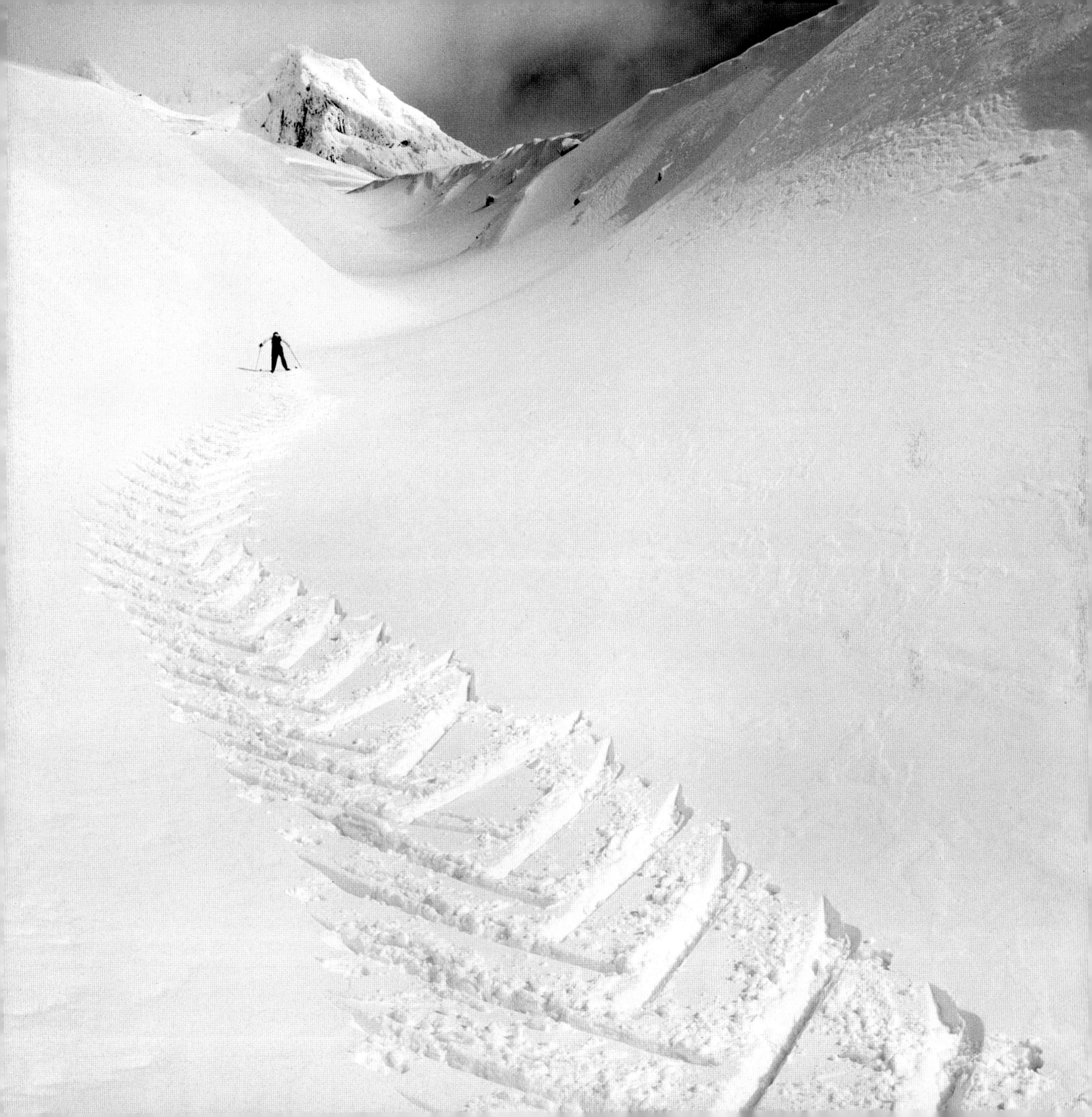

There is nothing in the world like going out onto an untouched, open, virgin mountain slope drenched under a thick blanket of new powder snow. It gives a supreme feeling of freedom, mobility. A great sense of flying, moving anywhere in a great white paradise.

HANS GMOSER

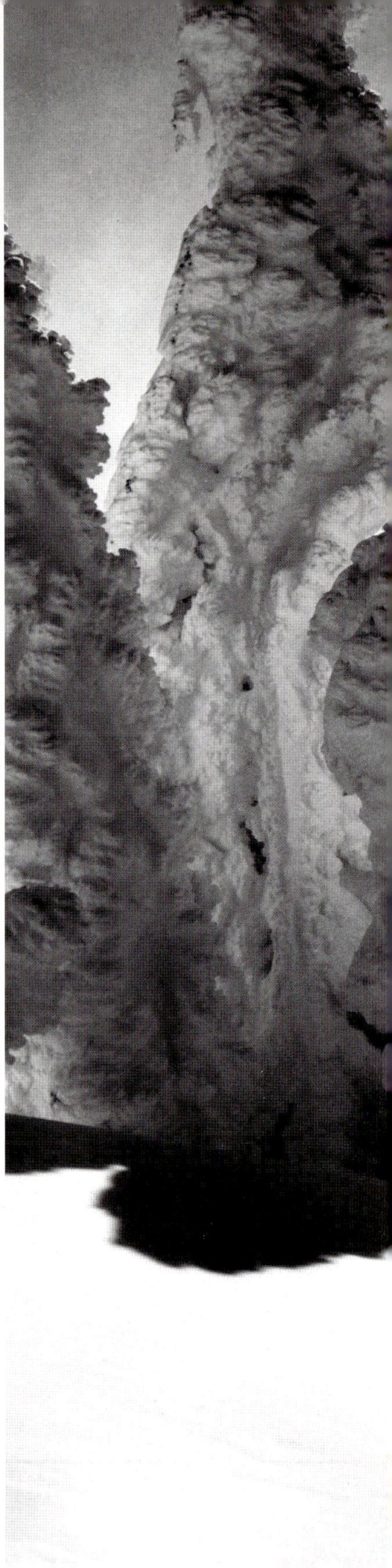

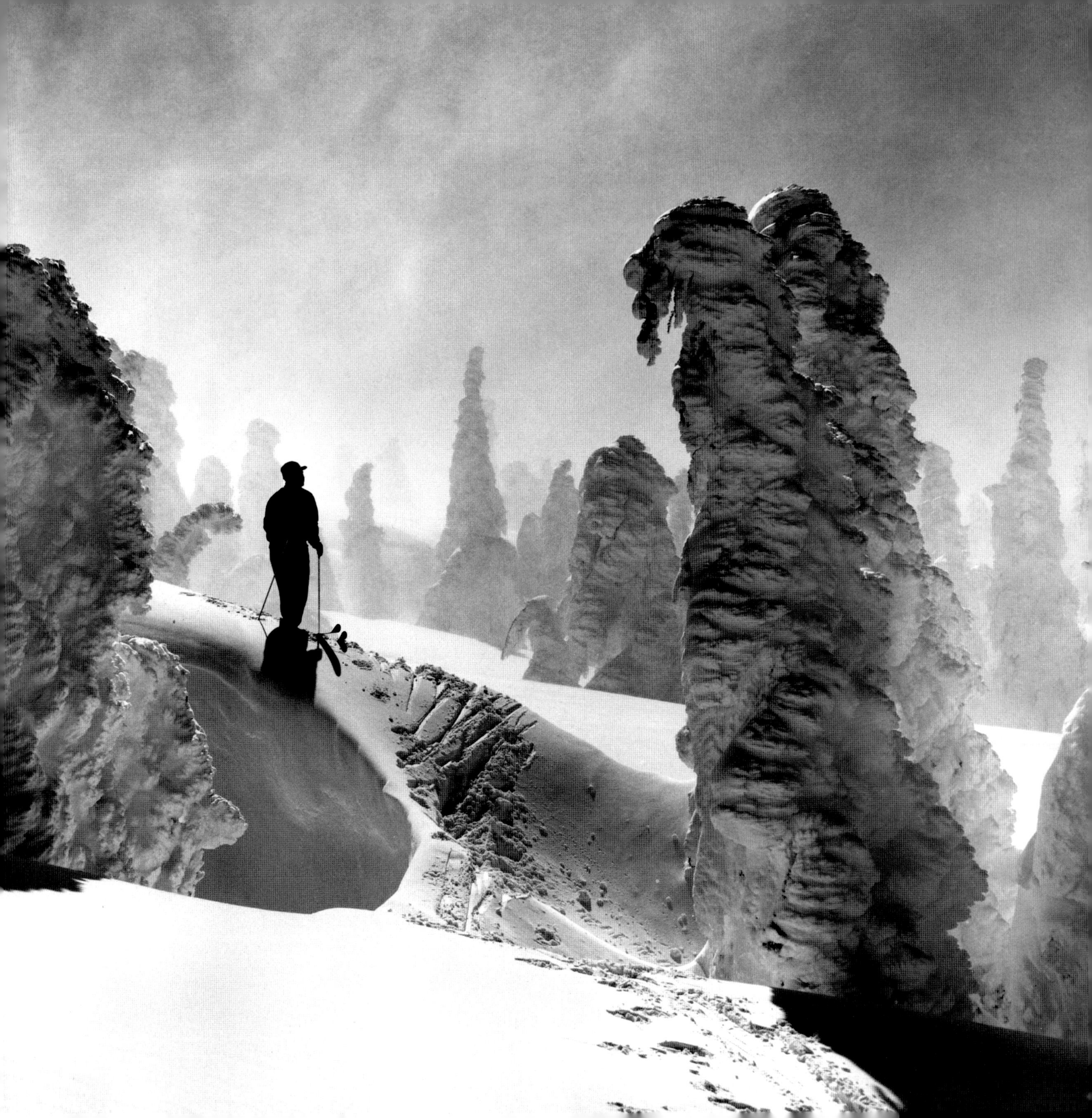

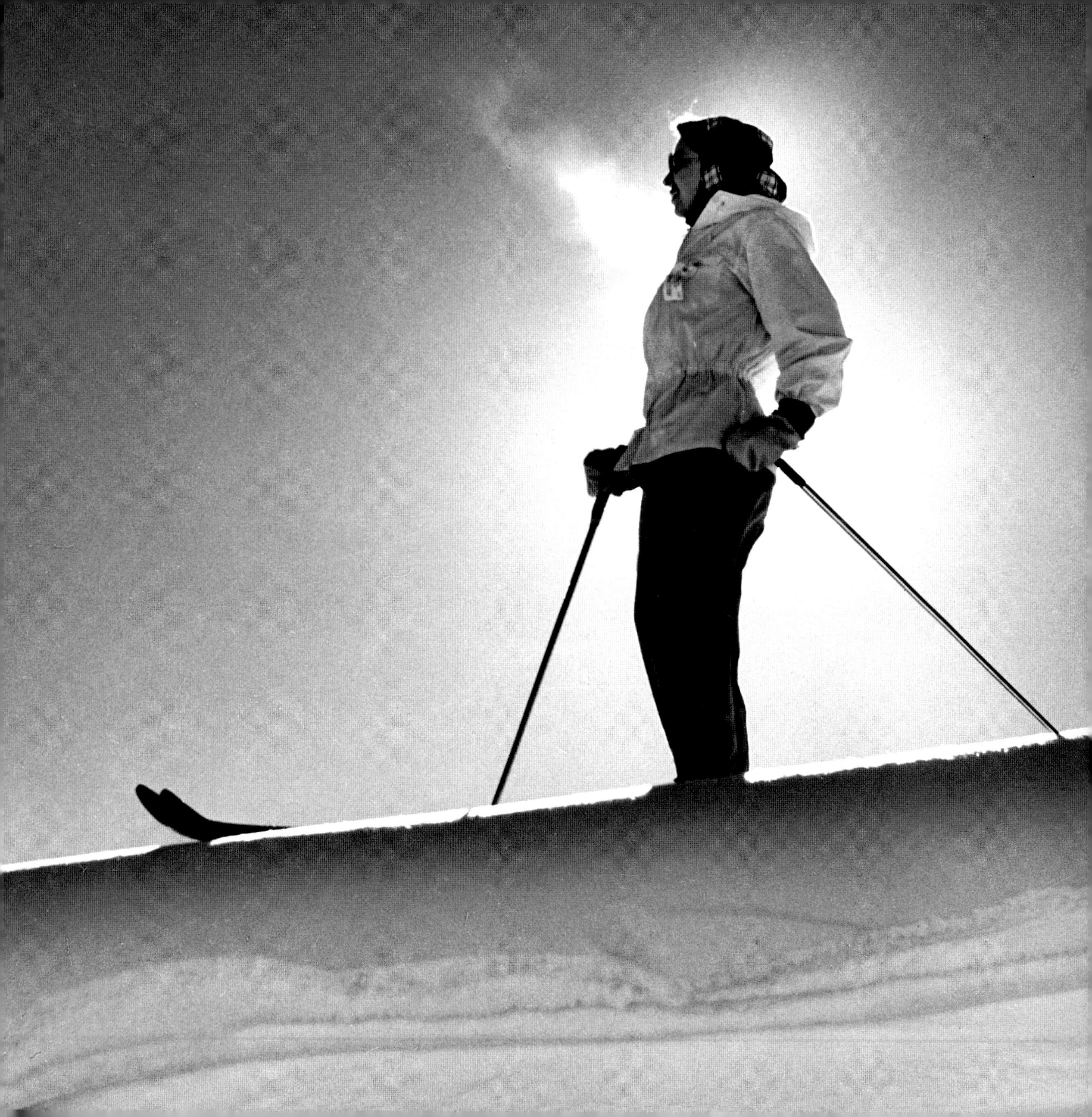

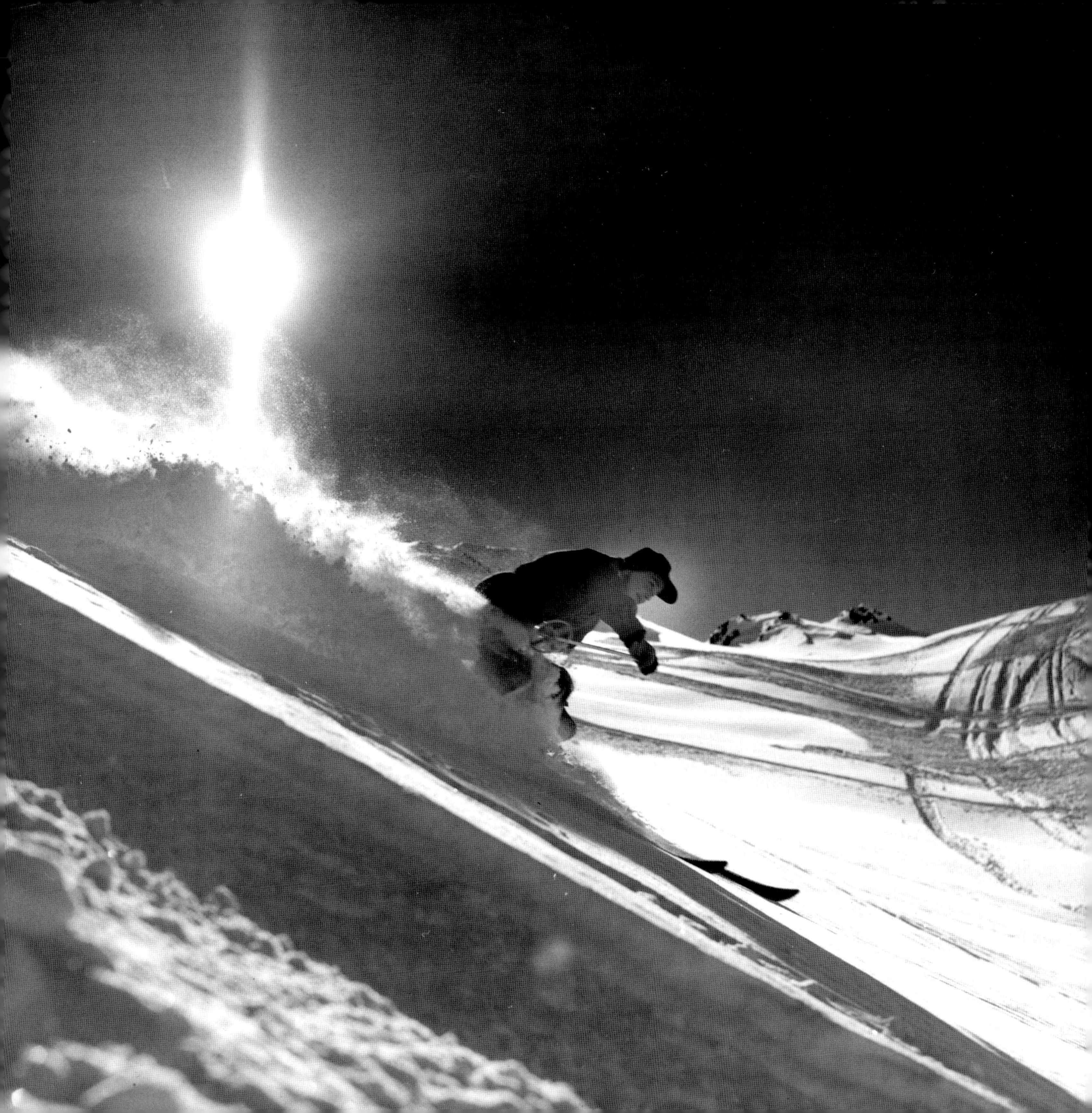

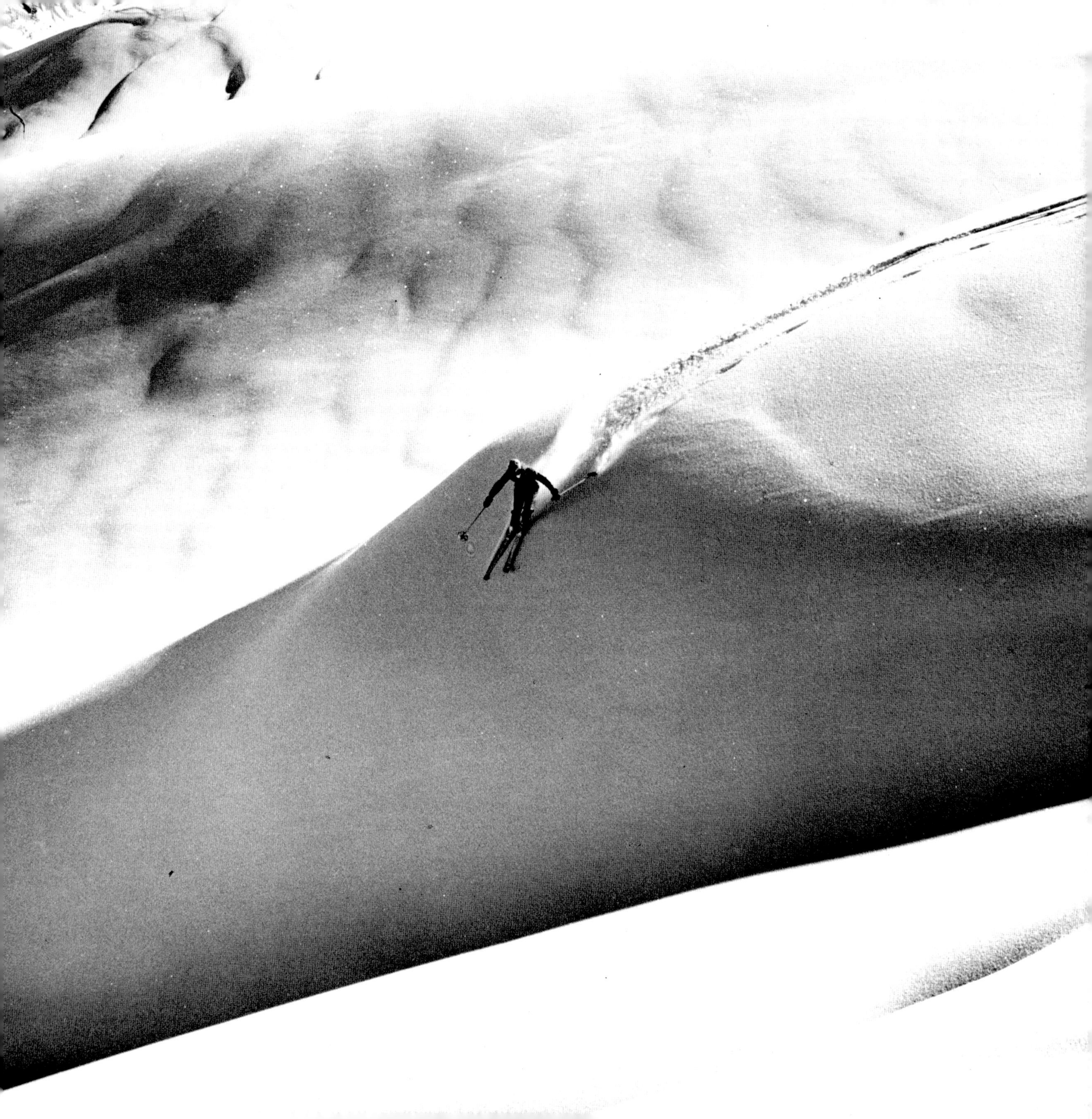

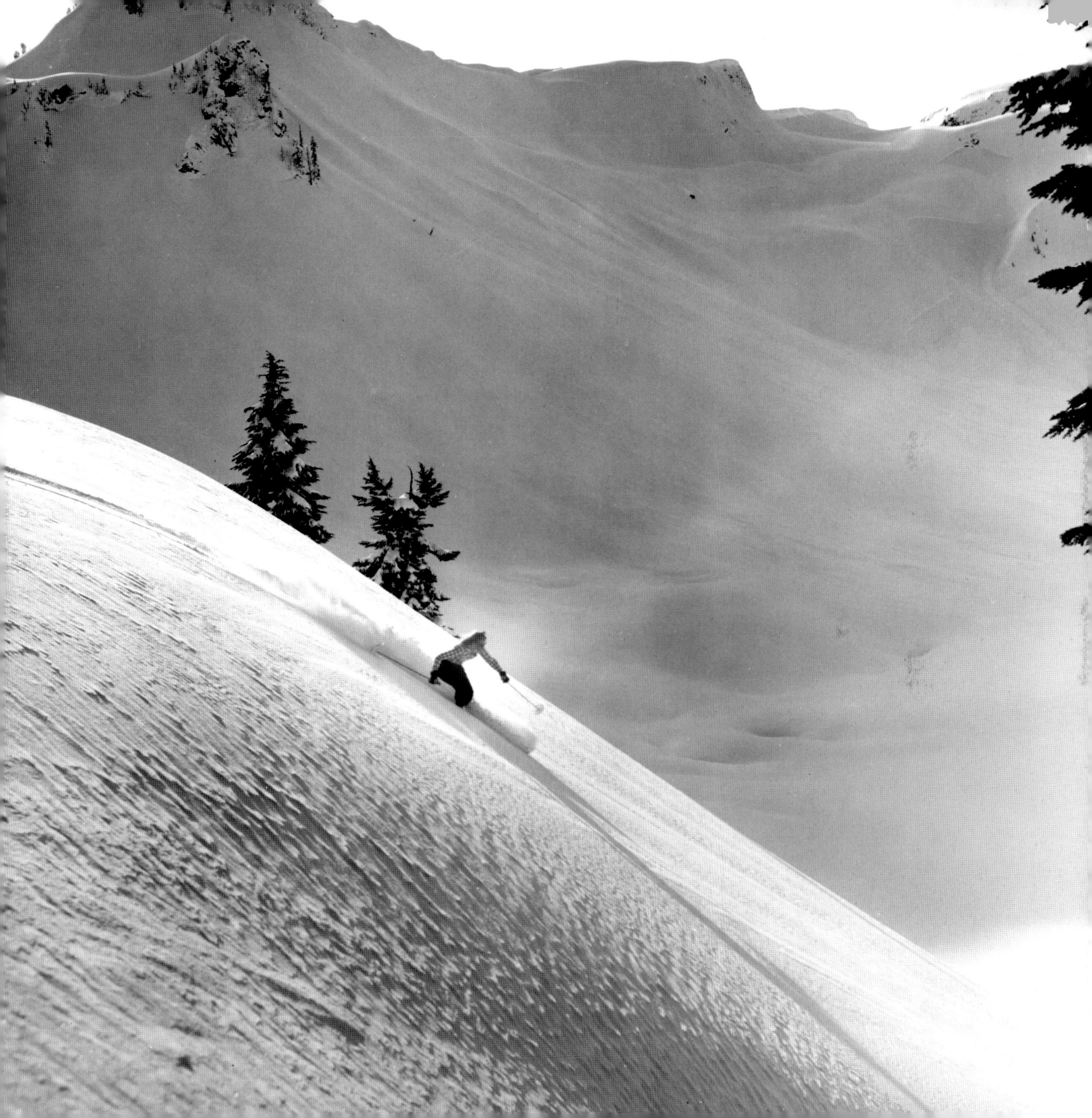

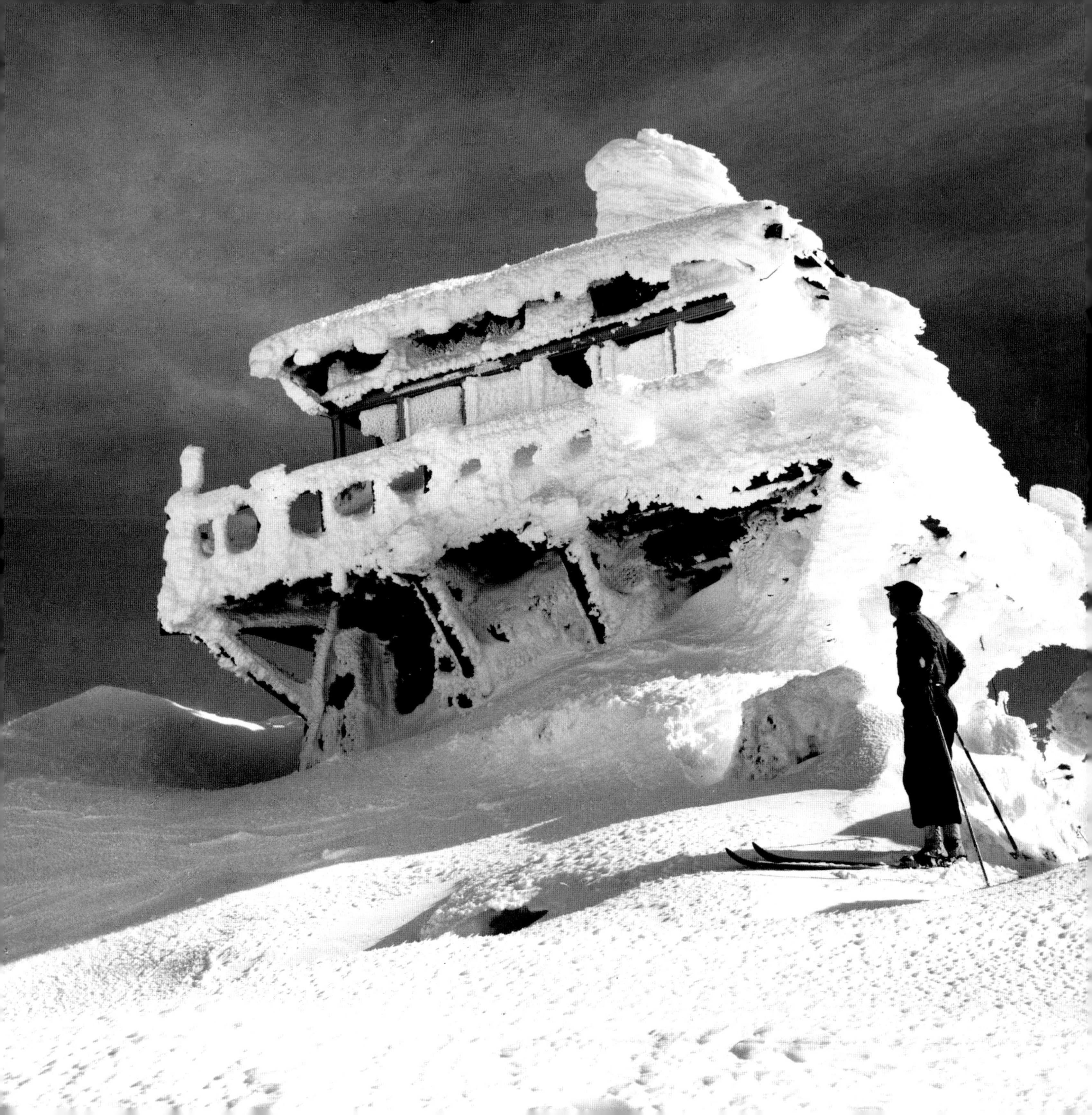

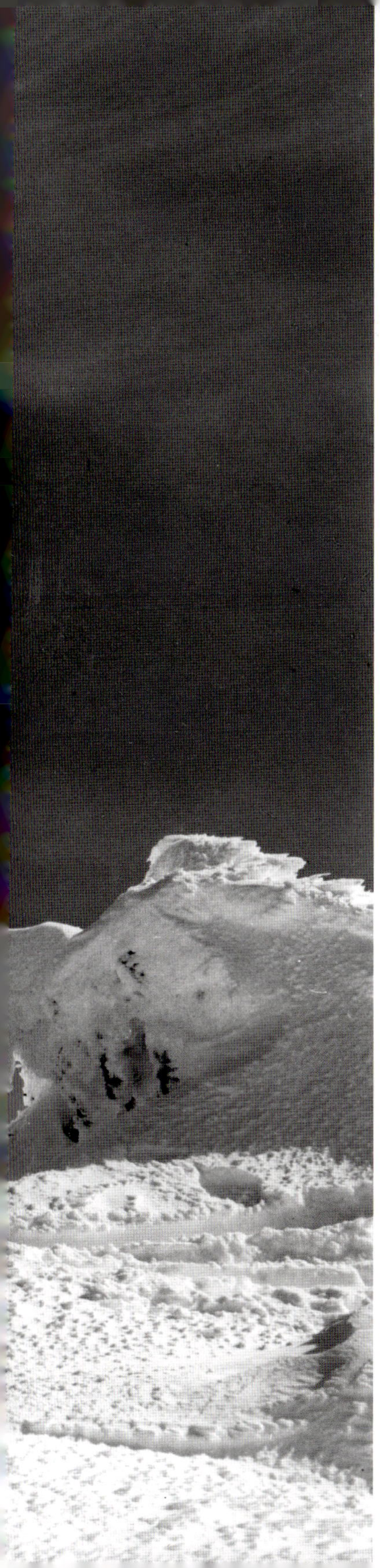

Backcountry skiing is full of surprises.

DAVID GOODMAN

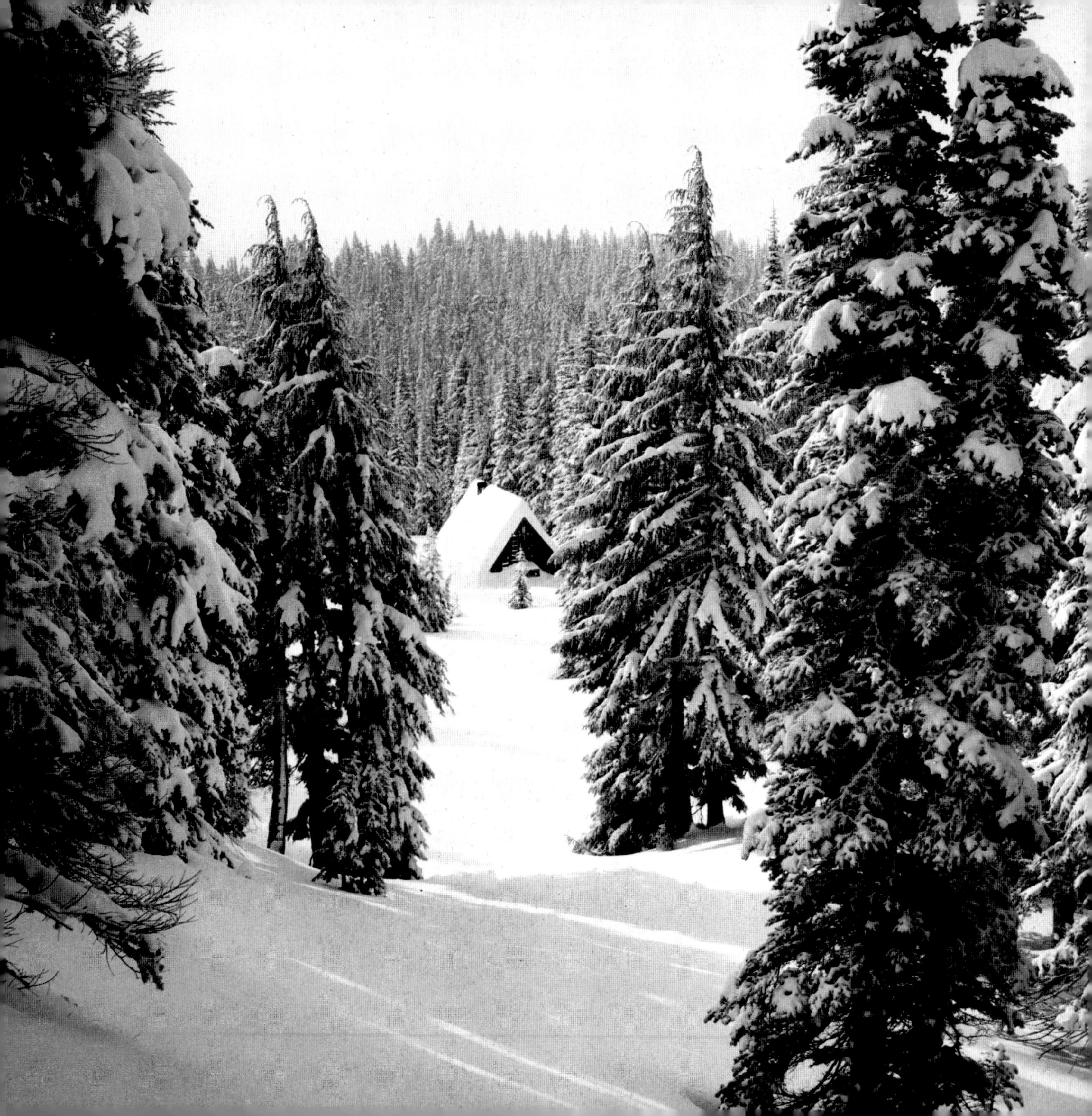

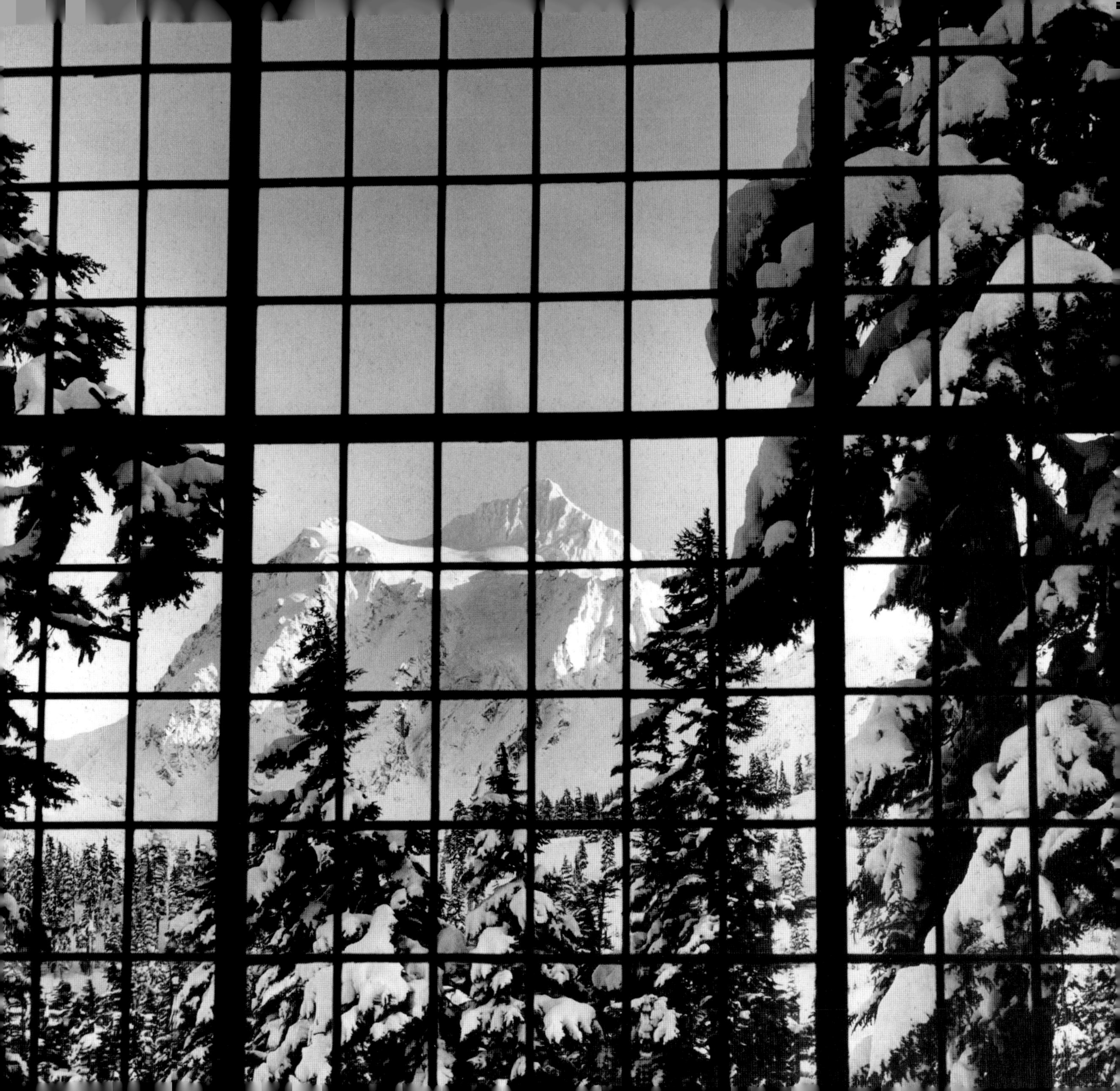

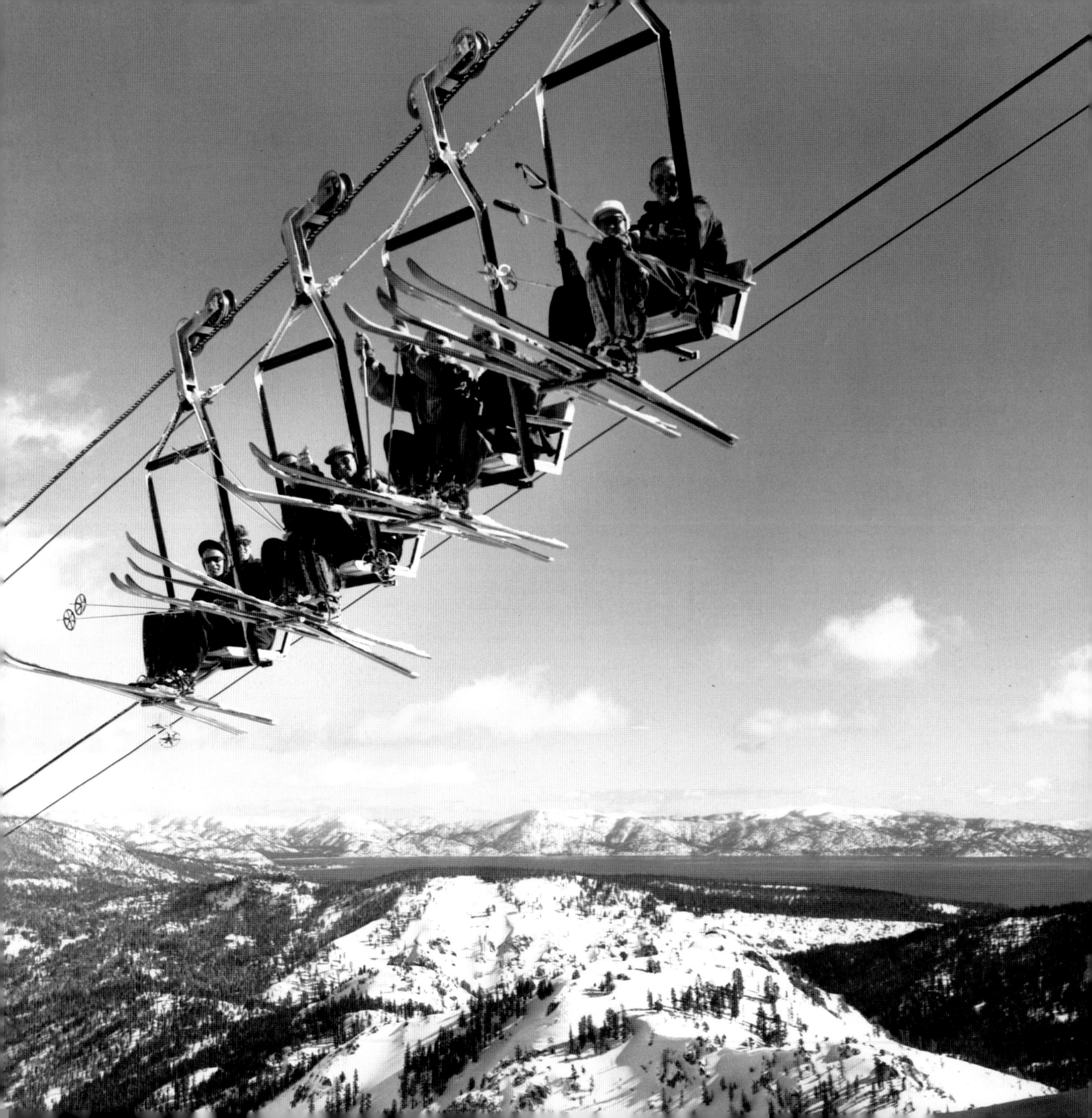

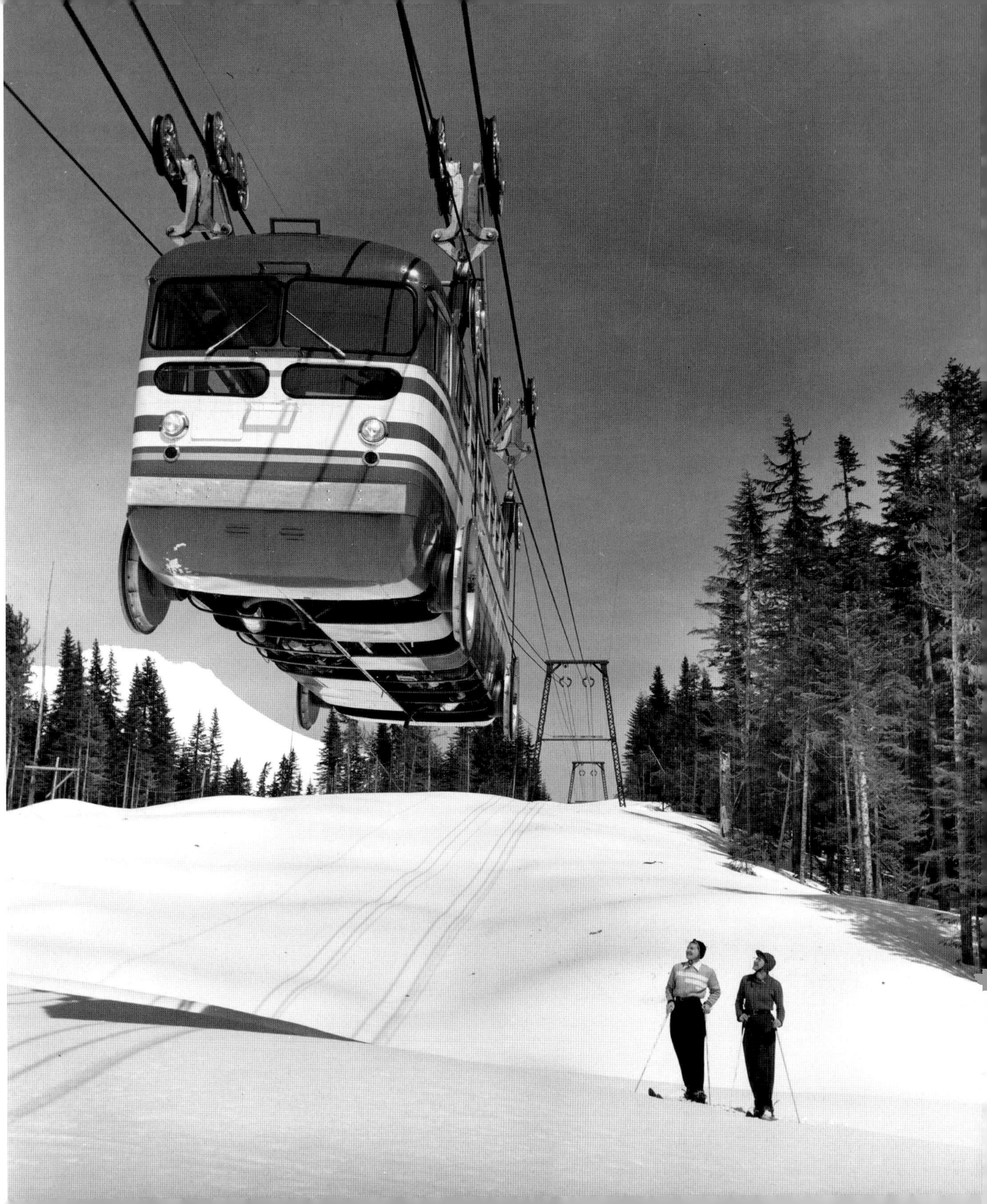

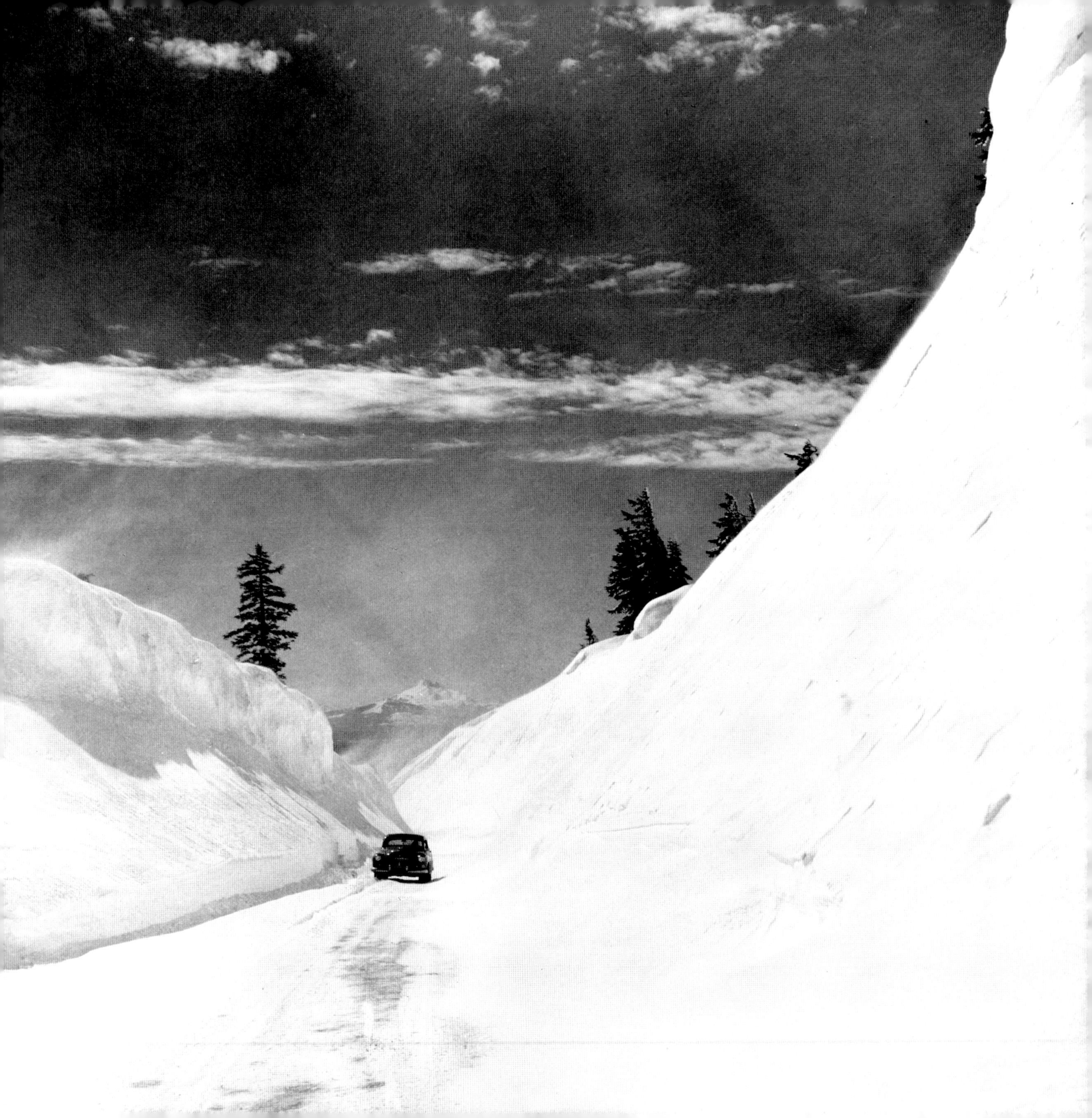

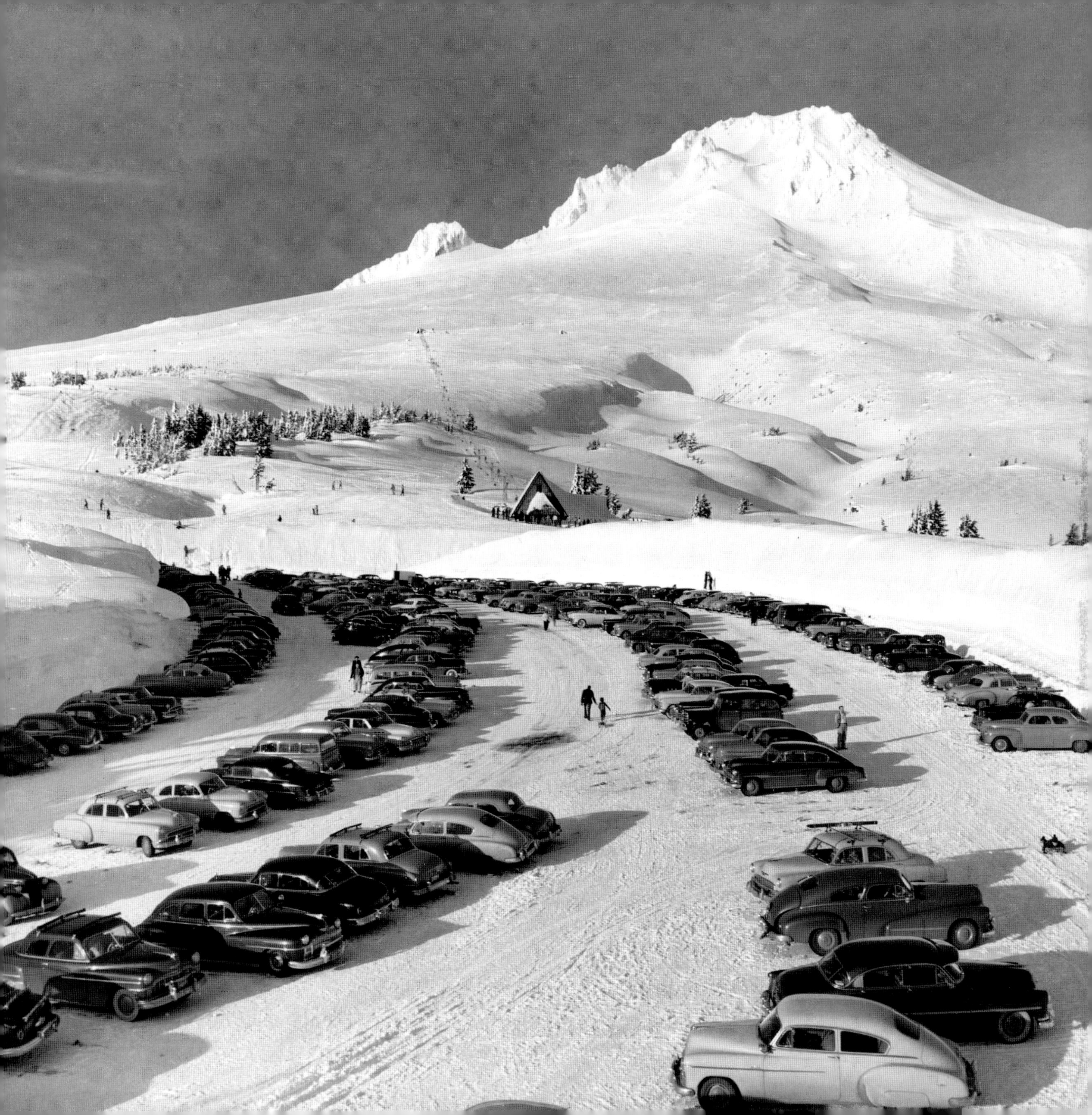

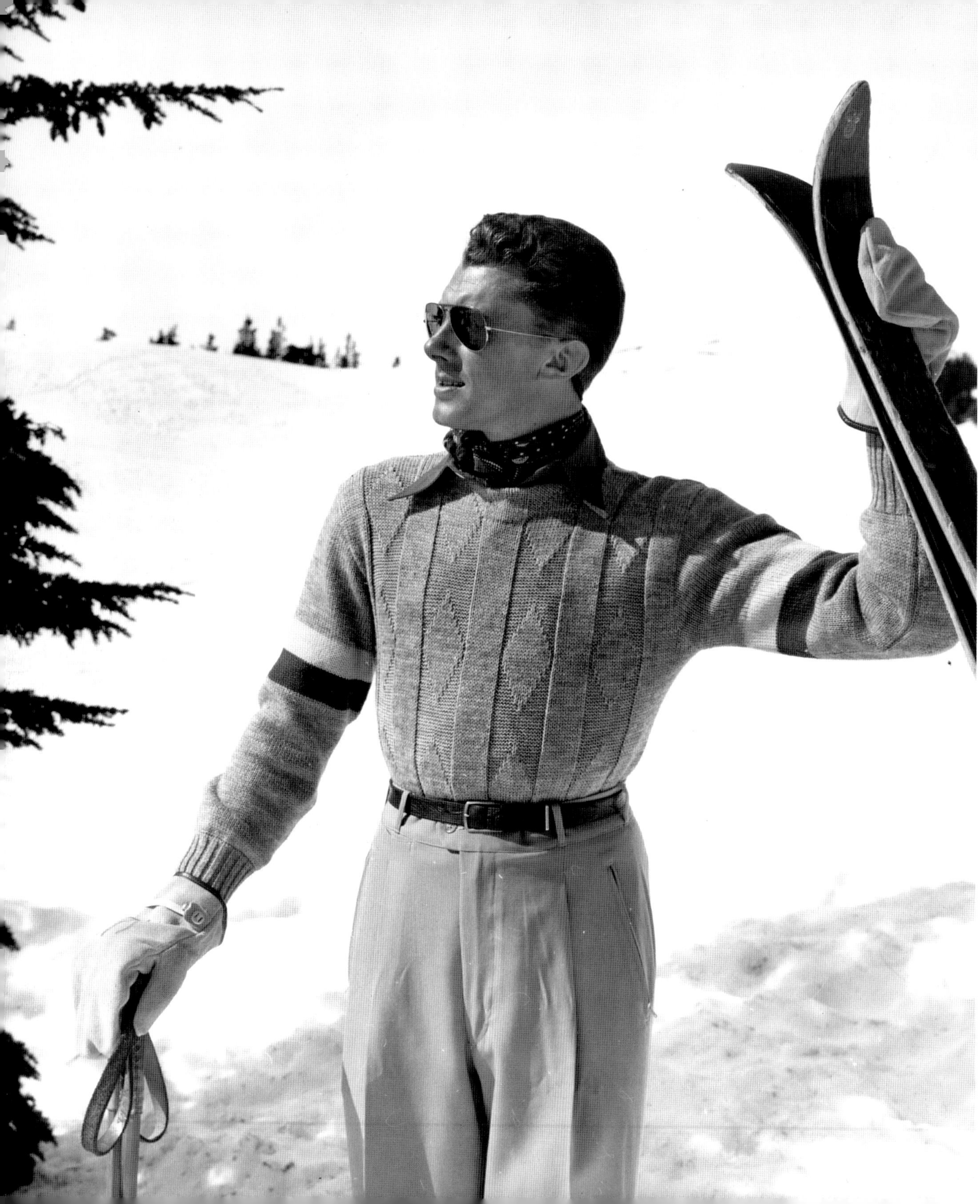

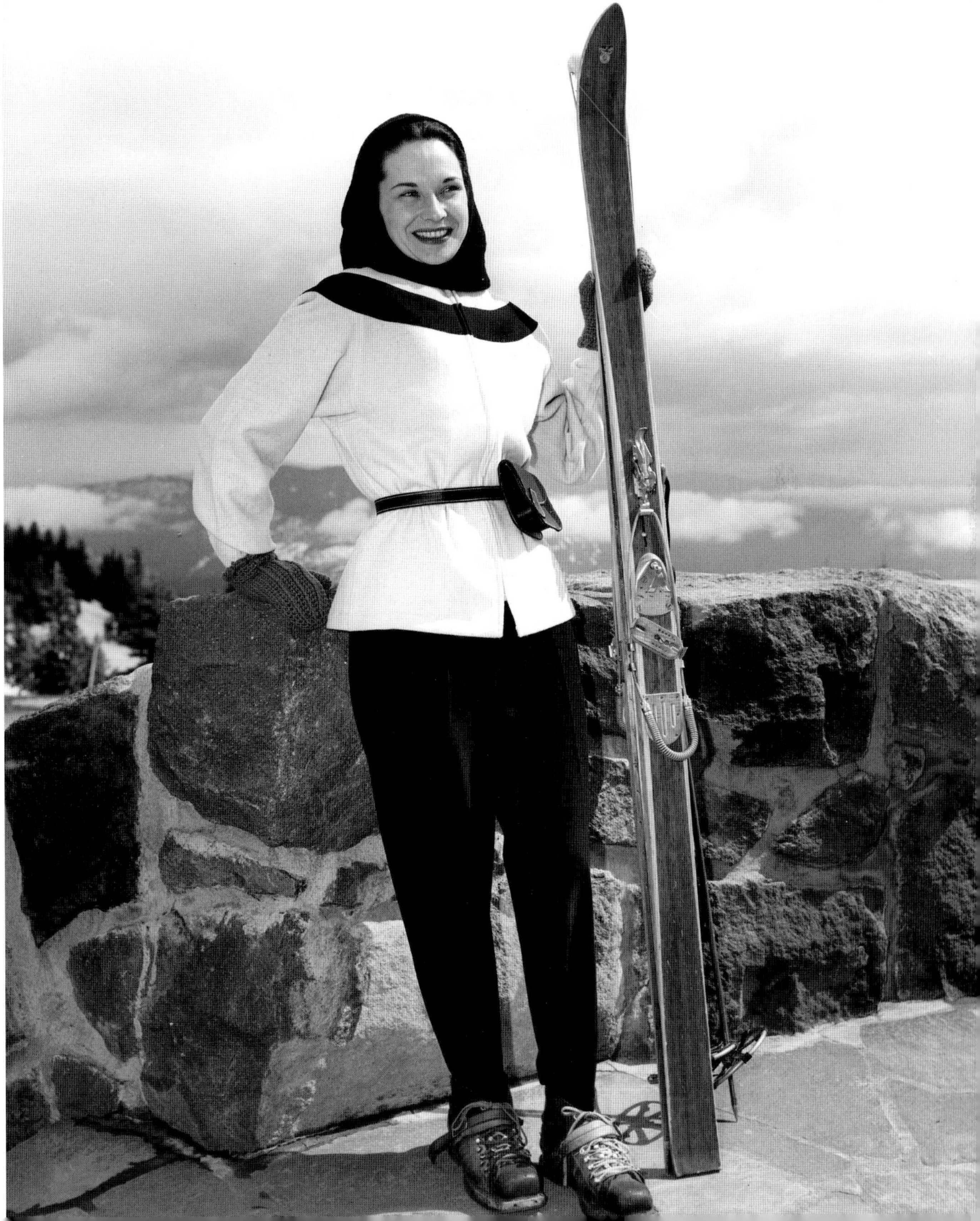

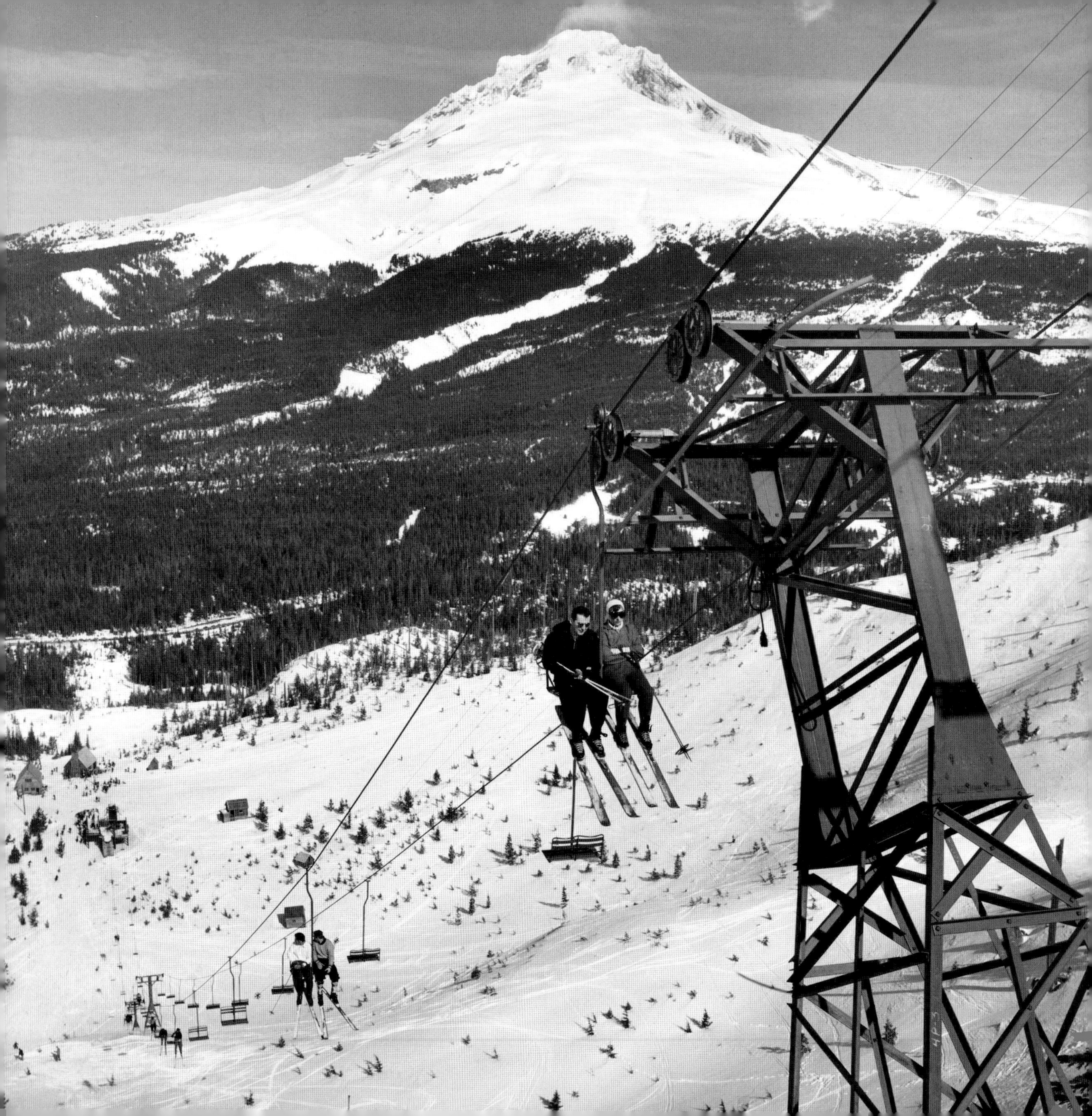

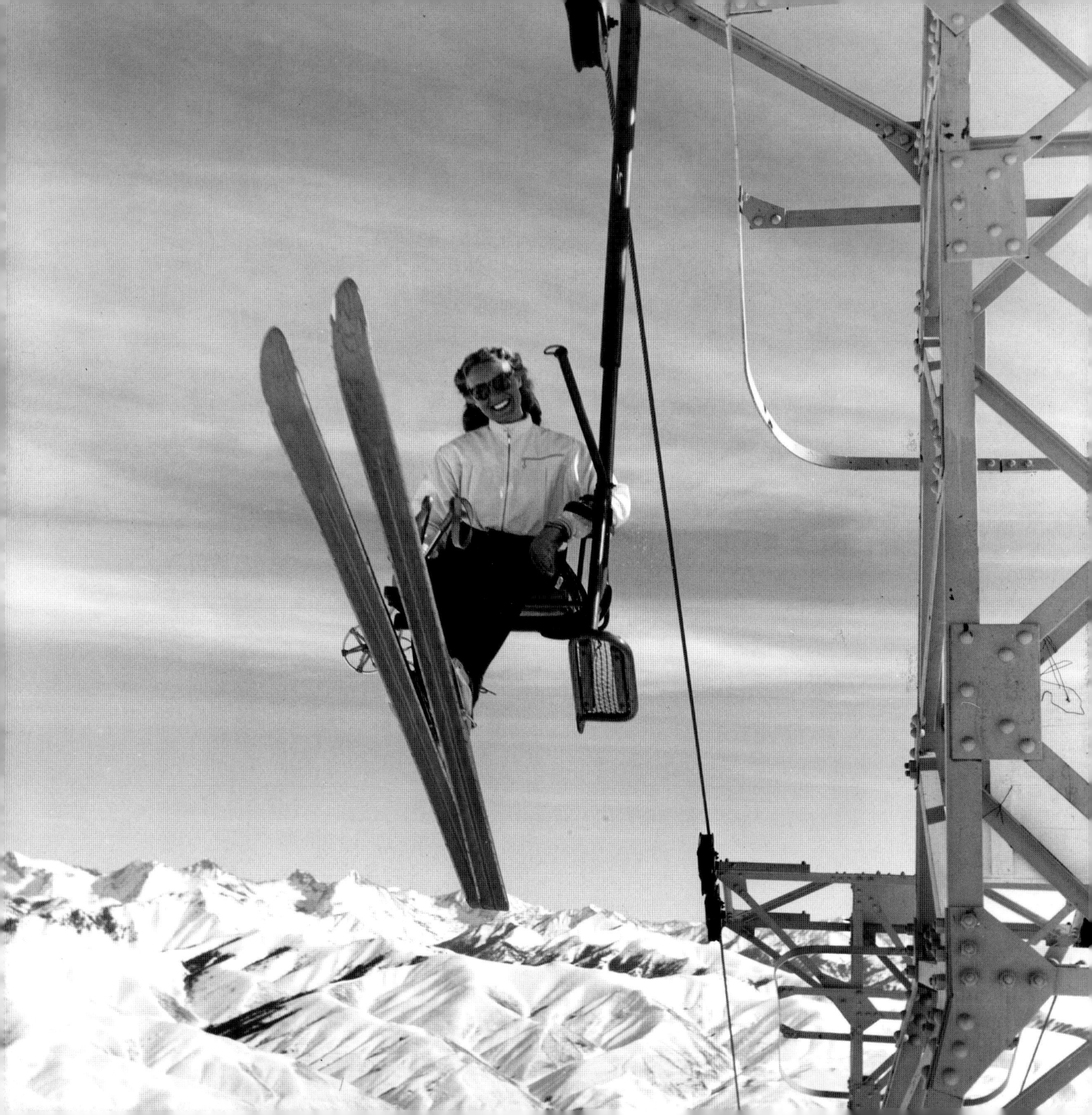

Skiing is a dance, and
the mountain always leads.

AUTHOR UNKNOWN

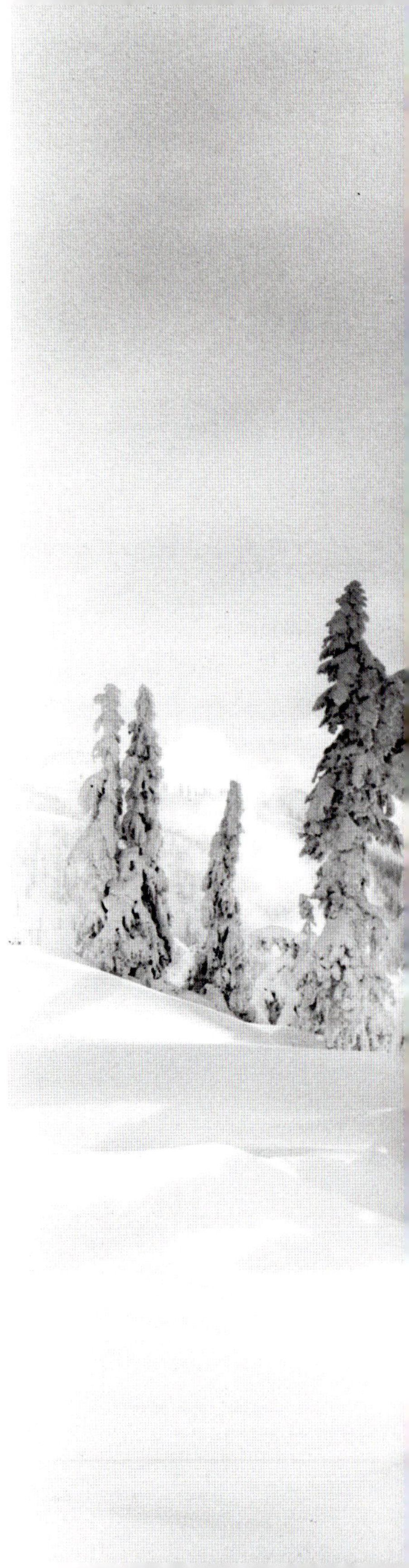

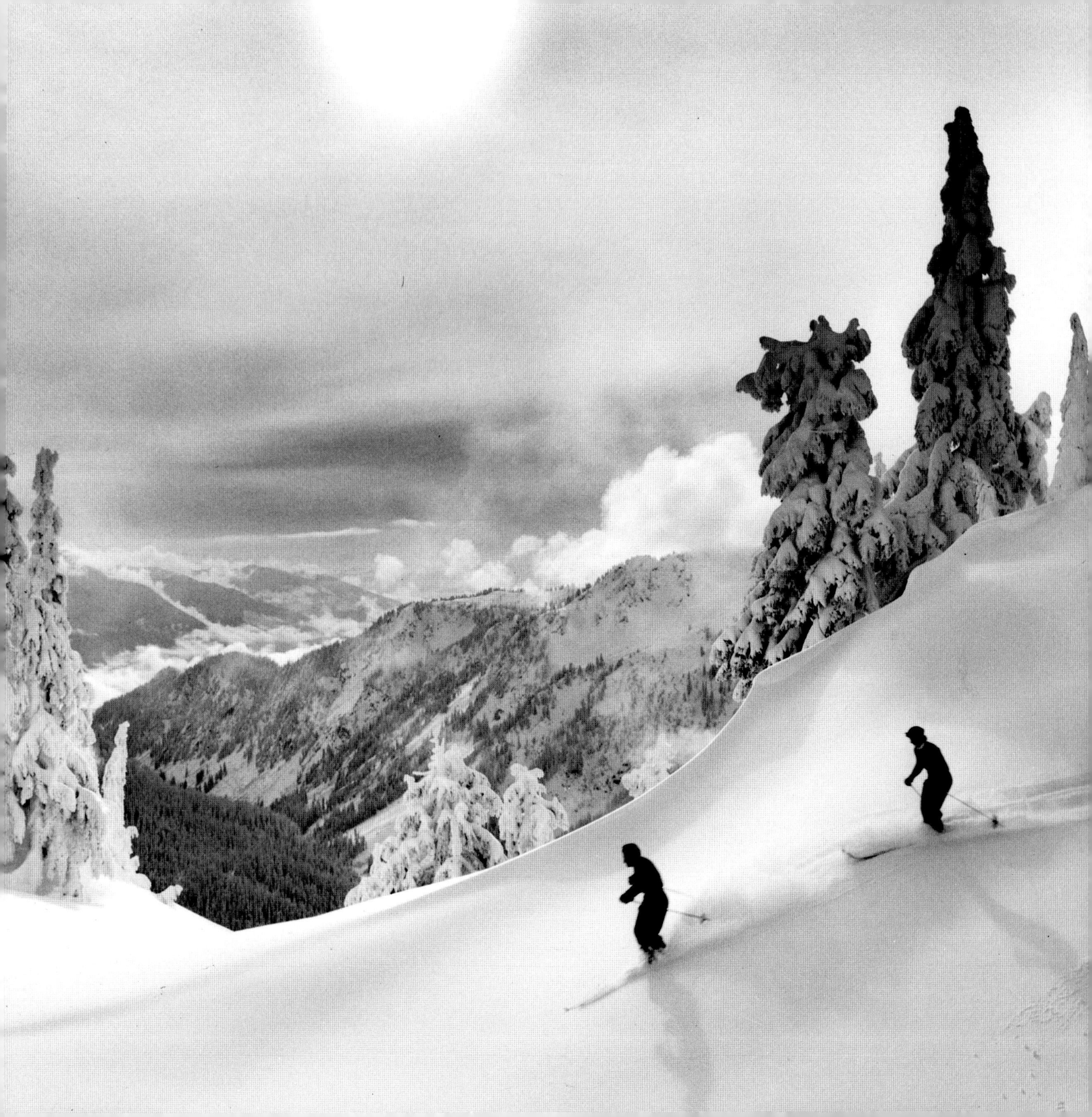

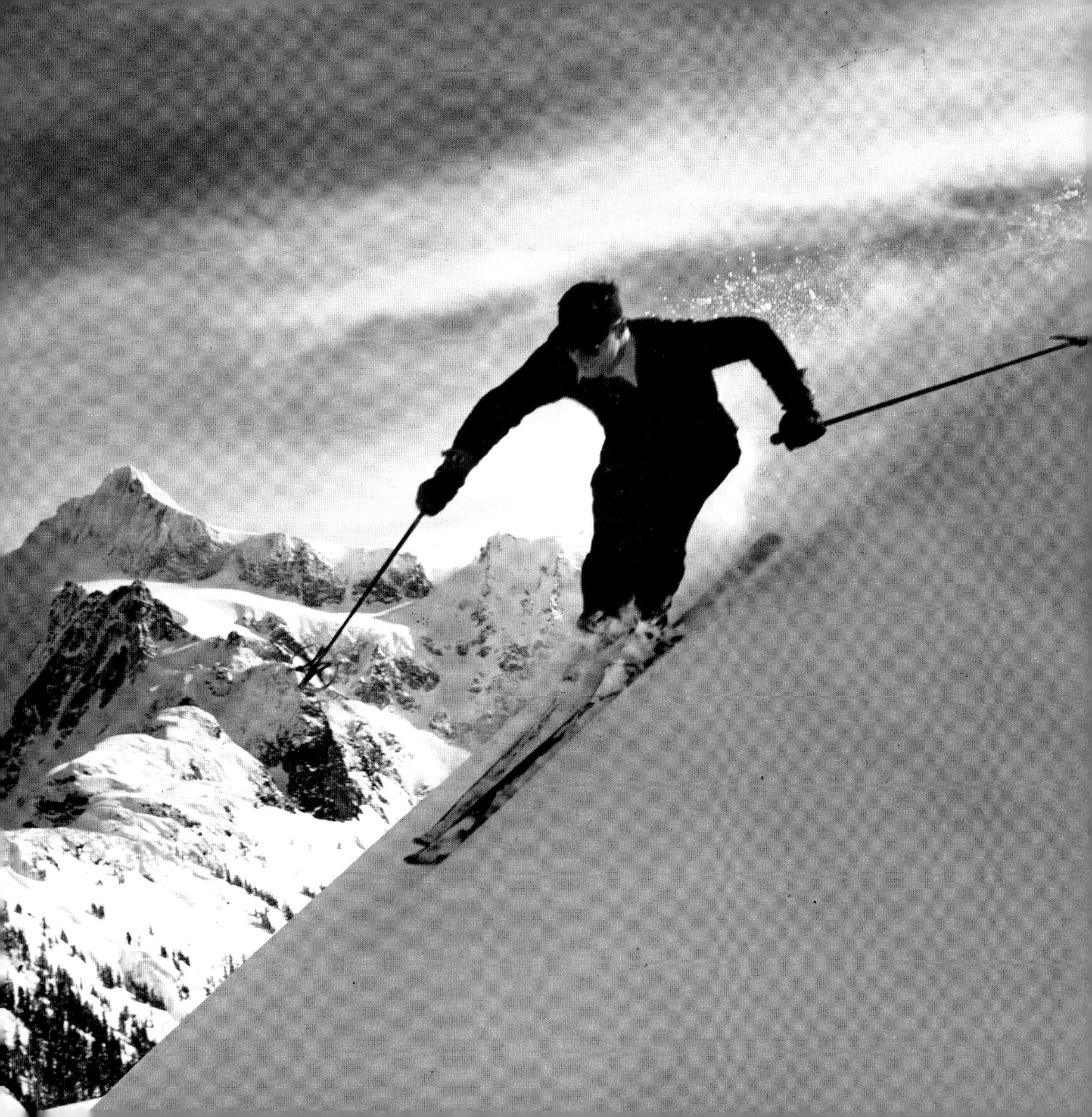

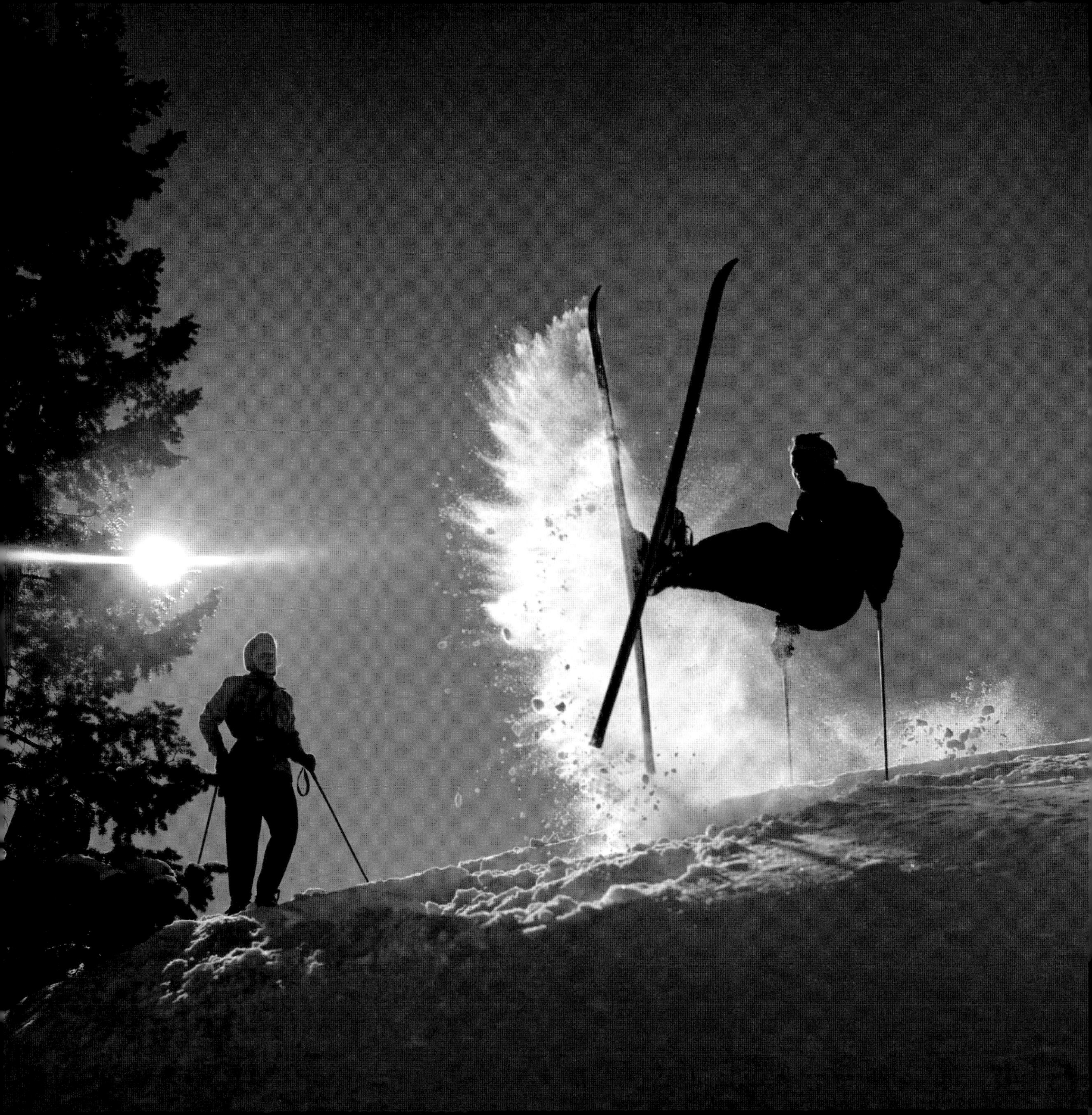

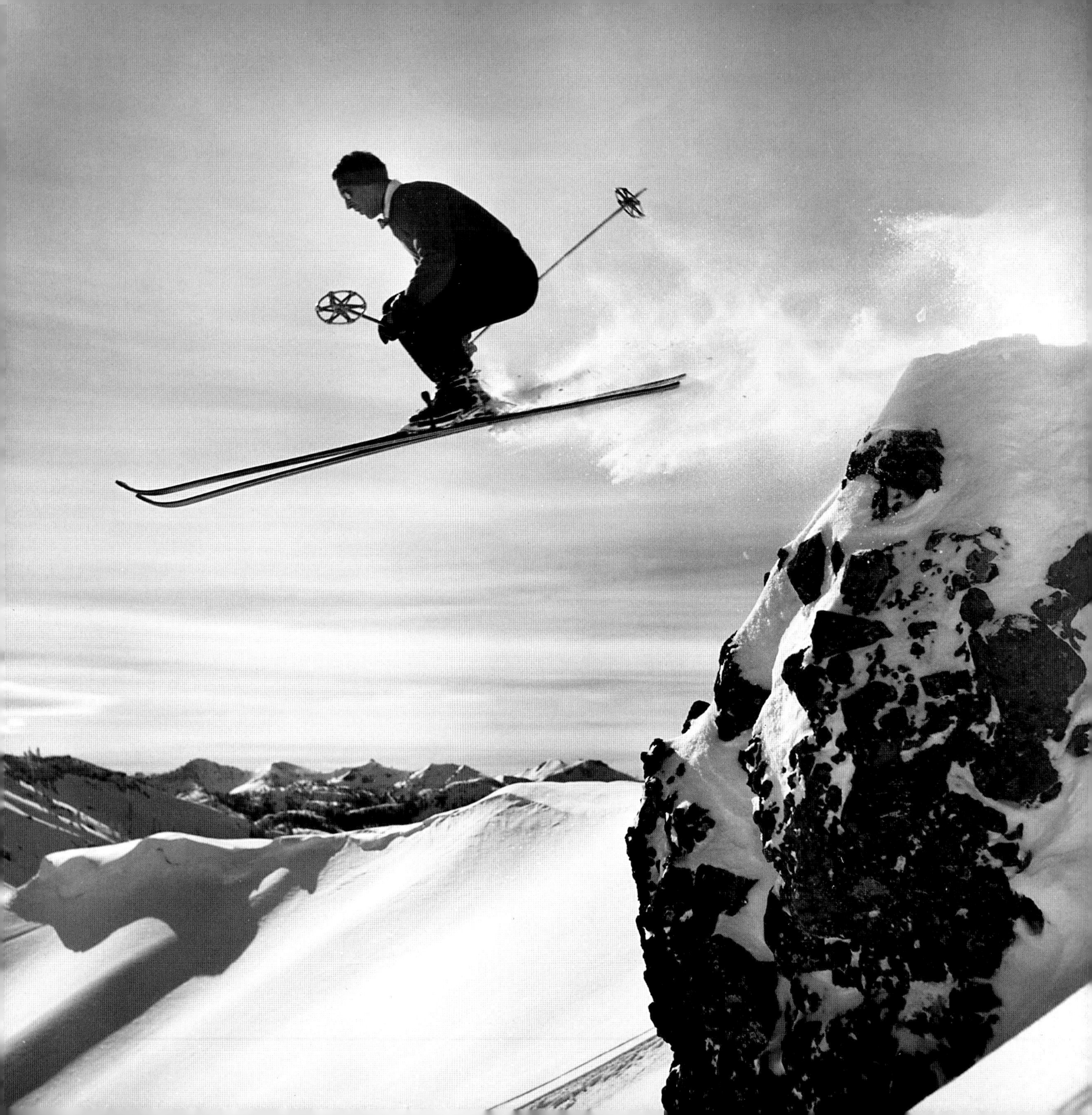

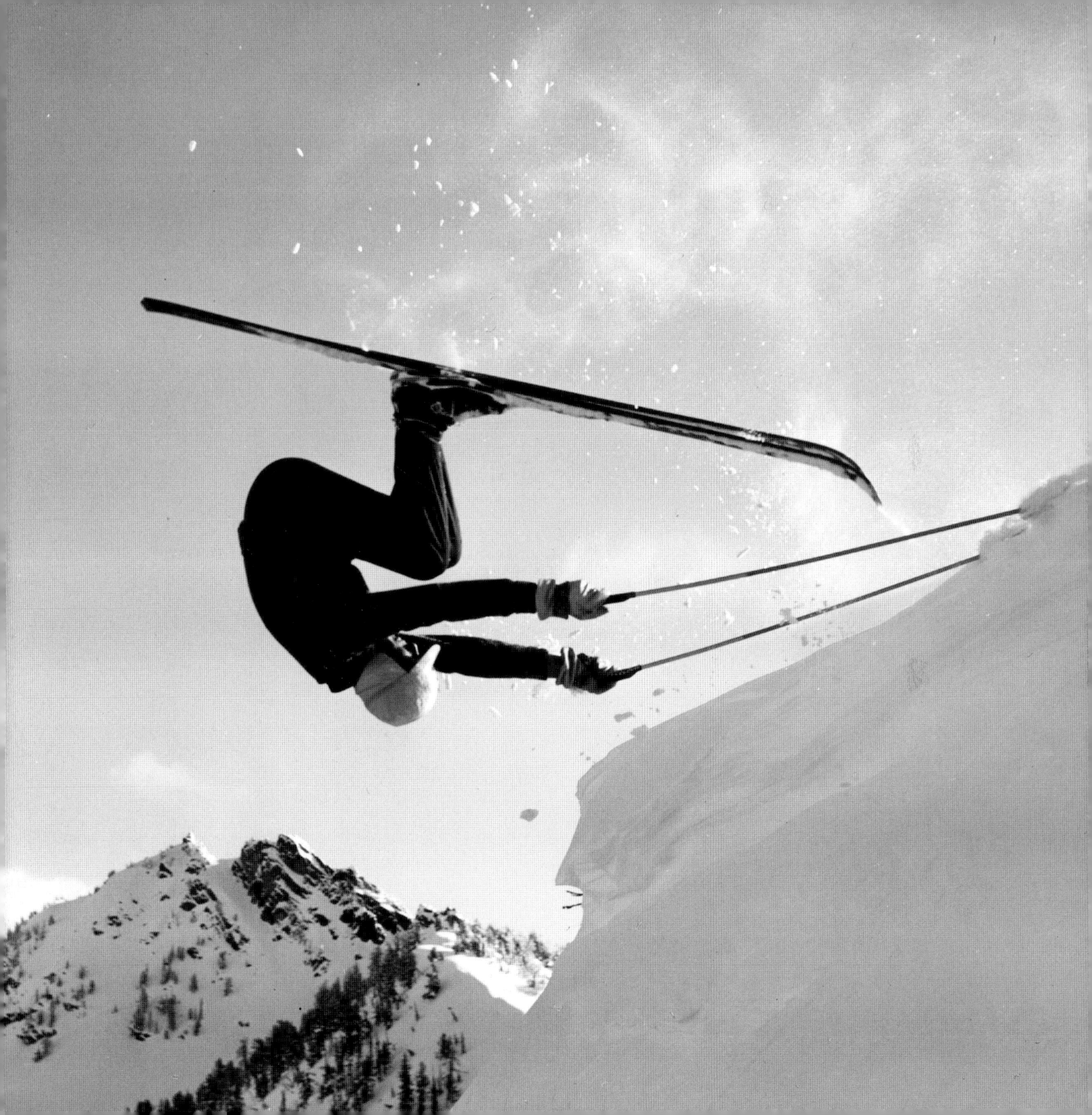

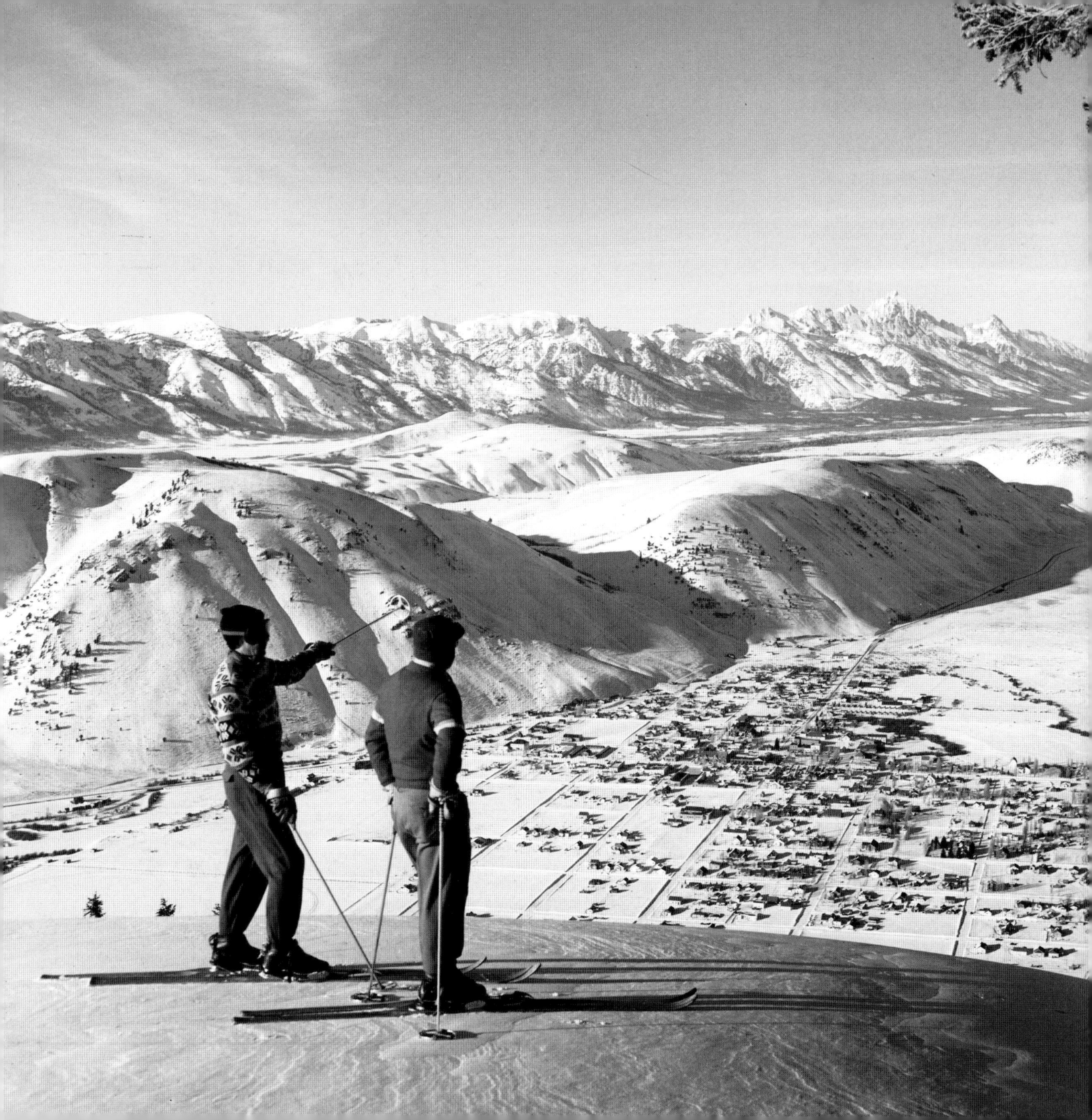

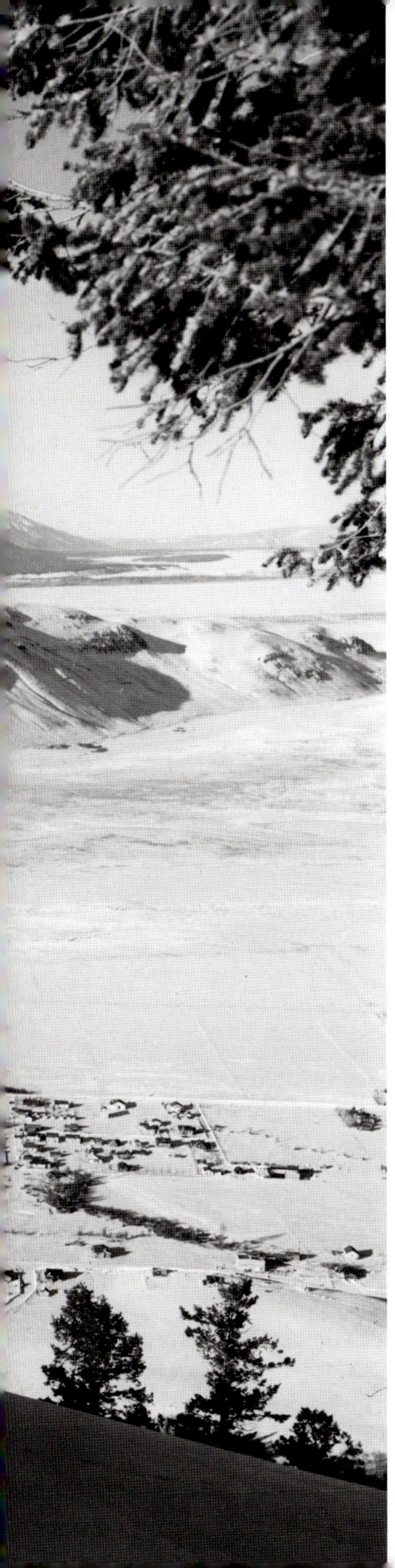

*Skiing is the best way
in the world to waste time.*

GLEN PLAKE

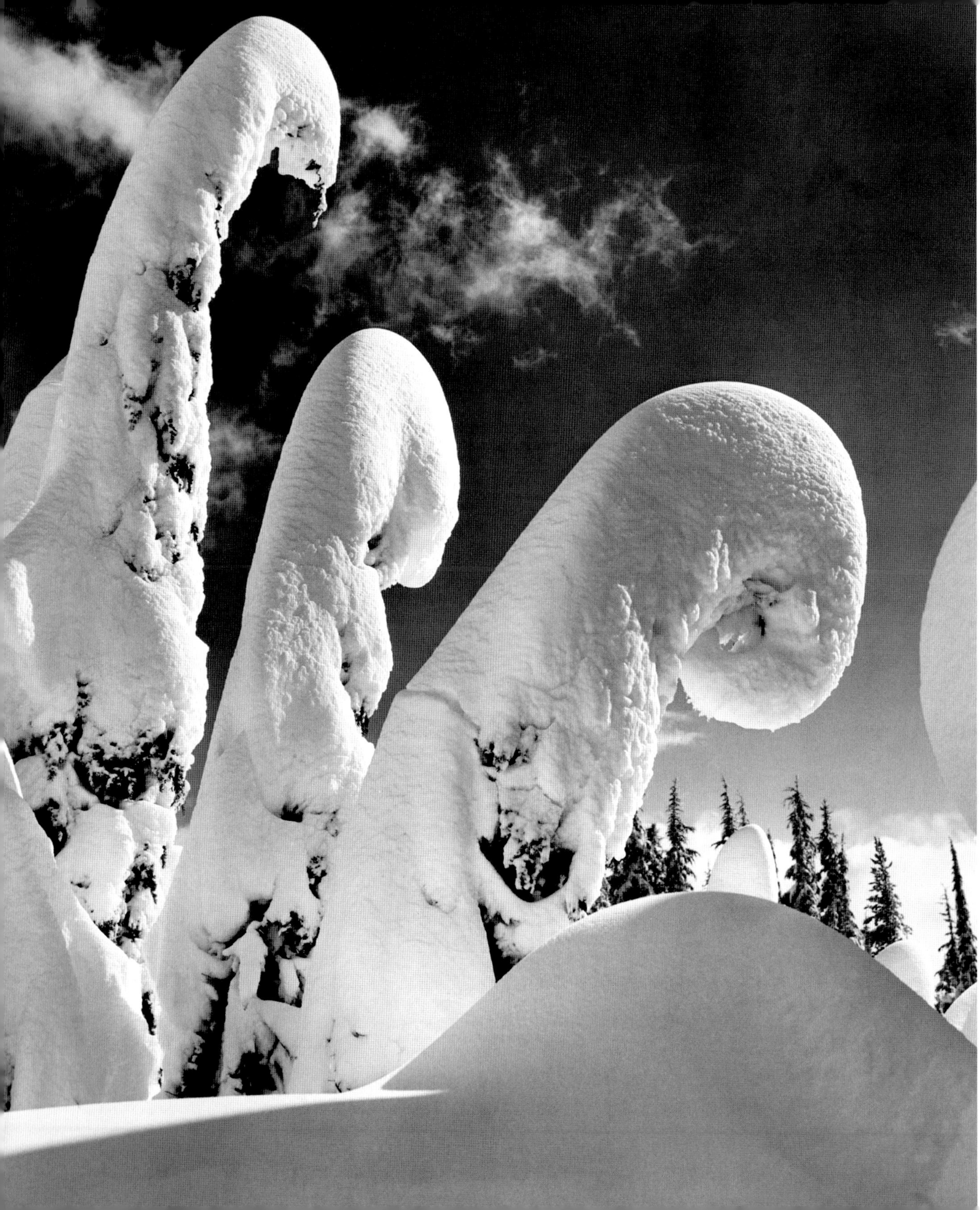

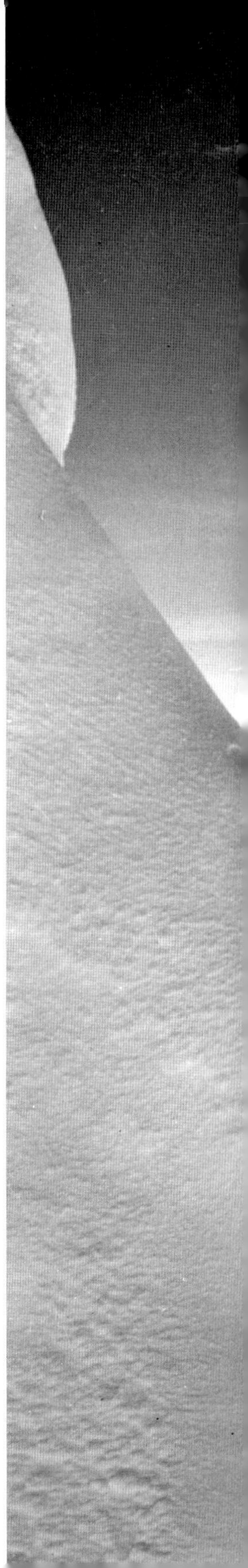

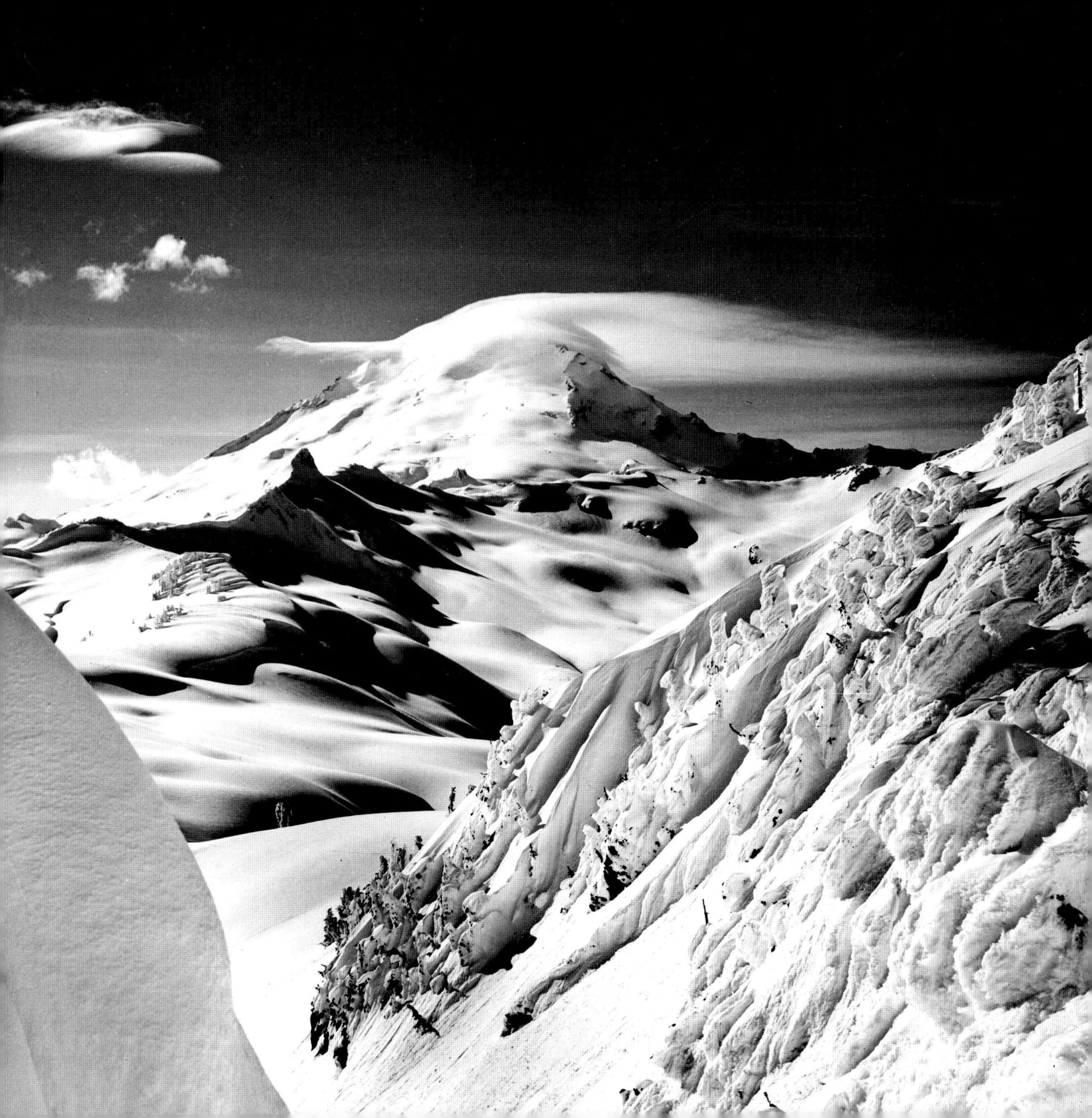

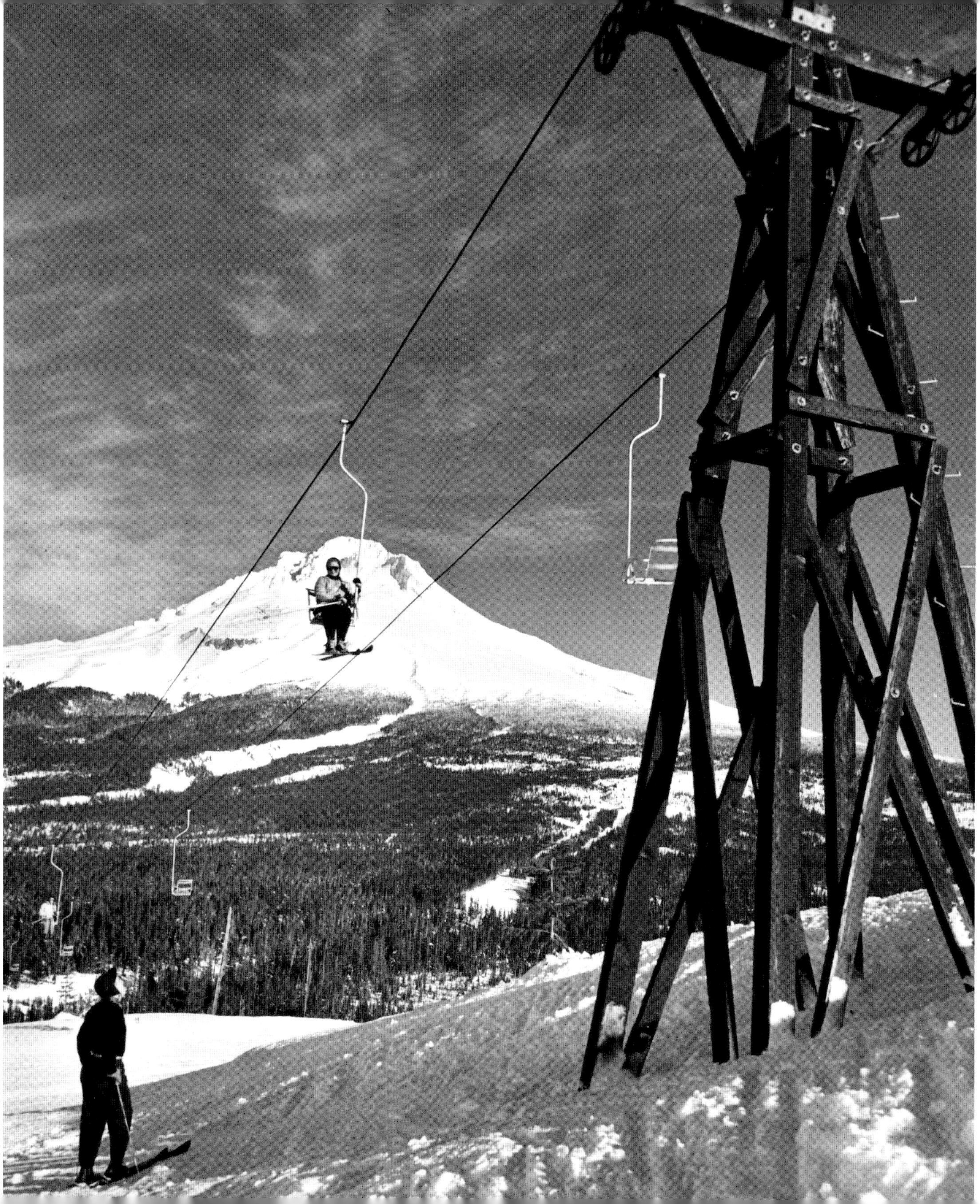

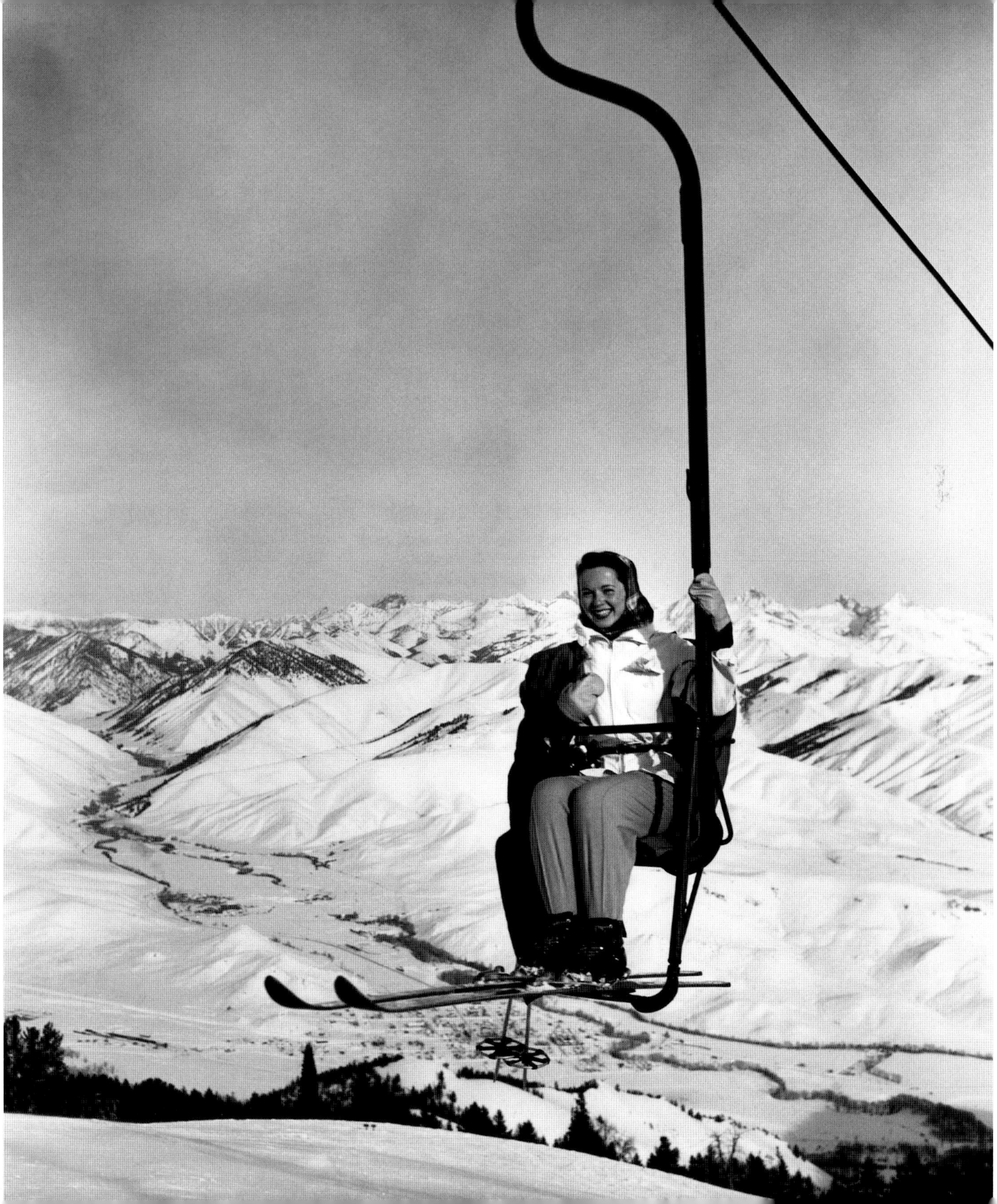

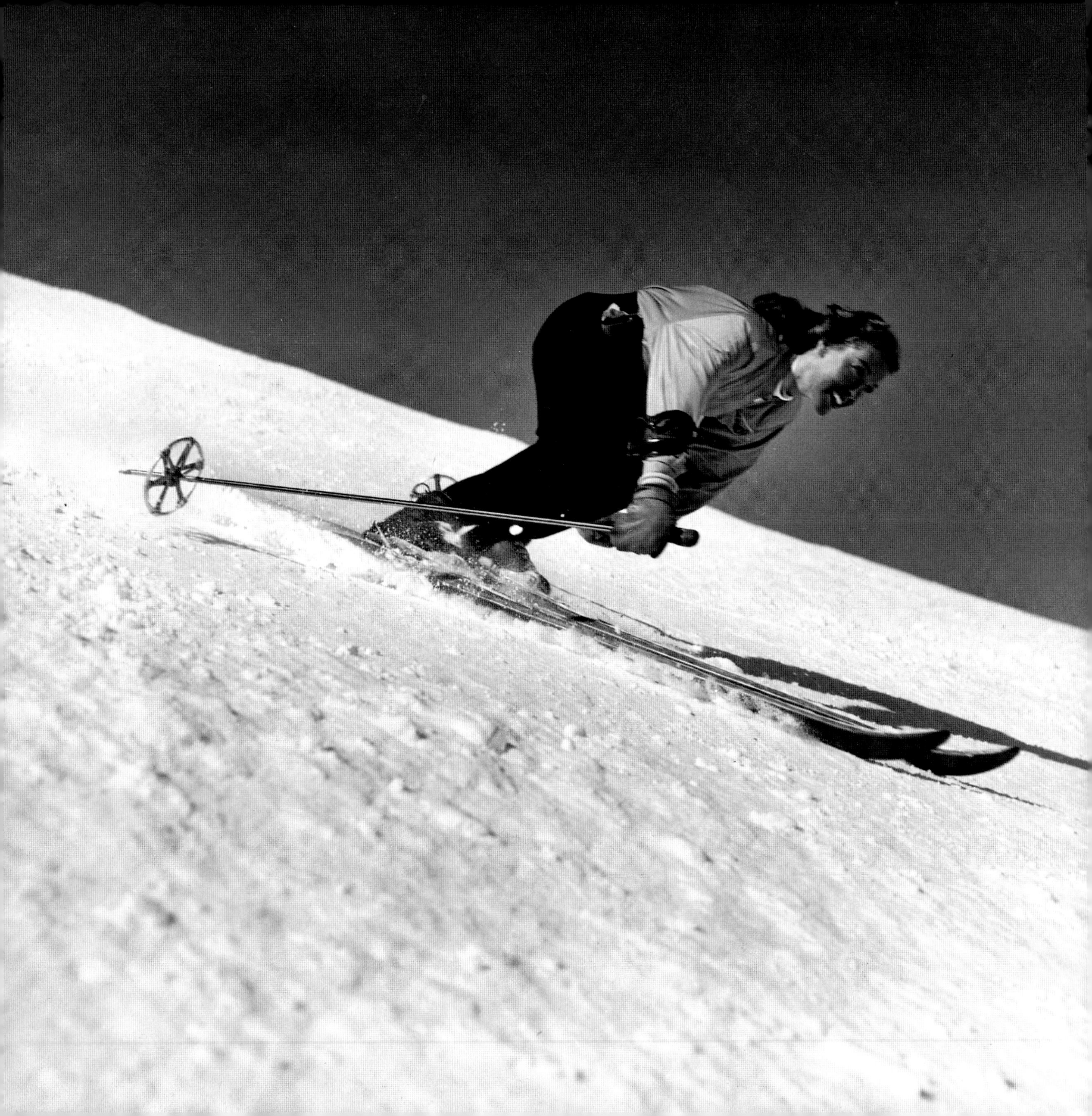

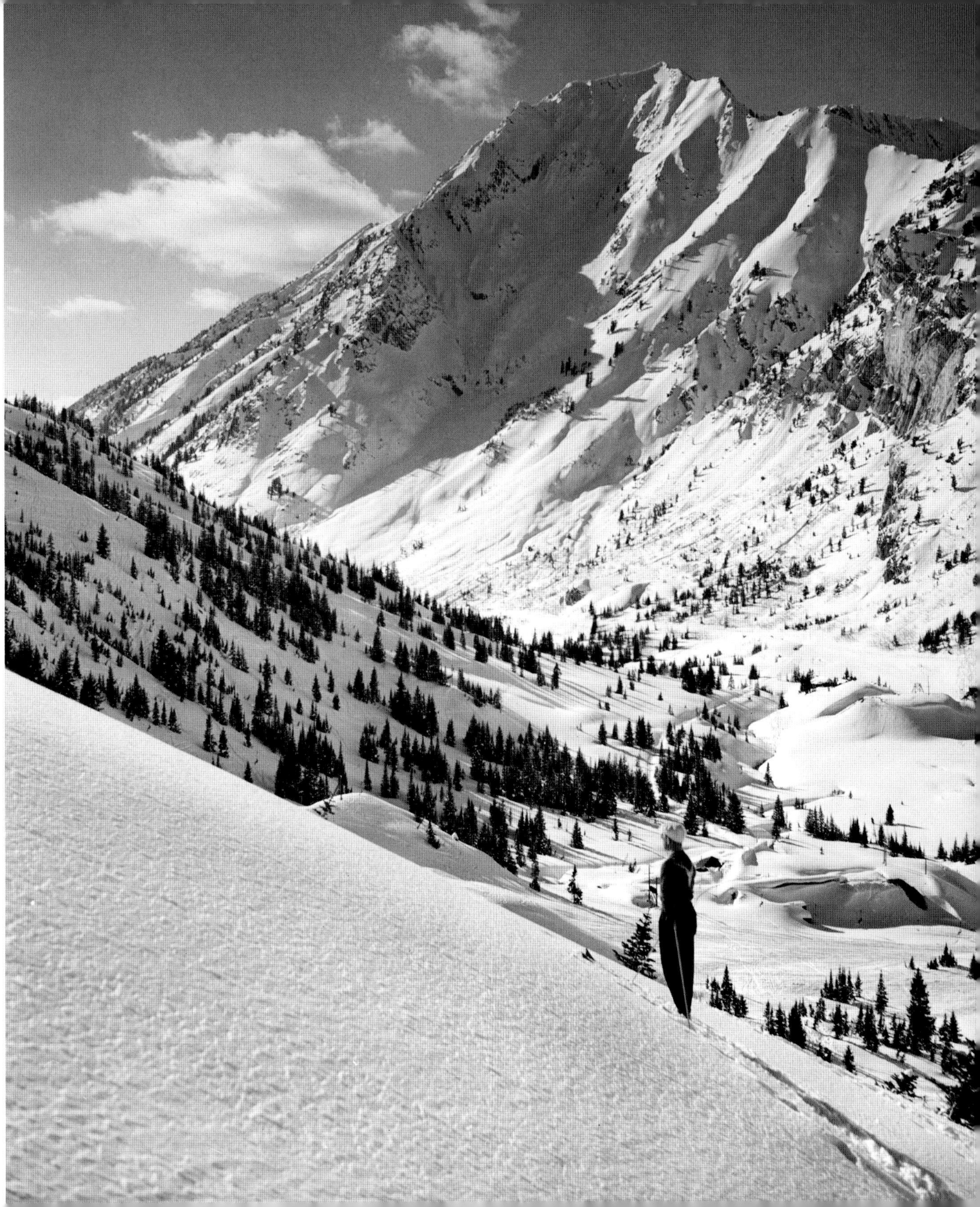

The history of skiing is important to me.

LINDSEY VONN

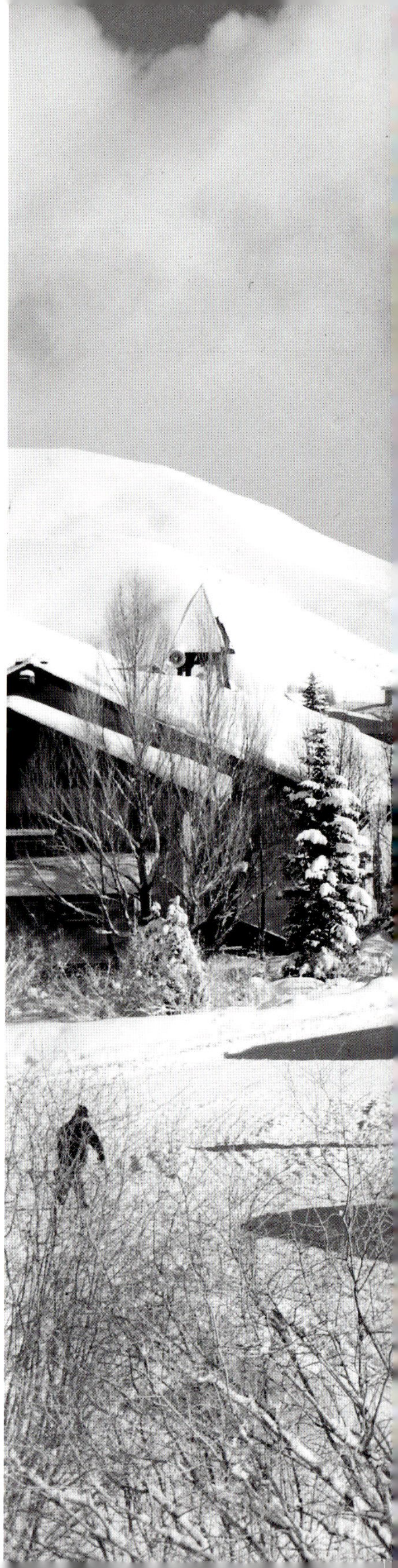

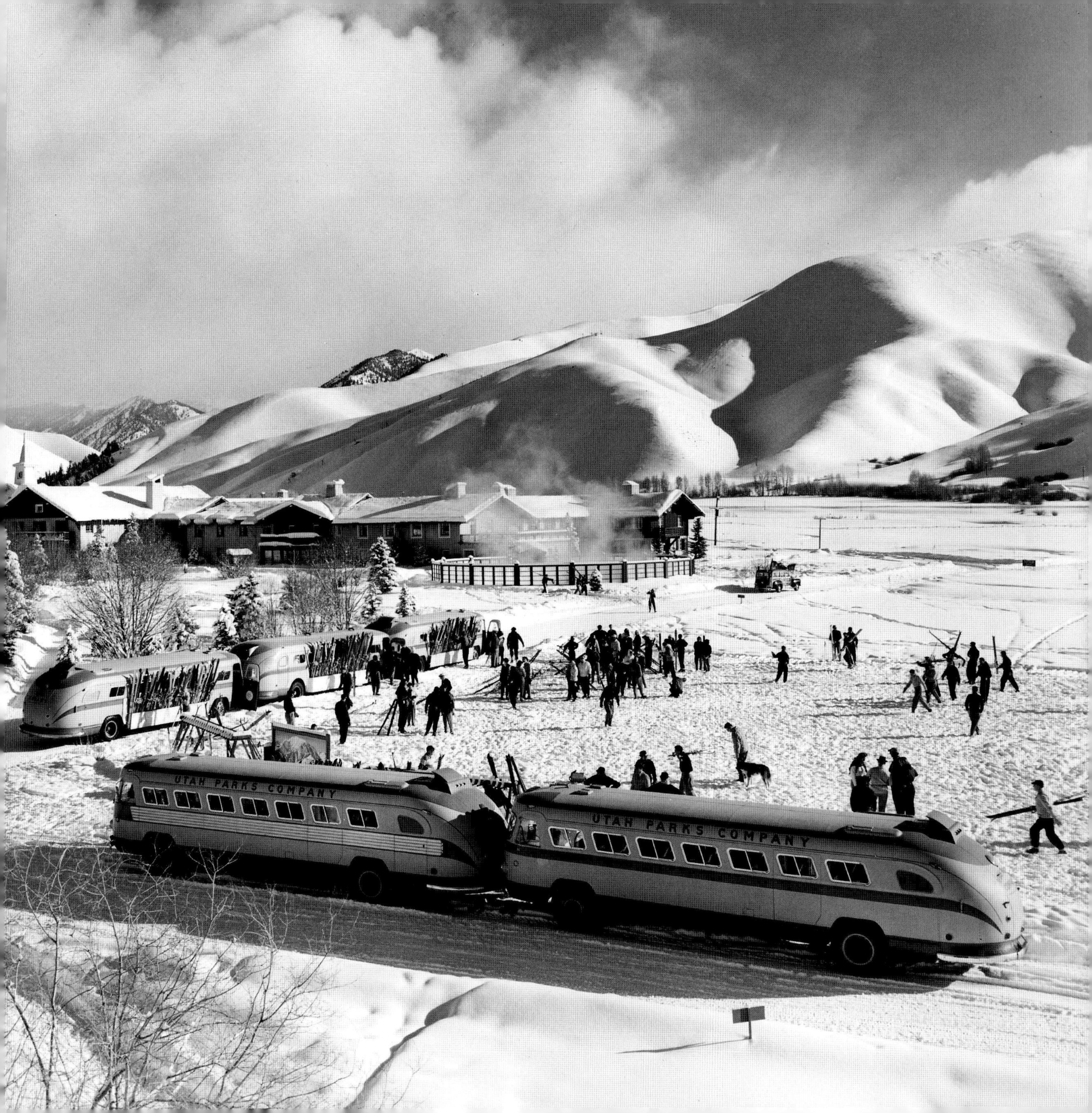
UTAH PARKS COMPANY
UTAH PARKS COMPANY

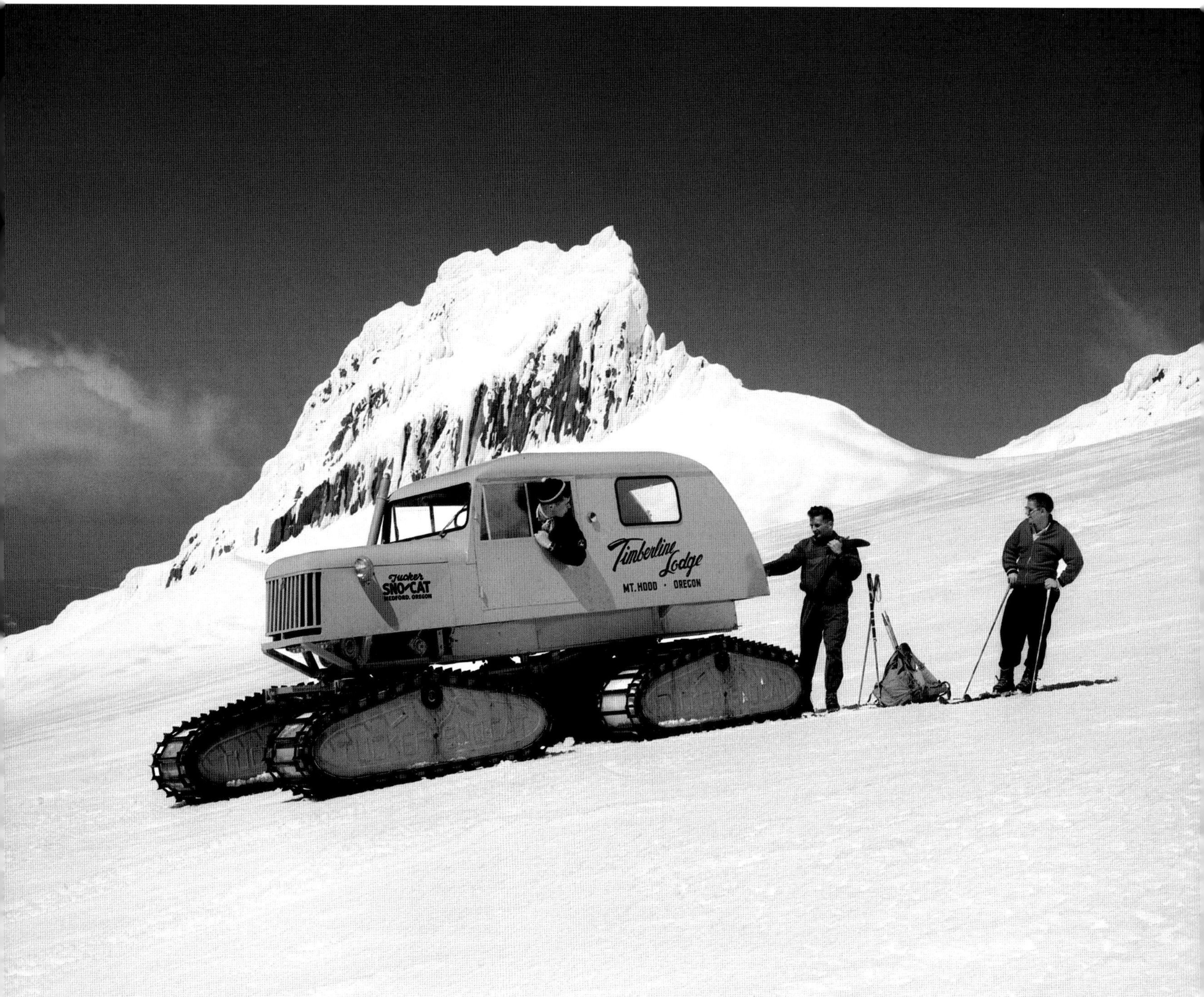
Tucker
SNO-CAT
MEDFORD, OREGON
Timberline
Lodge
MT. HOOD · OREGON

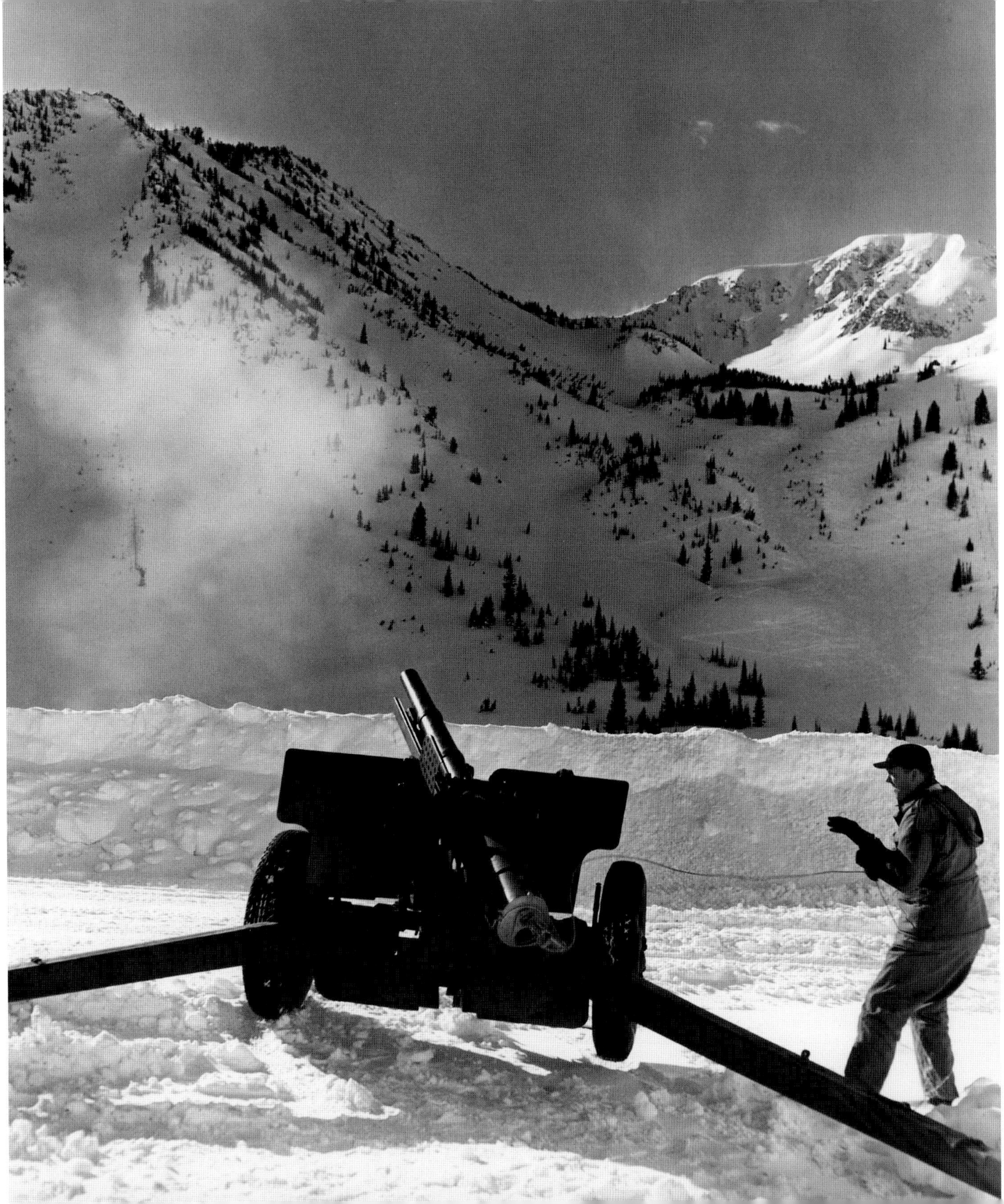

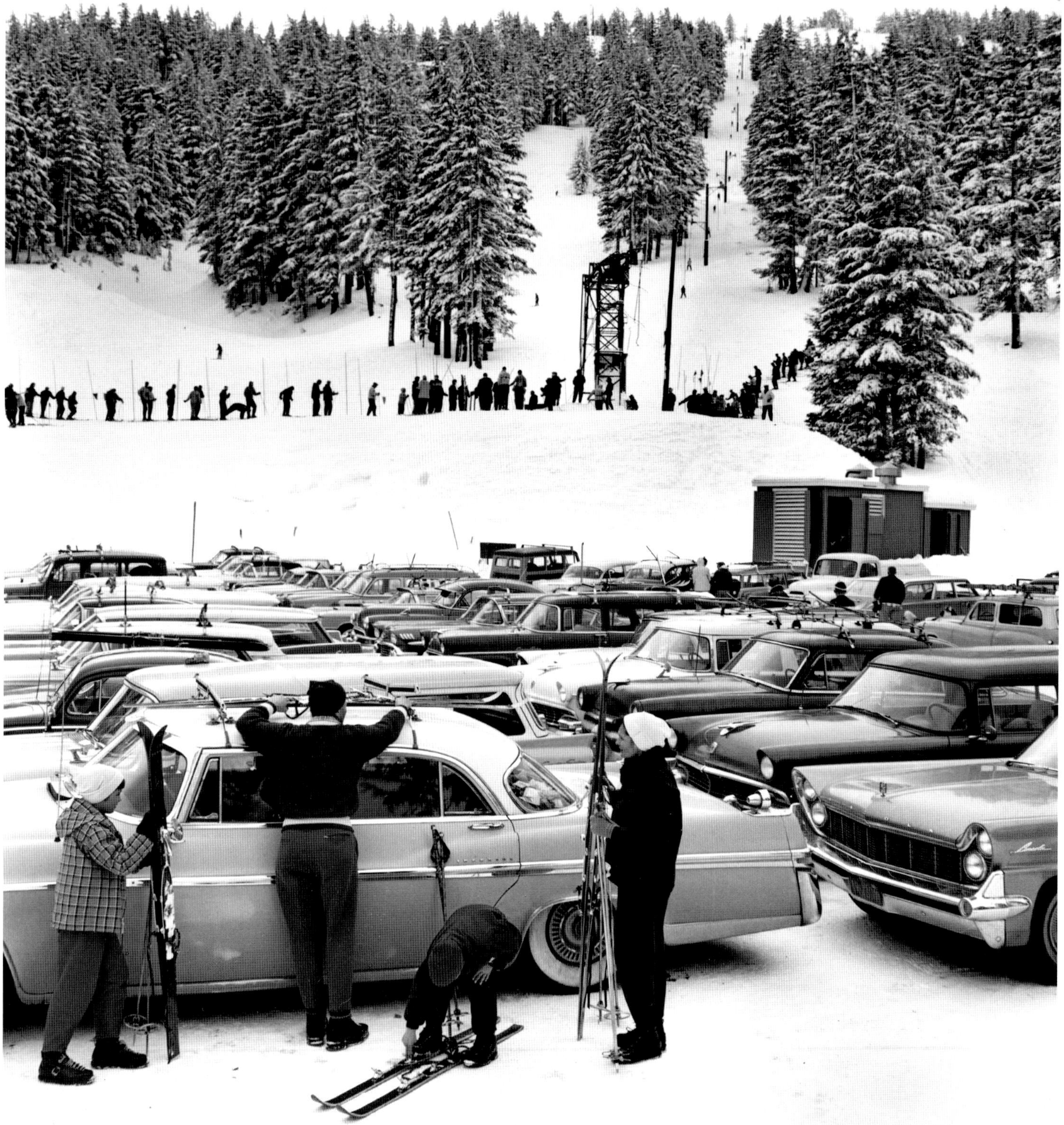

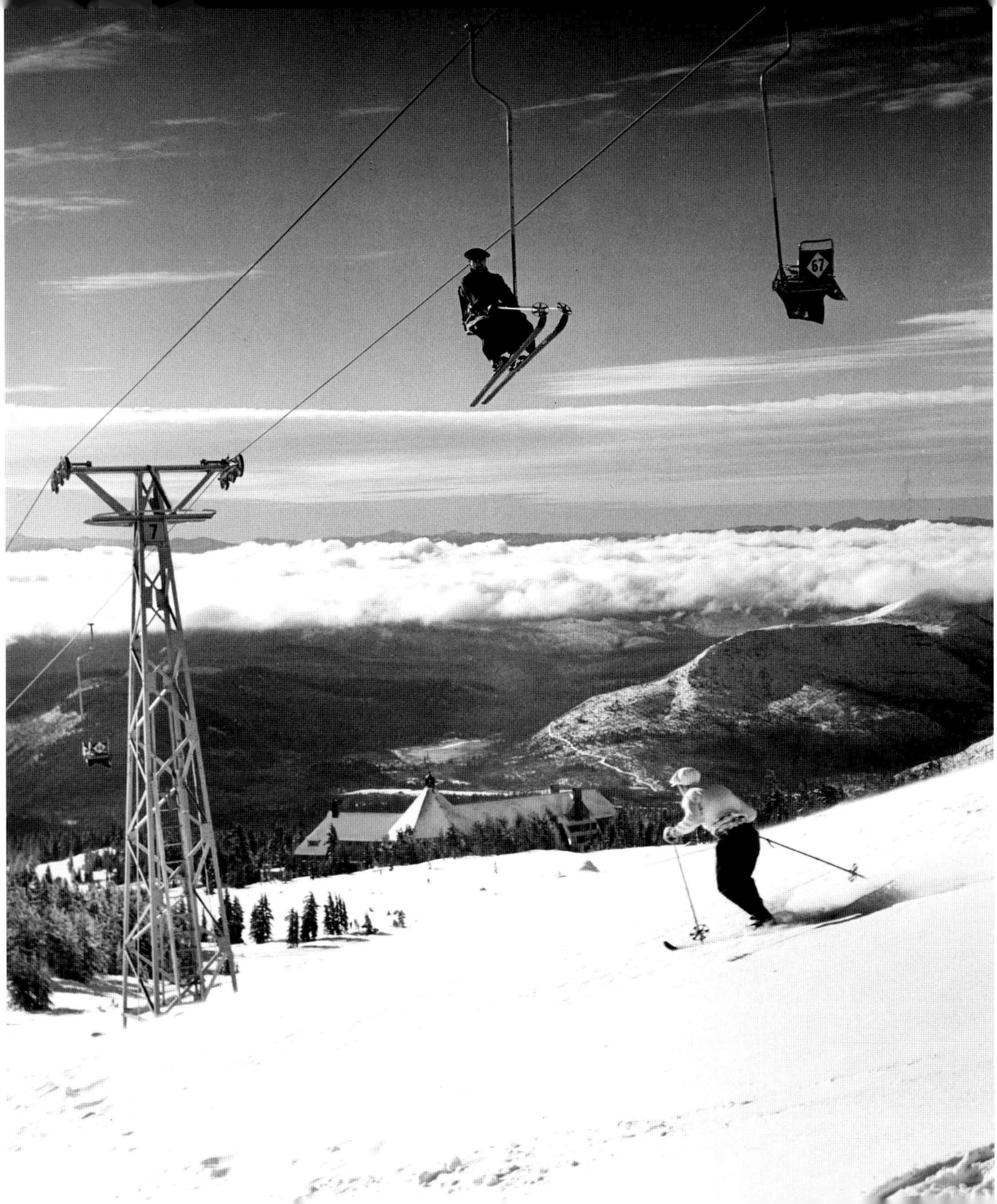
7
67

There's no waiting for friends on a powder day.

AUTHOR UNKNOWN

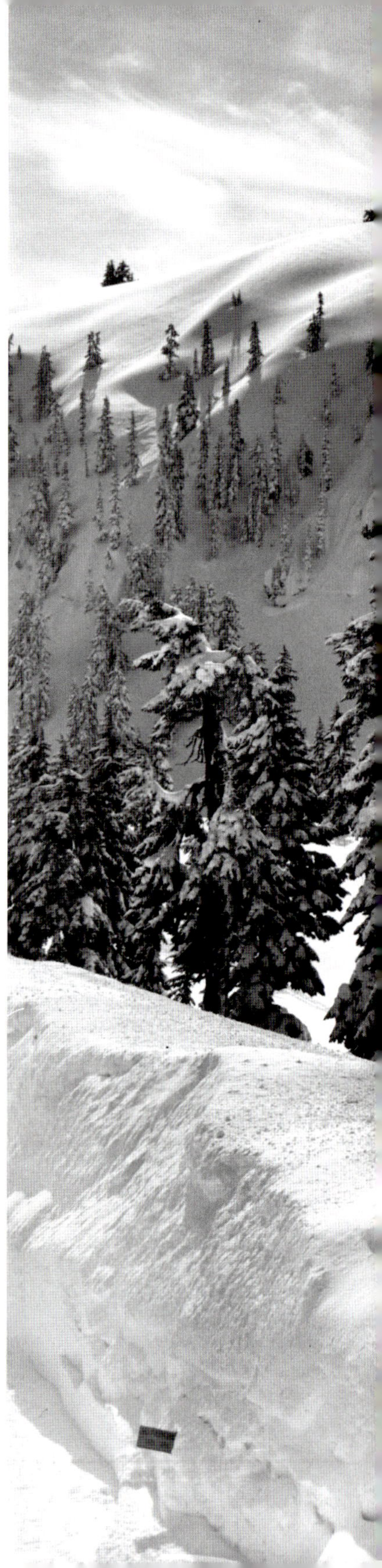

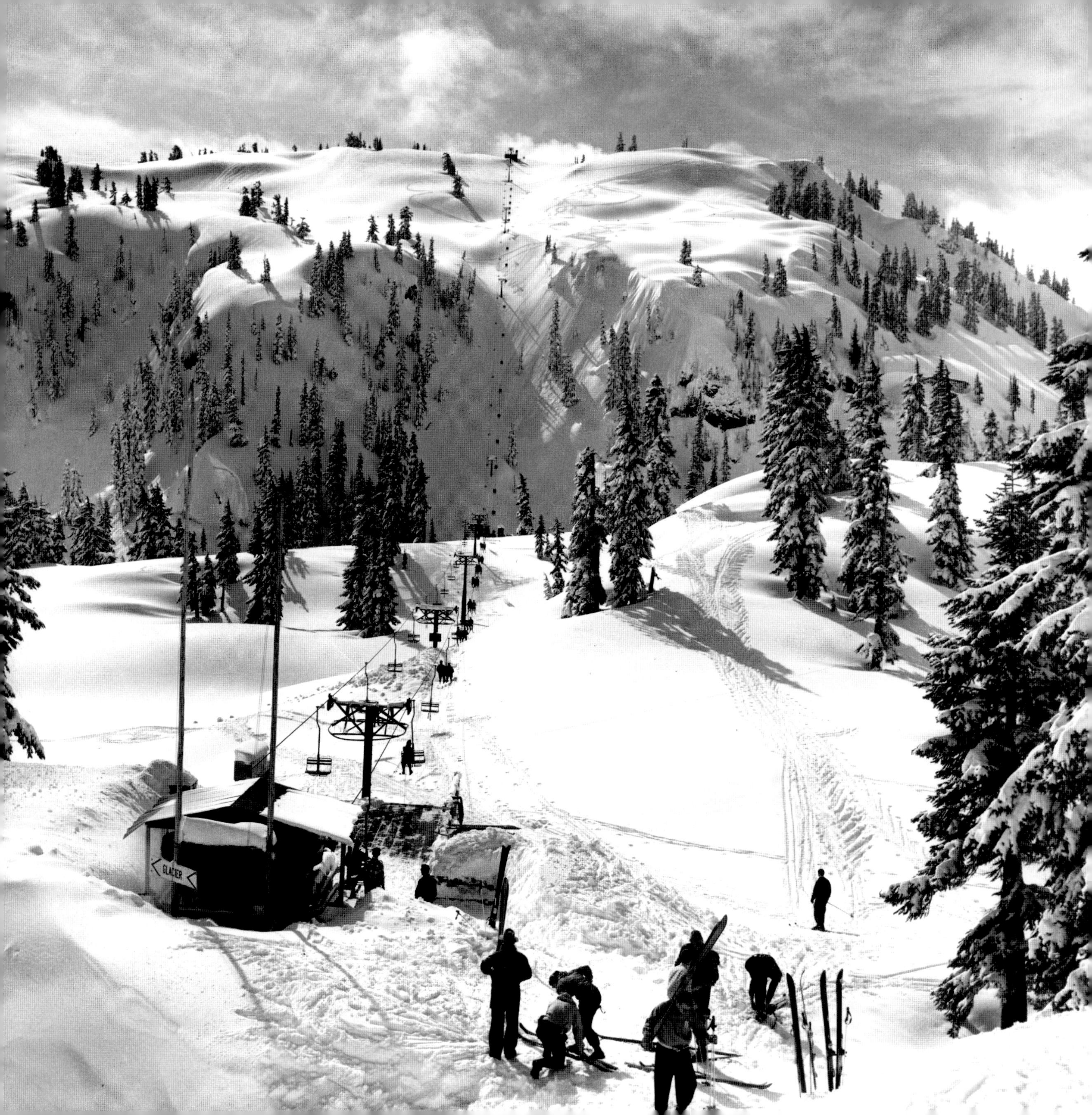
GLACIER

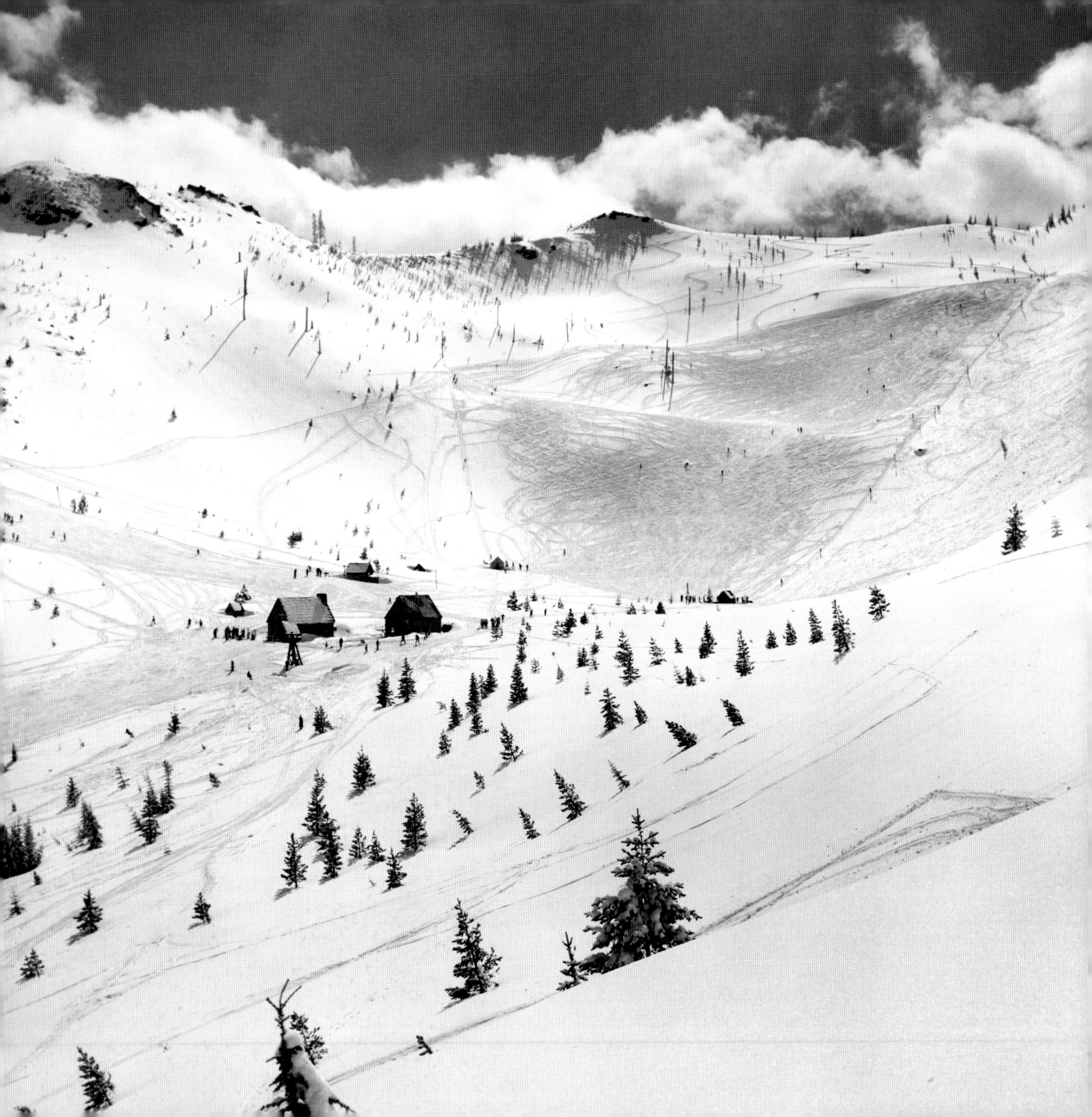

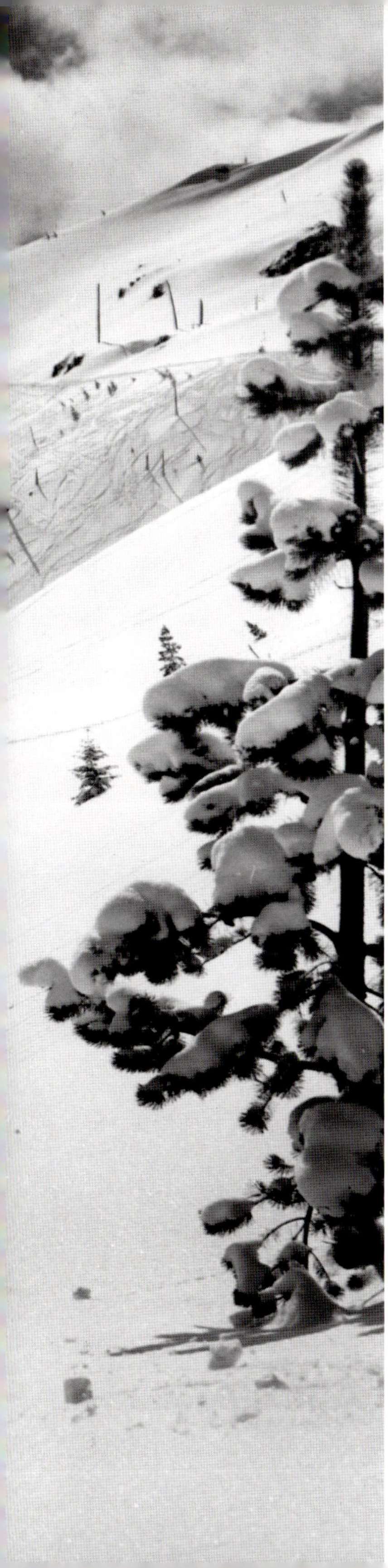

Skis are not just pieces of wood, steel, and fiberglass. They are tools for escape, a medium for personal expression, a way to challenge fears, push limits, and share incredible experiences with your friends.

AUTHOR UNKNOWN

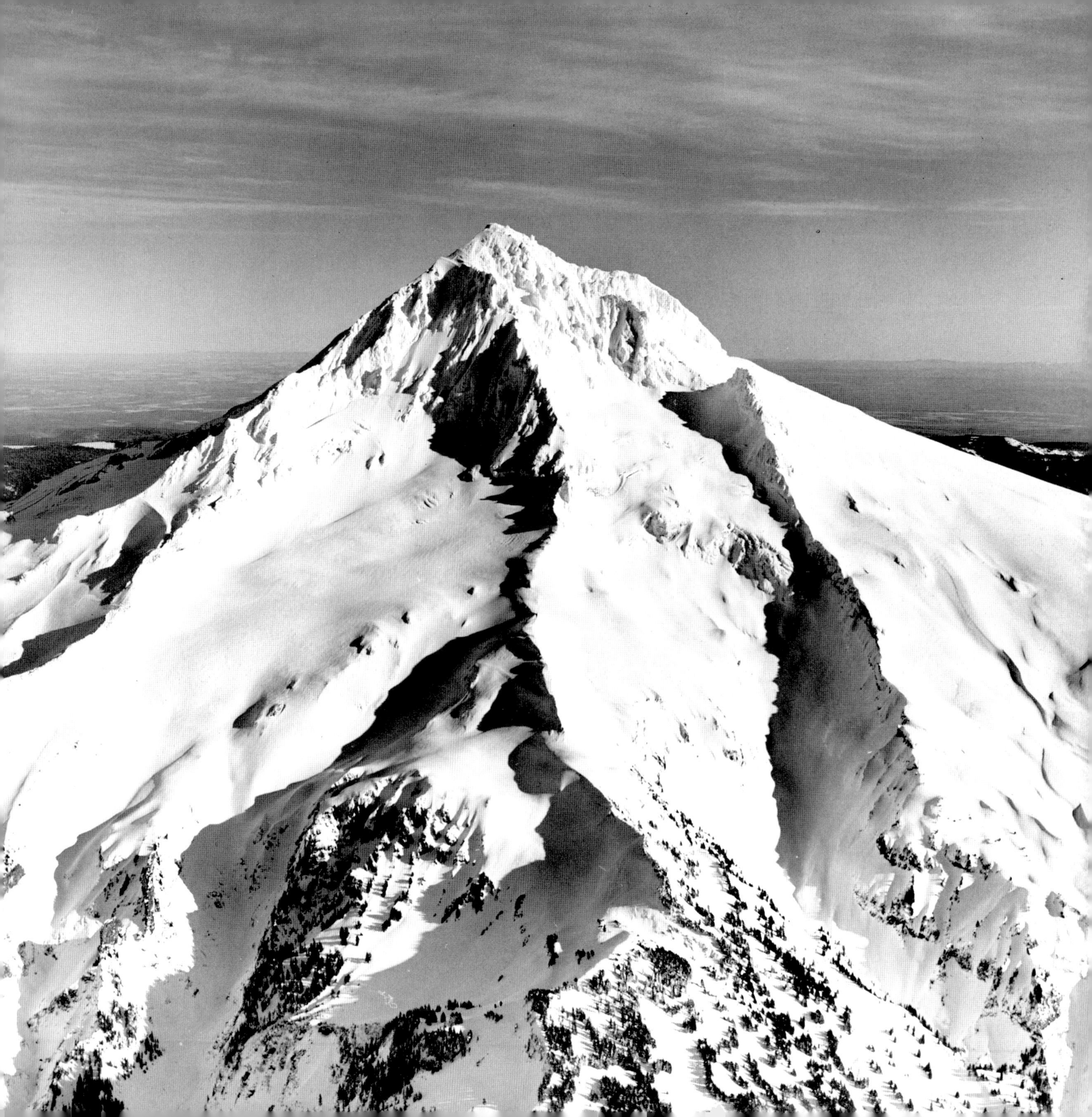

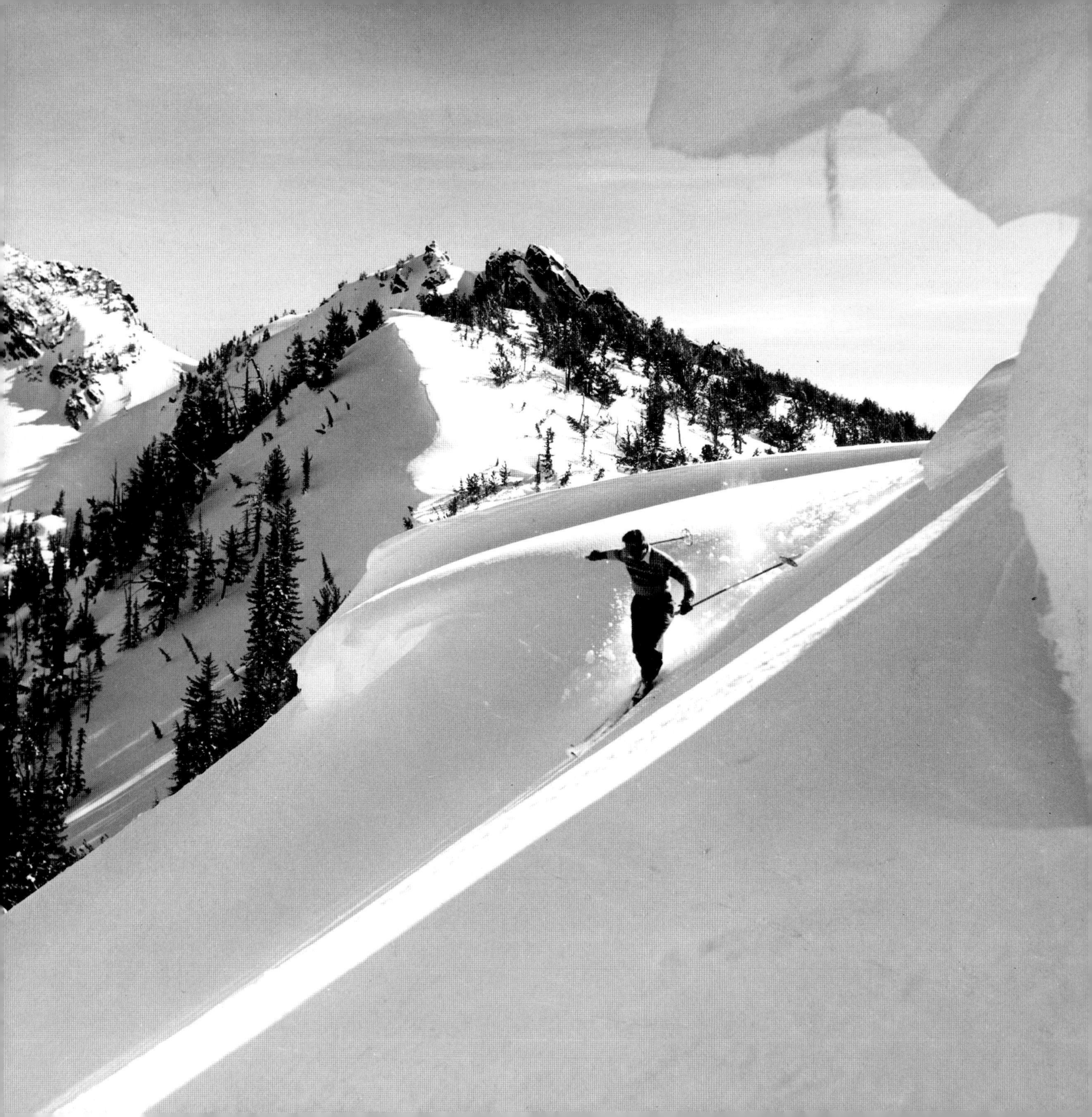

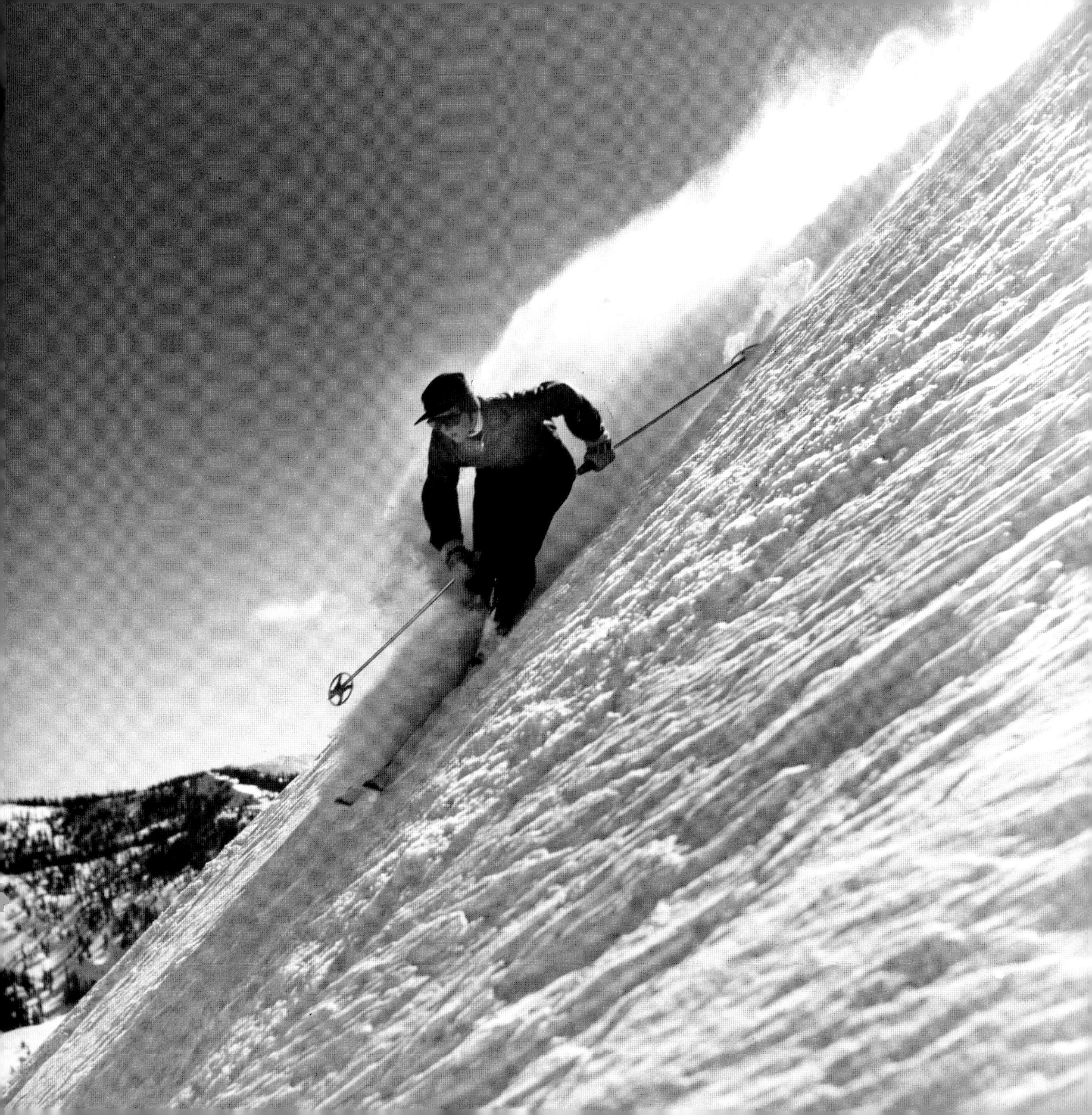

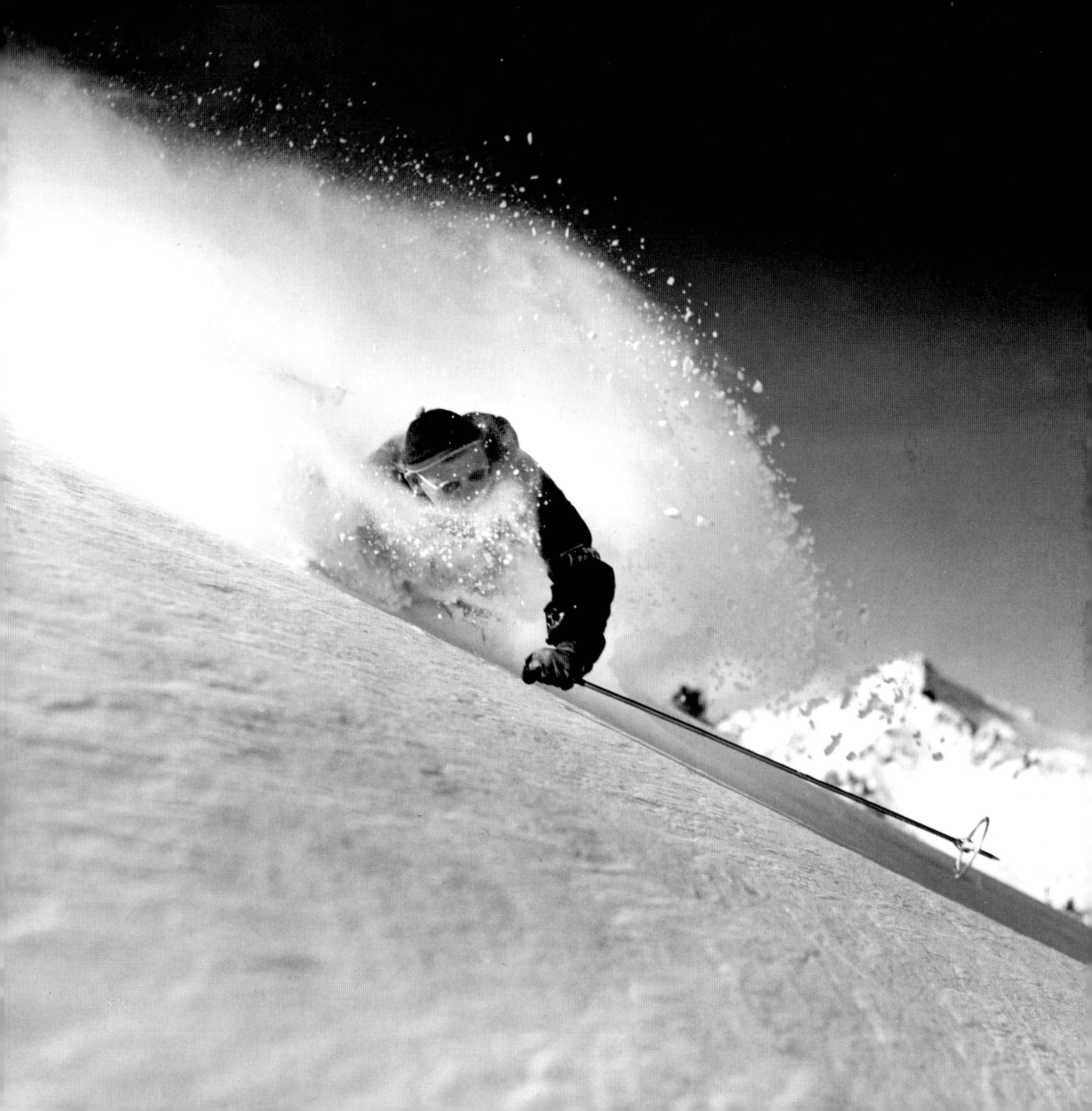

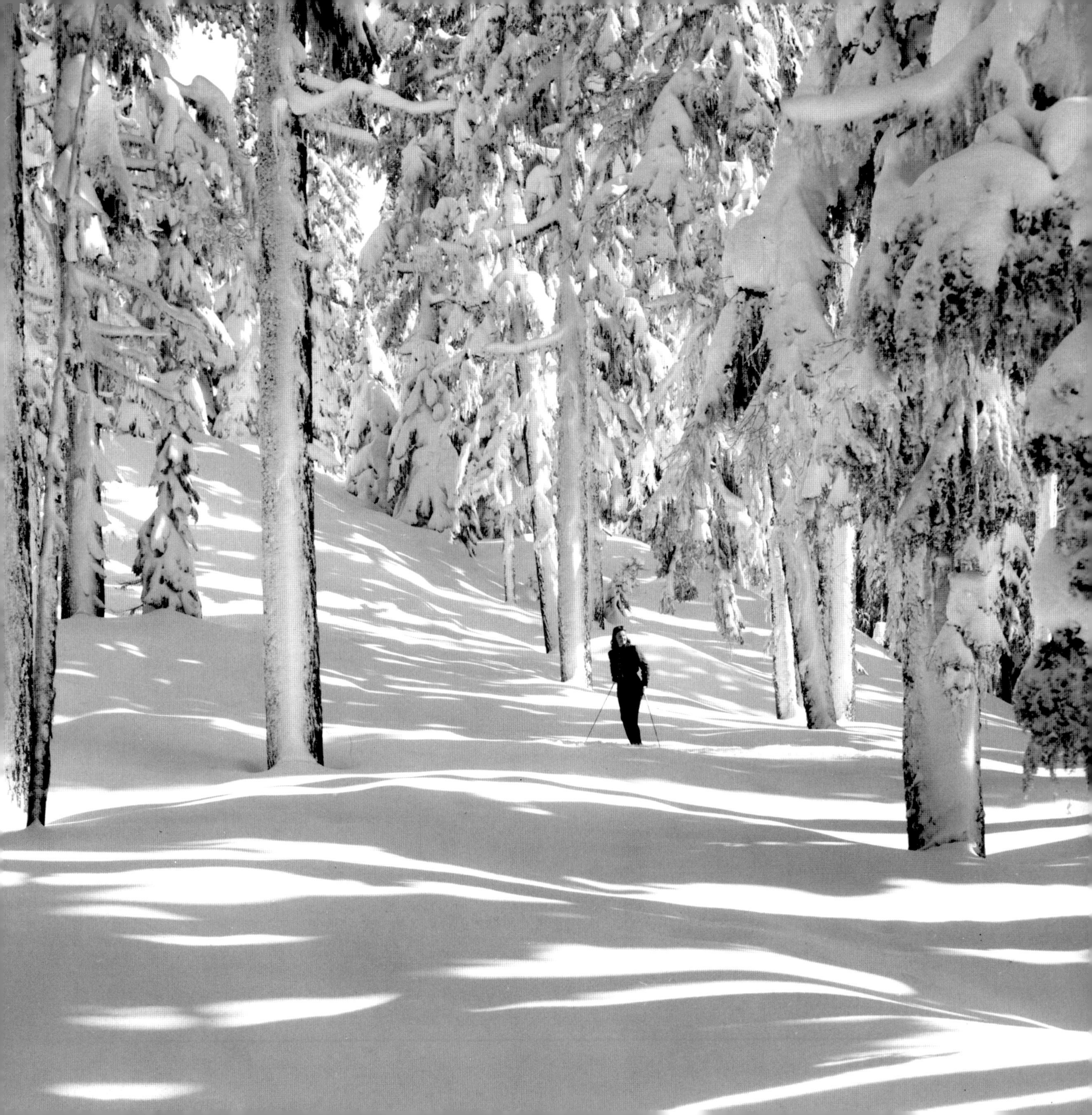

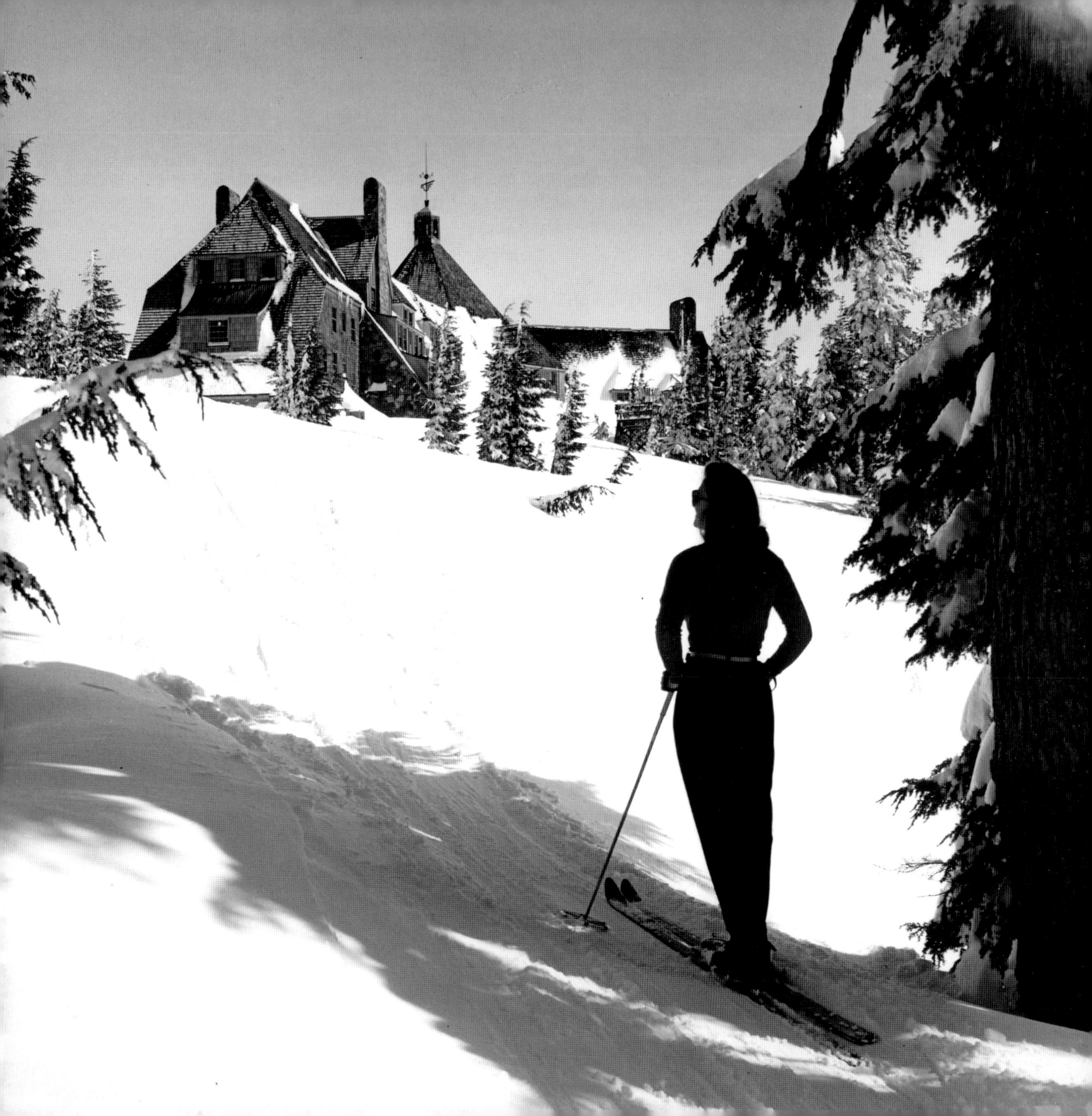

It is better to go skiing and think of God,
than go to church and think of sport.

FREDTJOF NANSEN

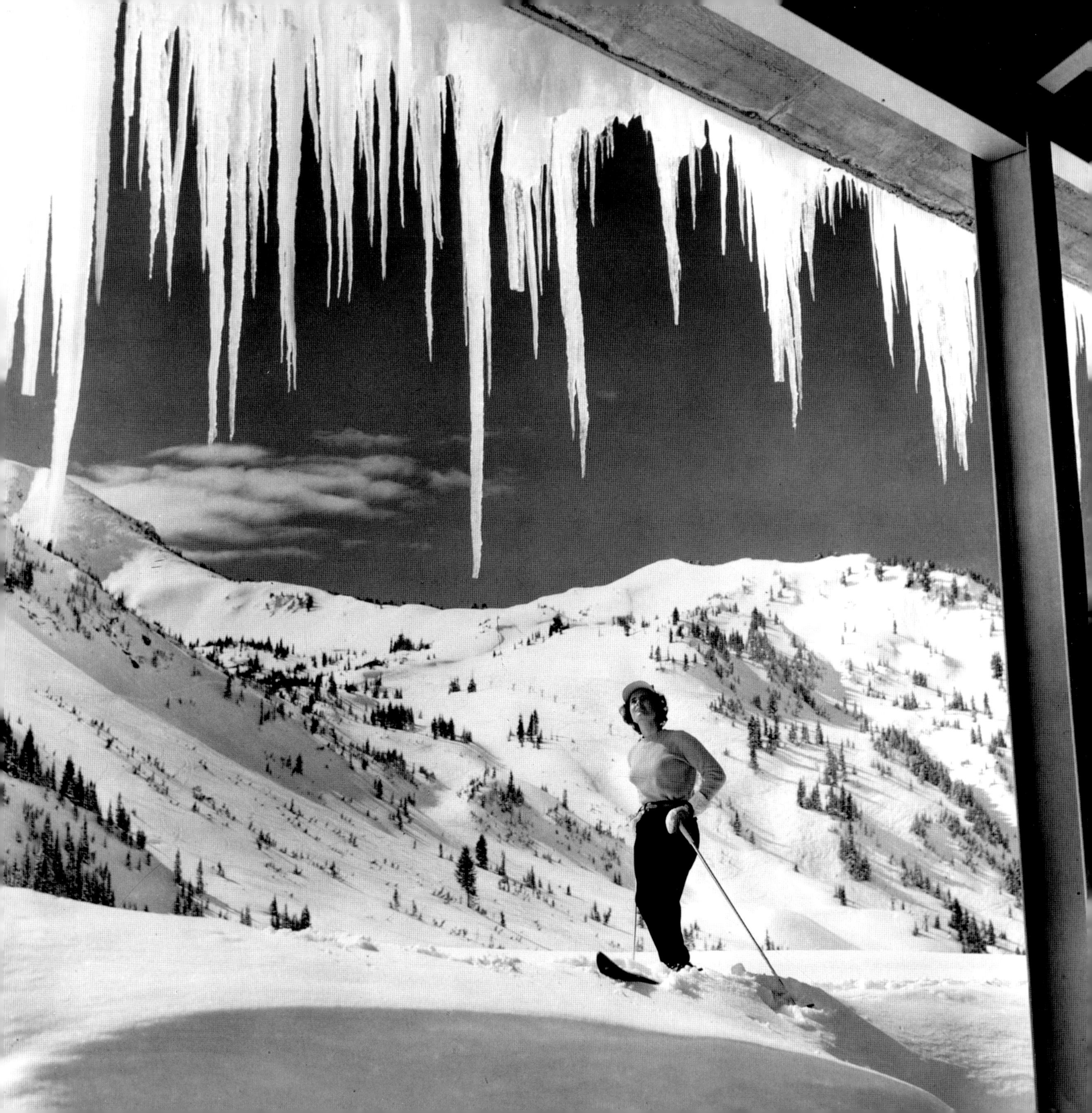

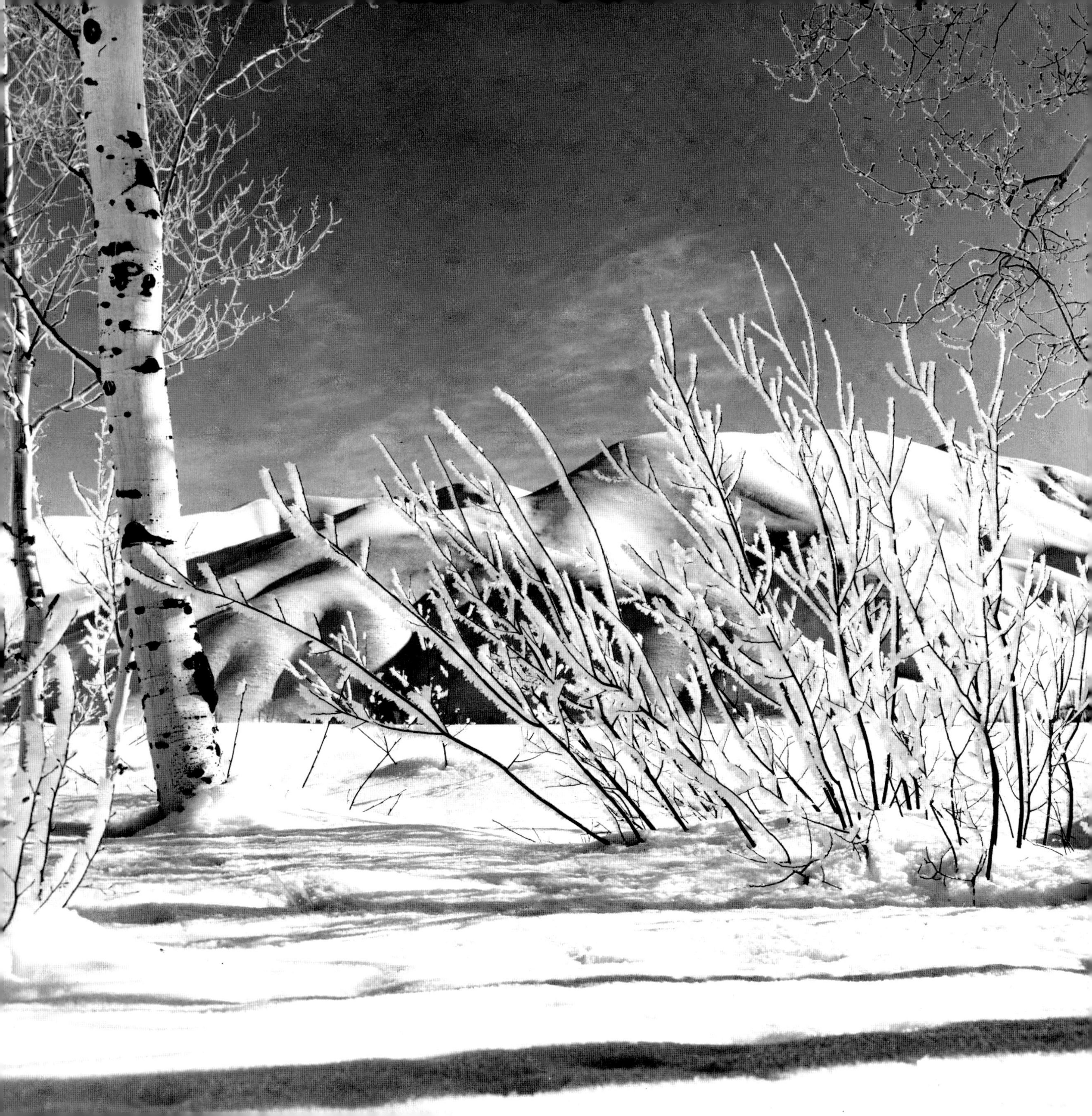

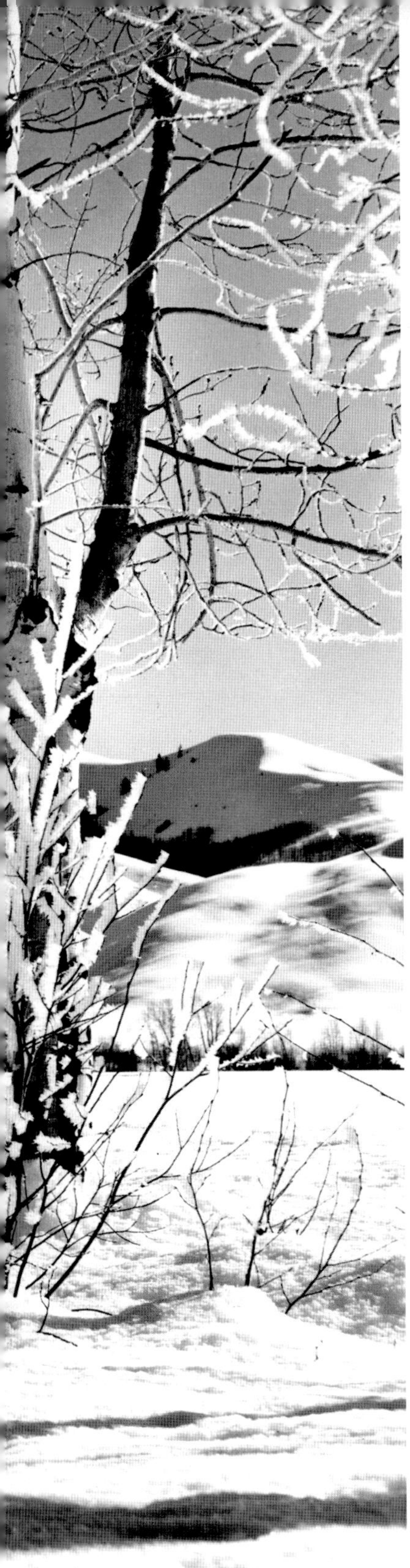
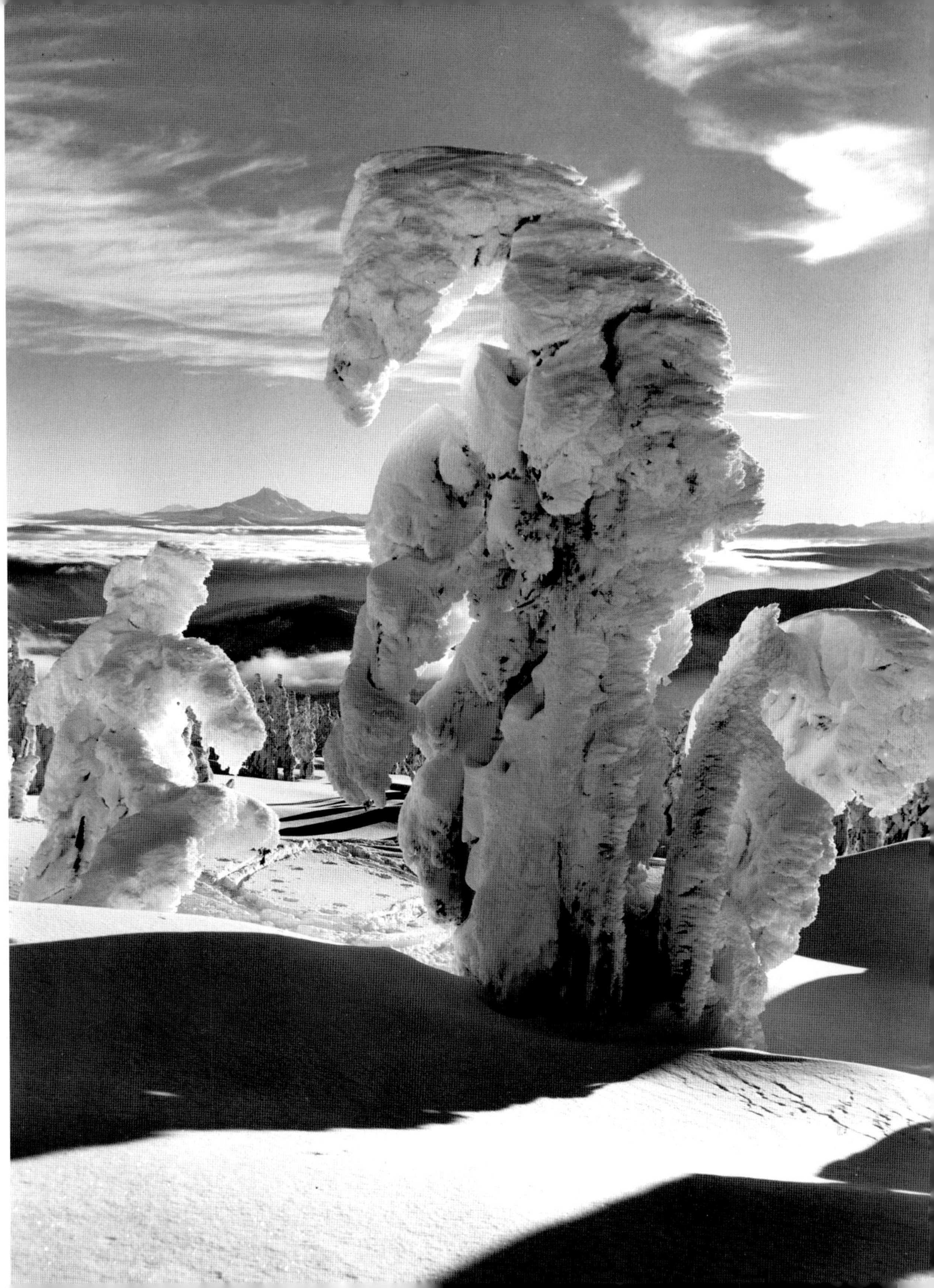

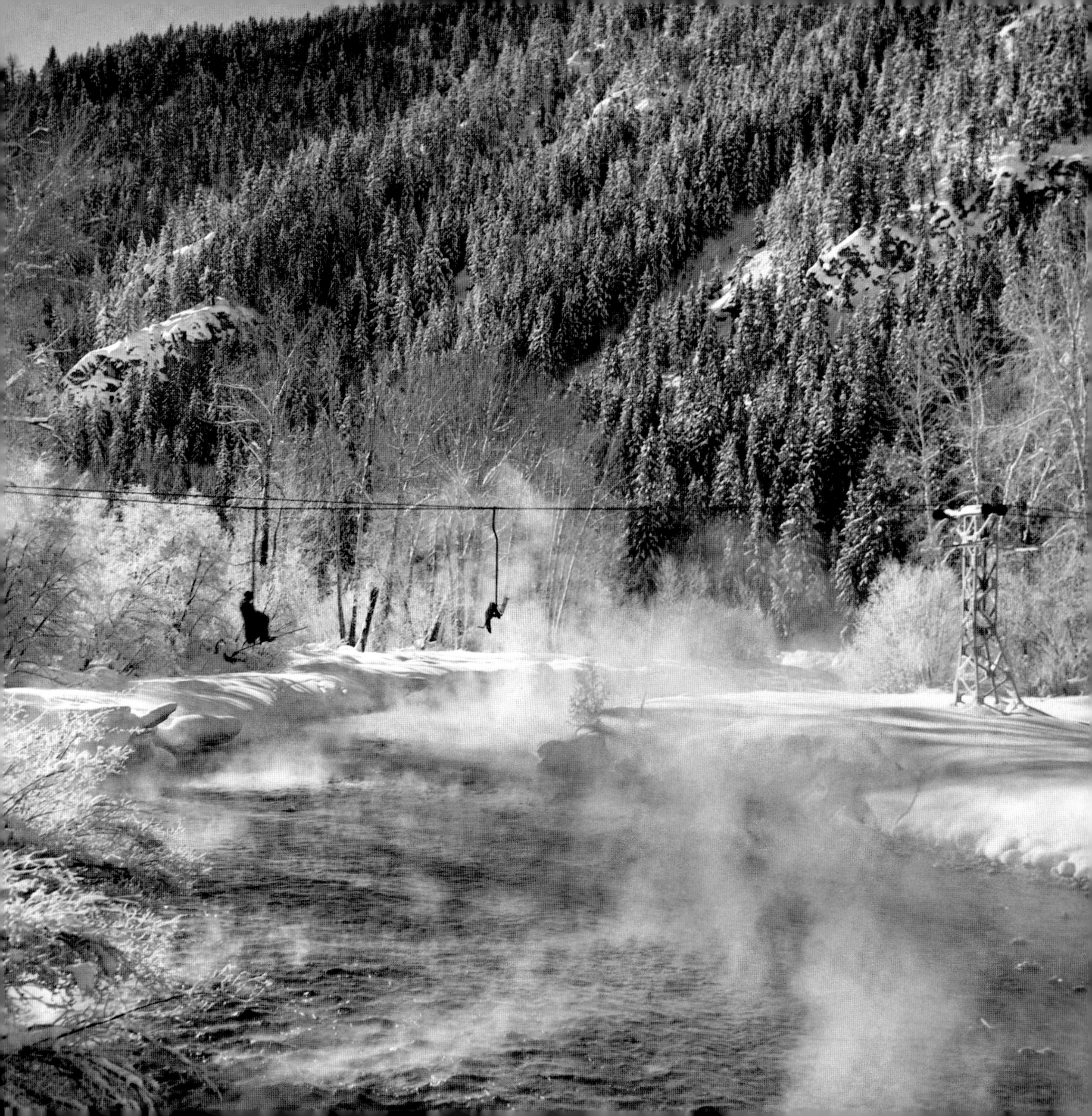

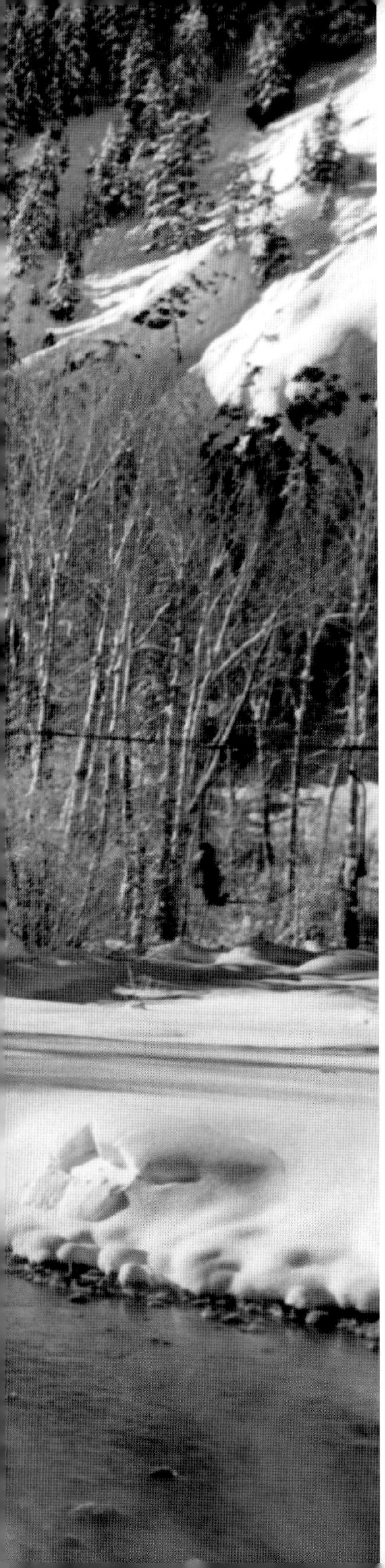
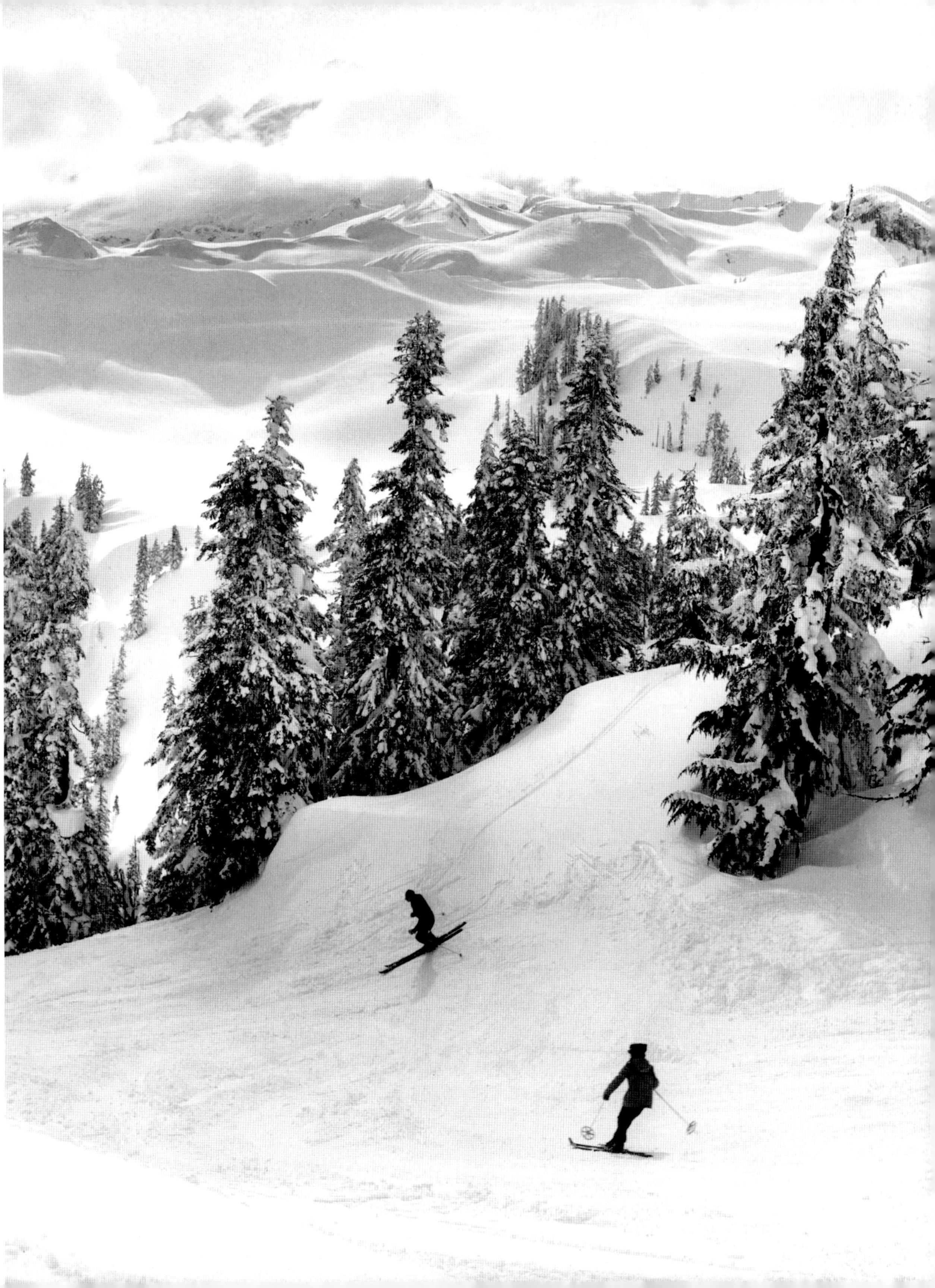

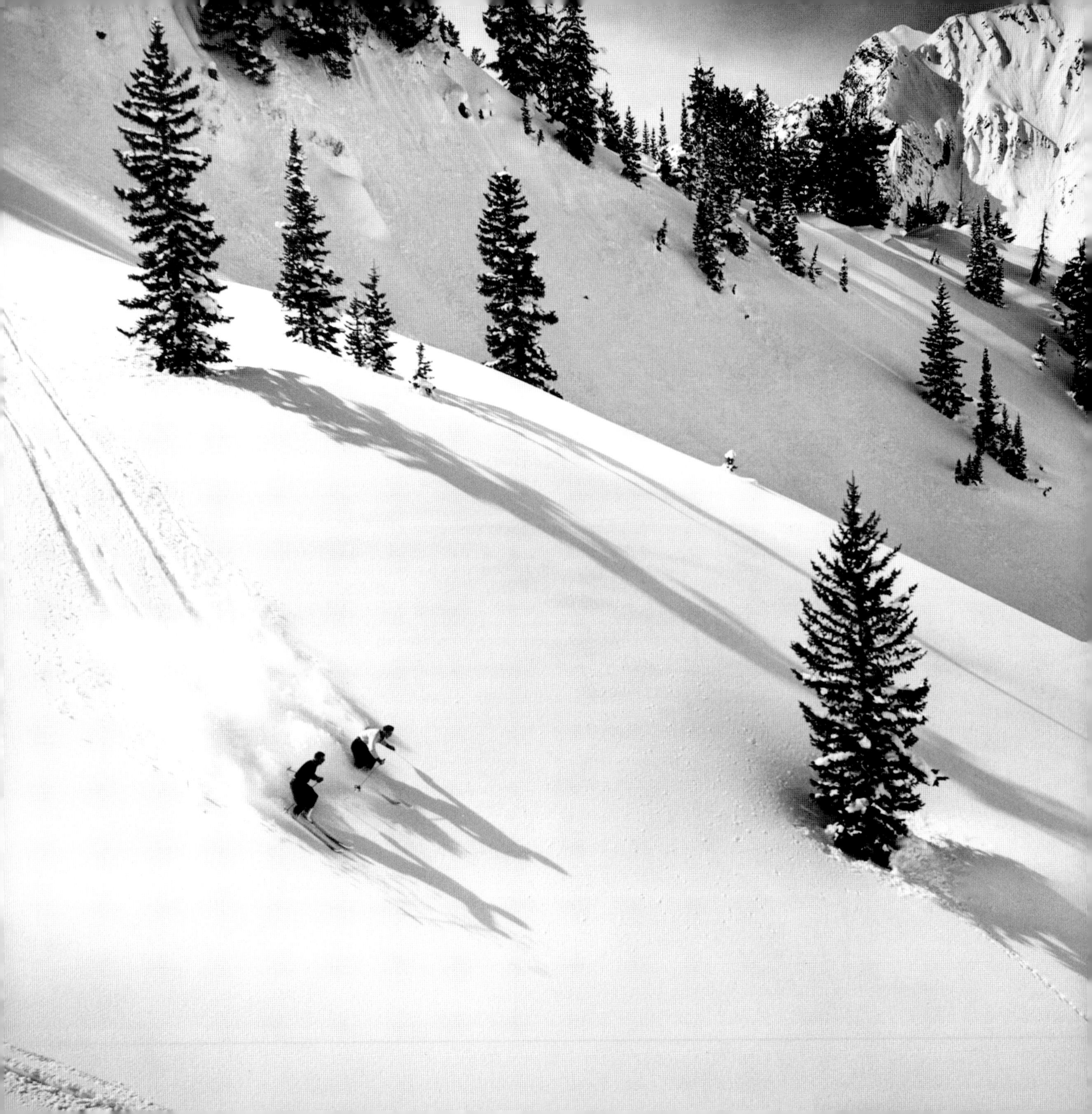

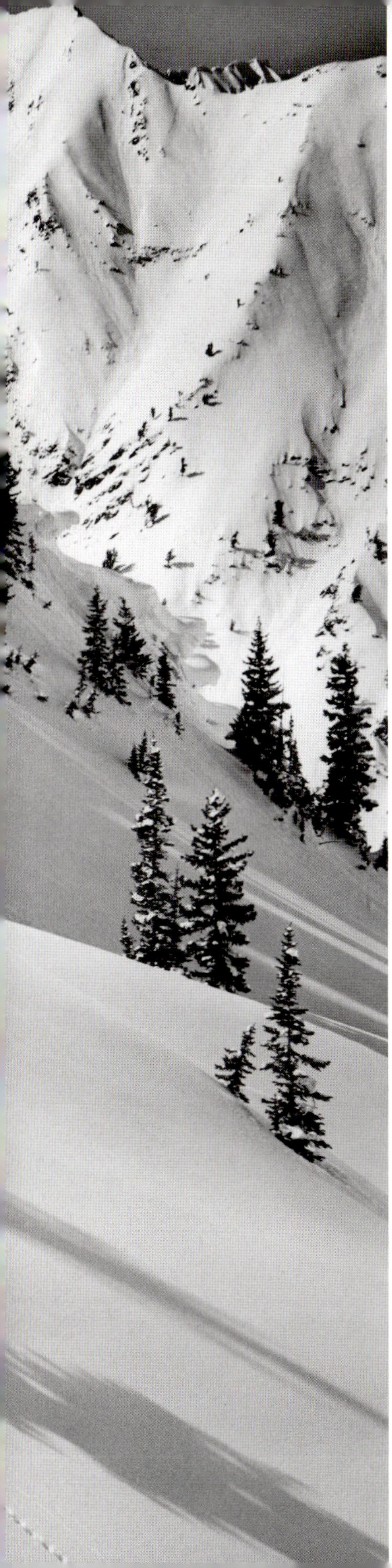

Powder skiing is not fun.
It's life fully lived,
life lived in a blaze of reality.

DOLORES LACHAPELLE

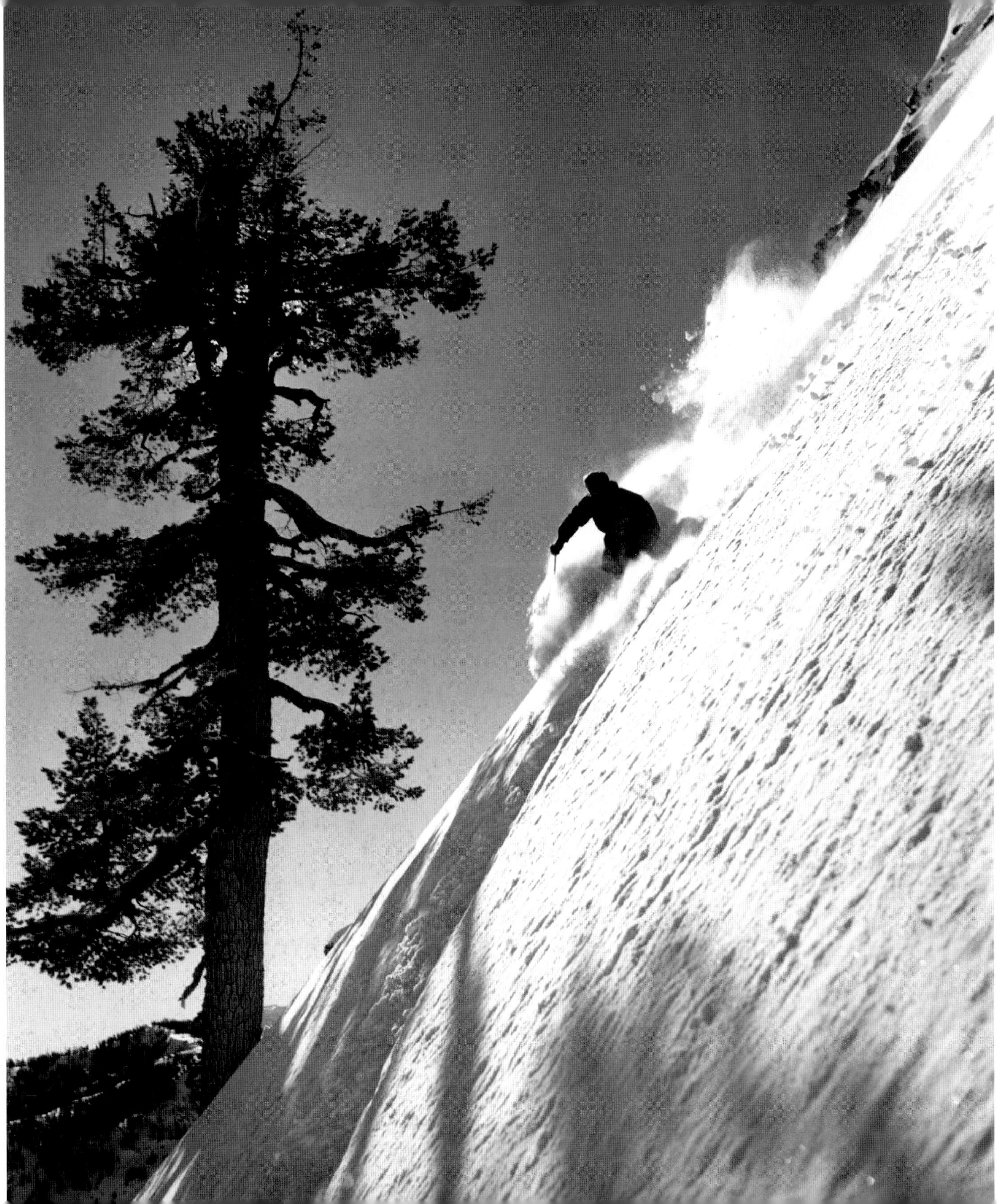

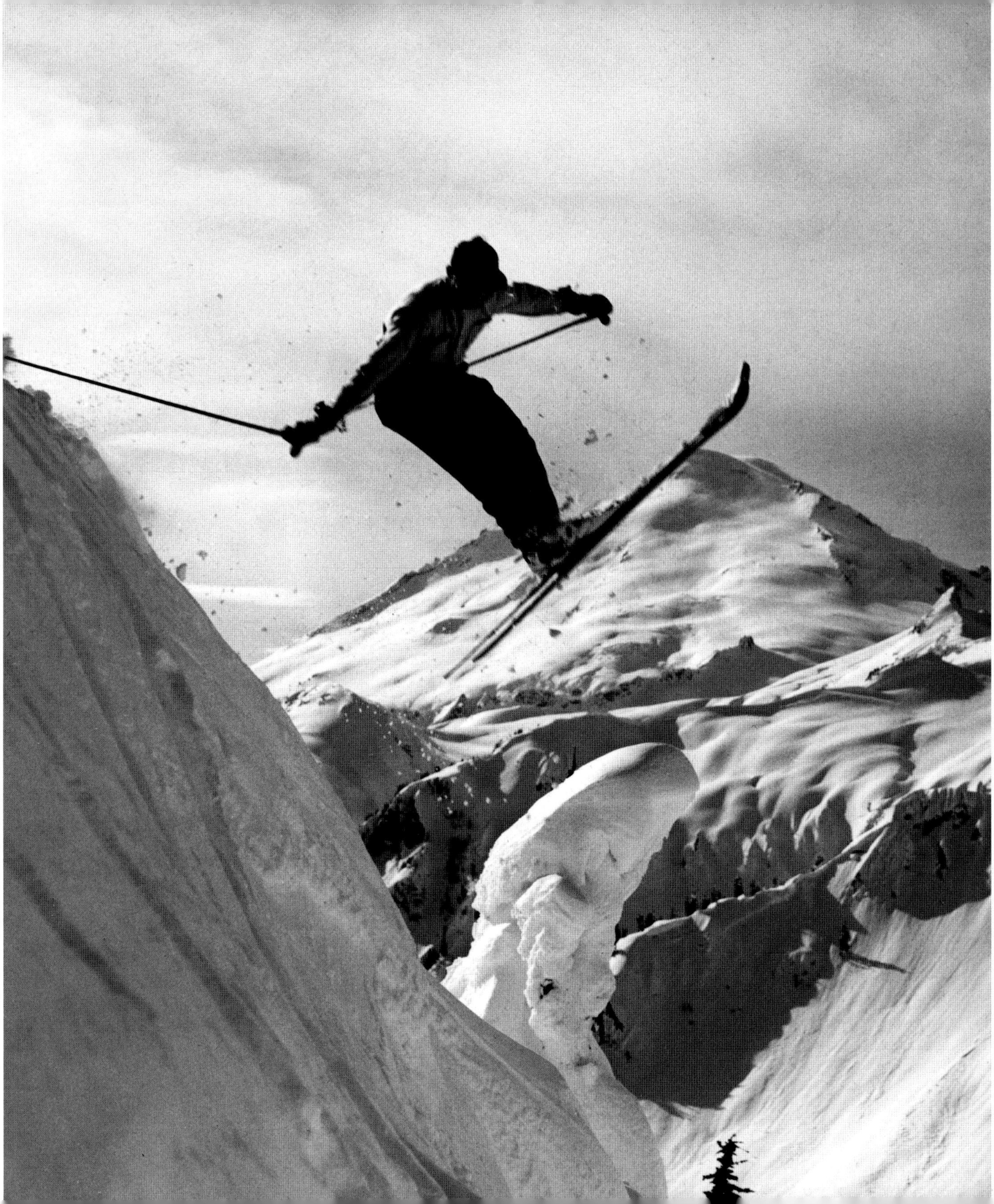

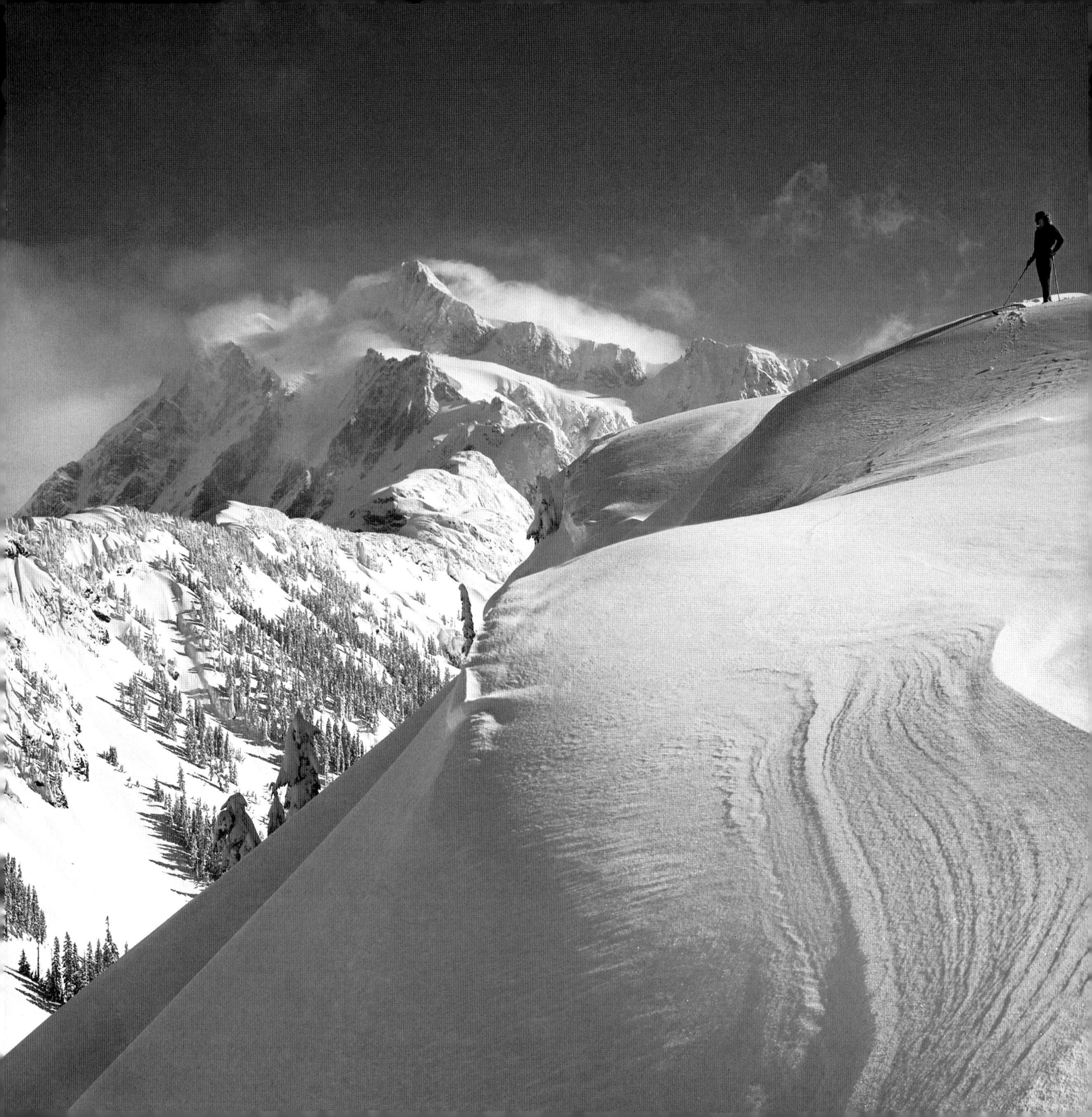

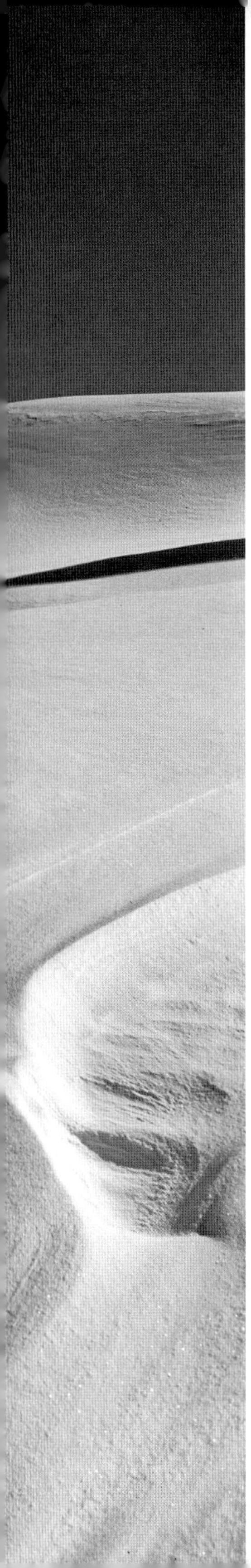

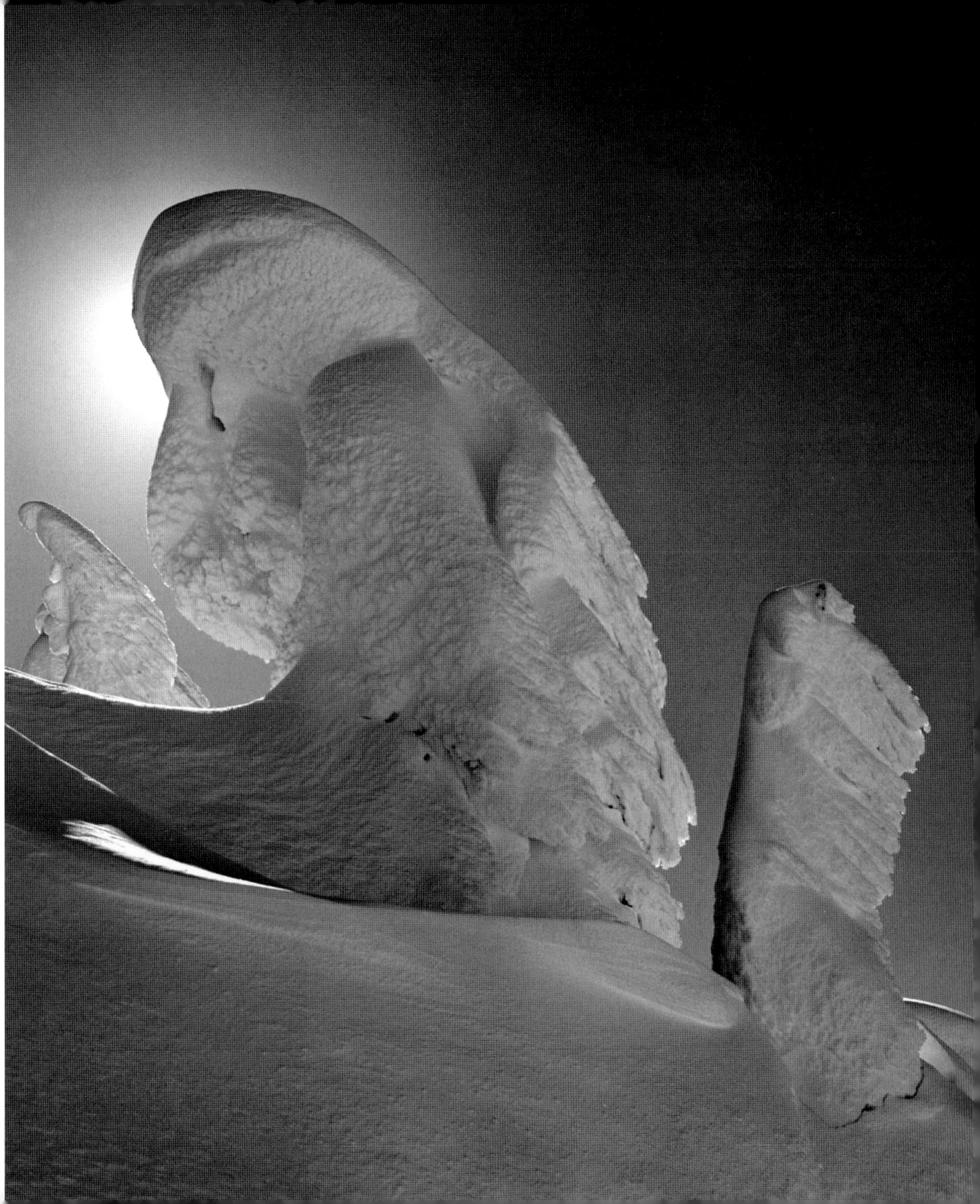

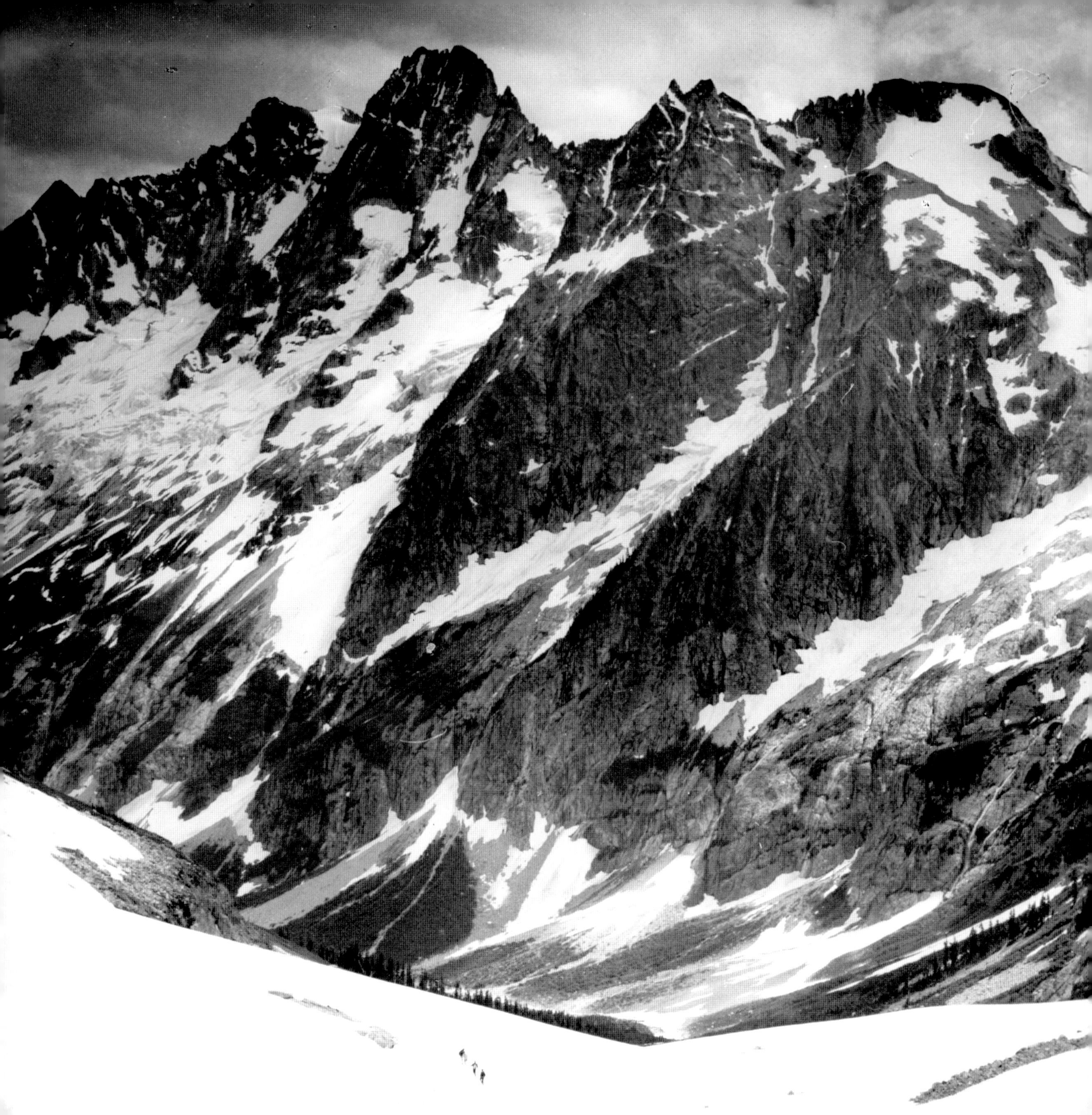

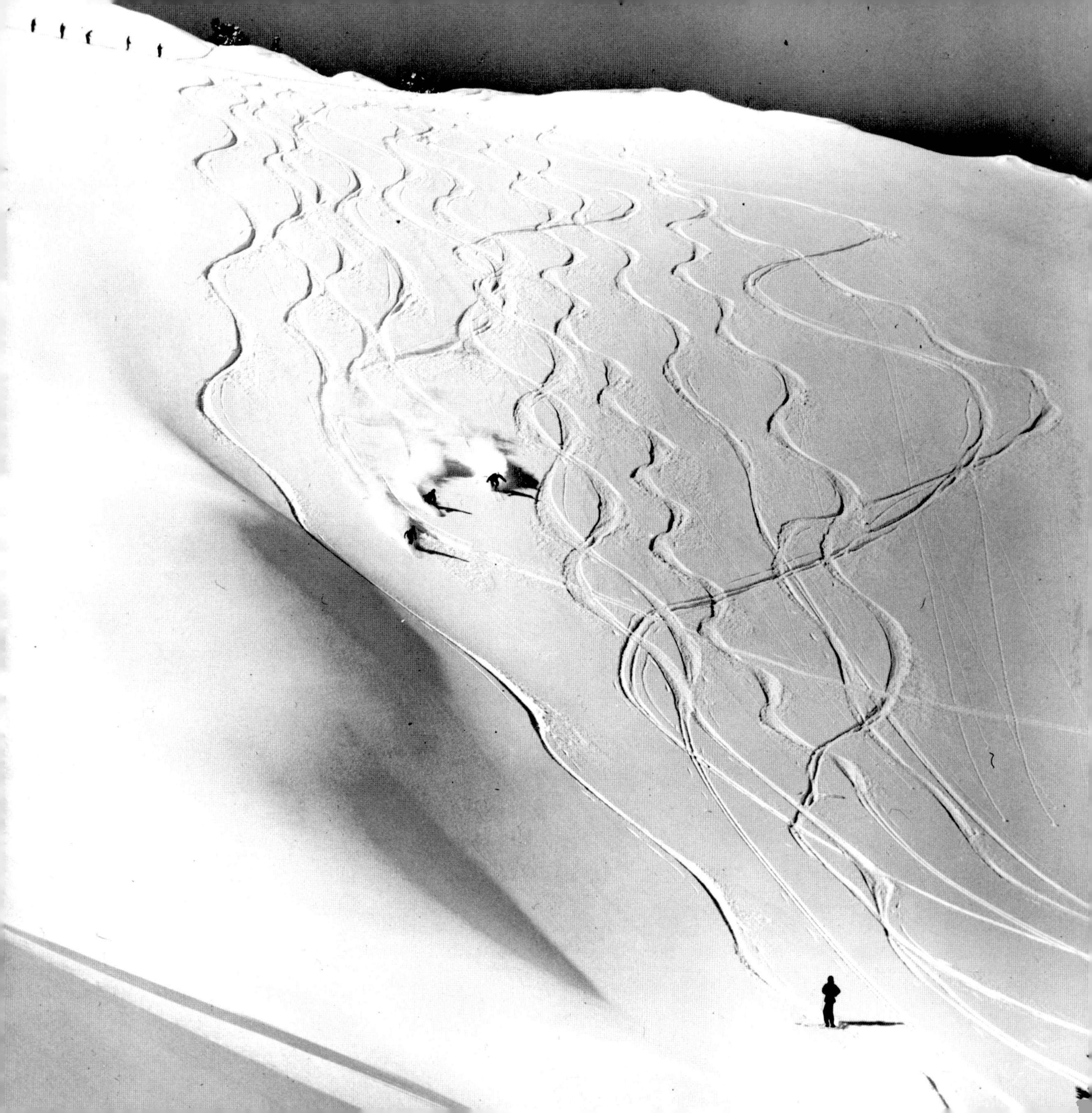

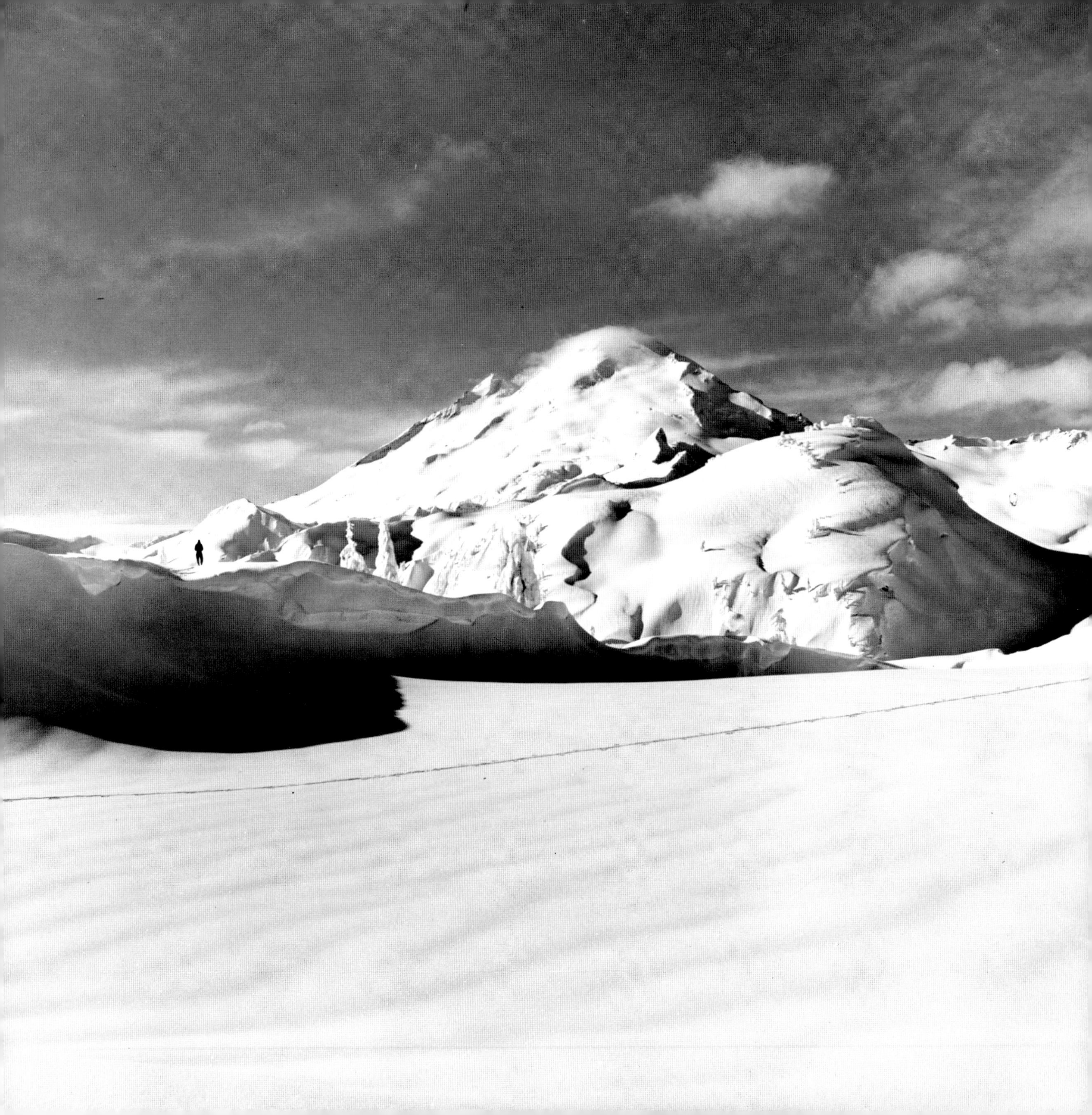

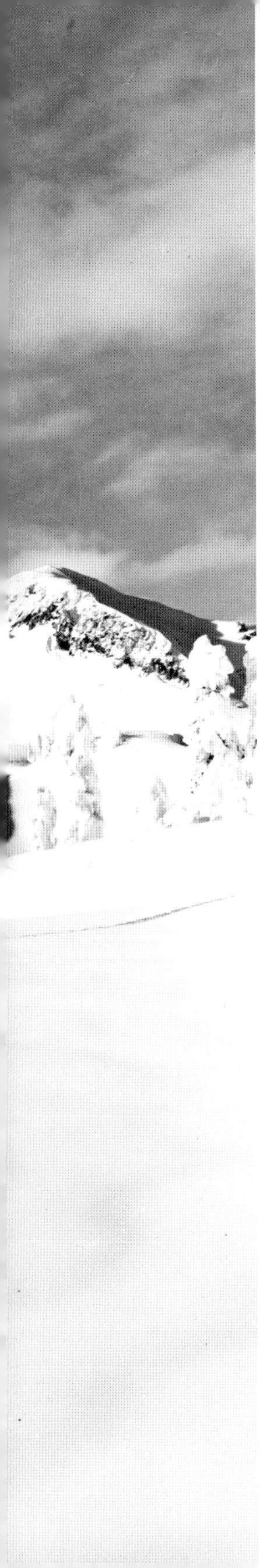

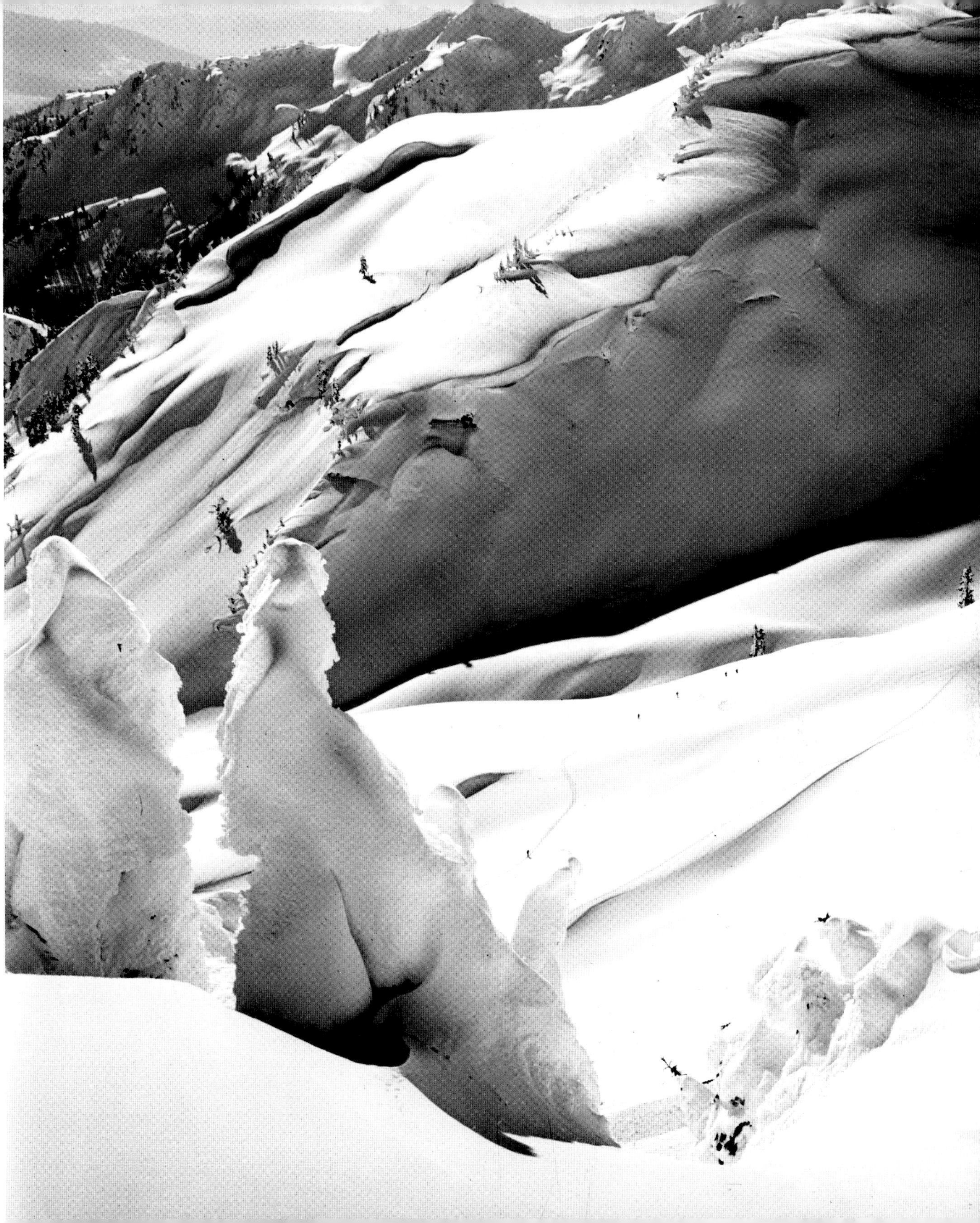

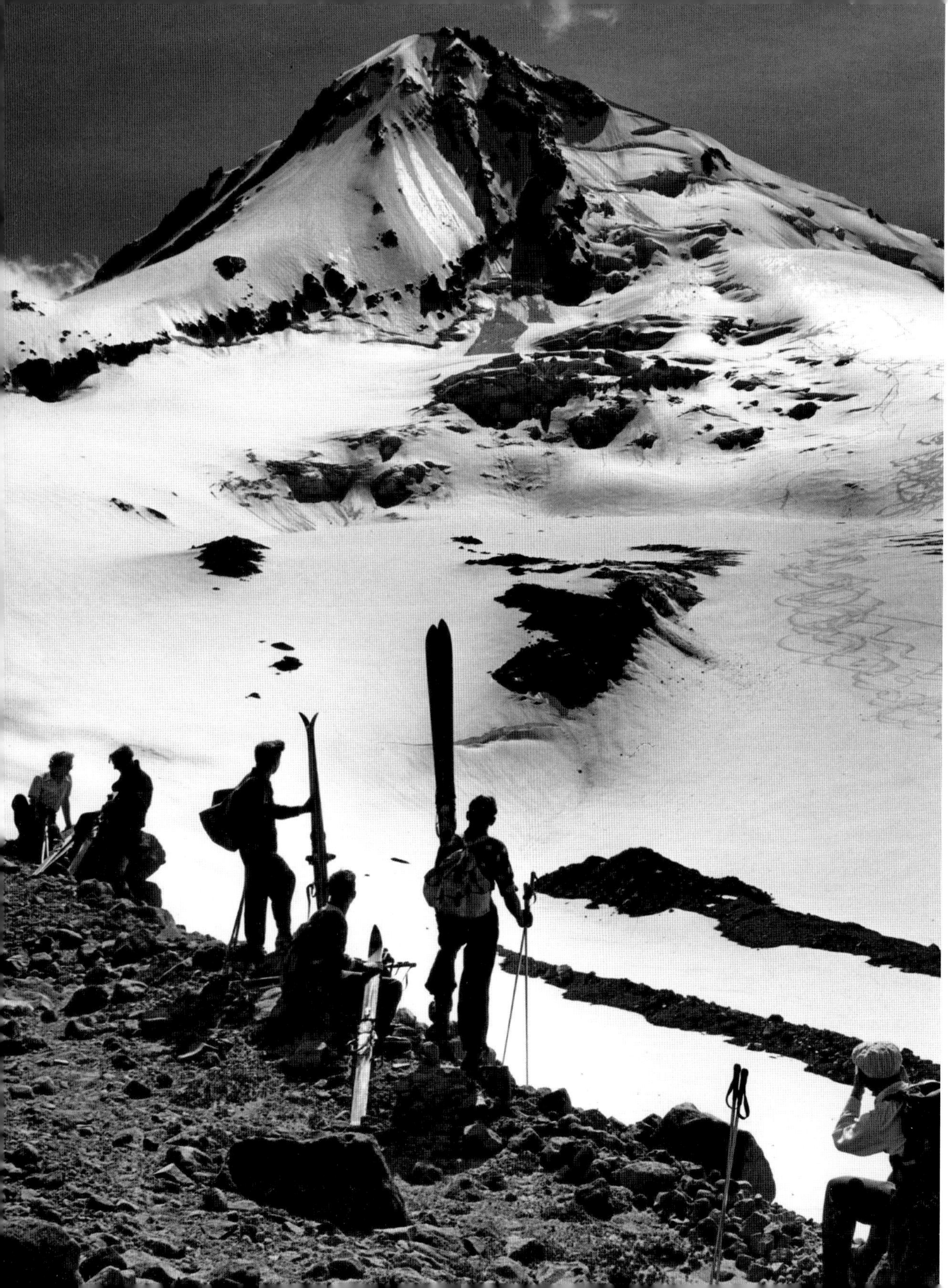

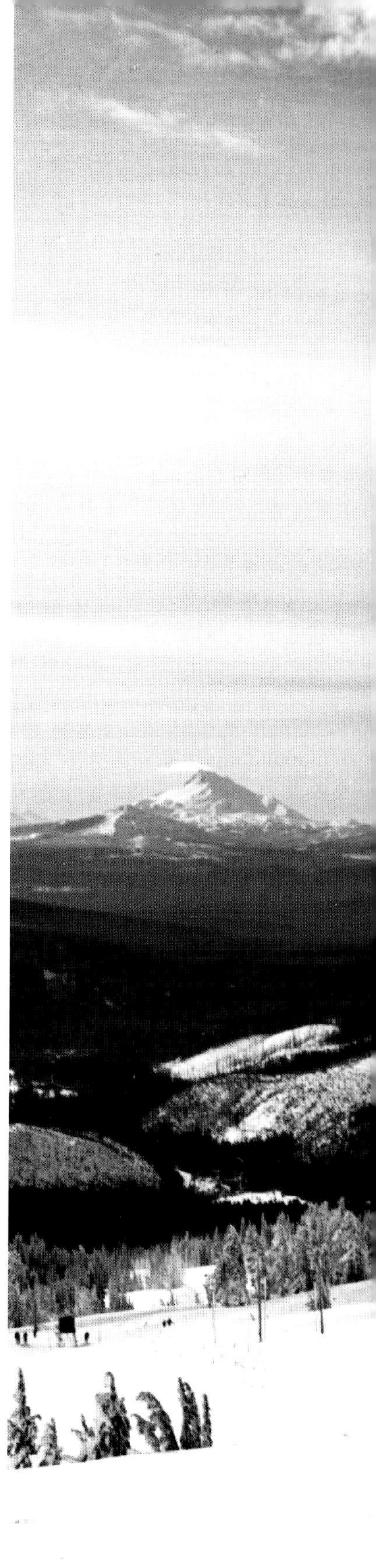

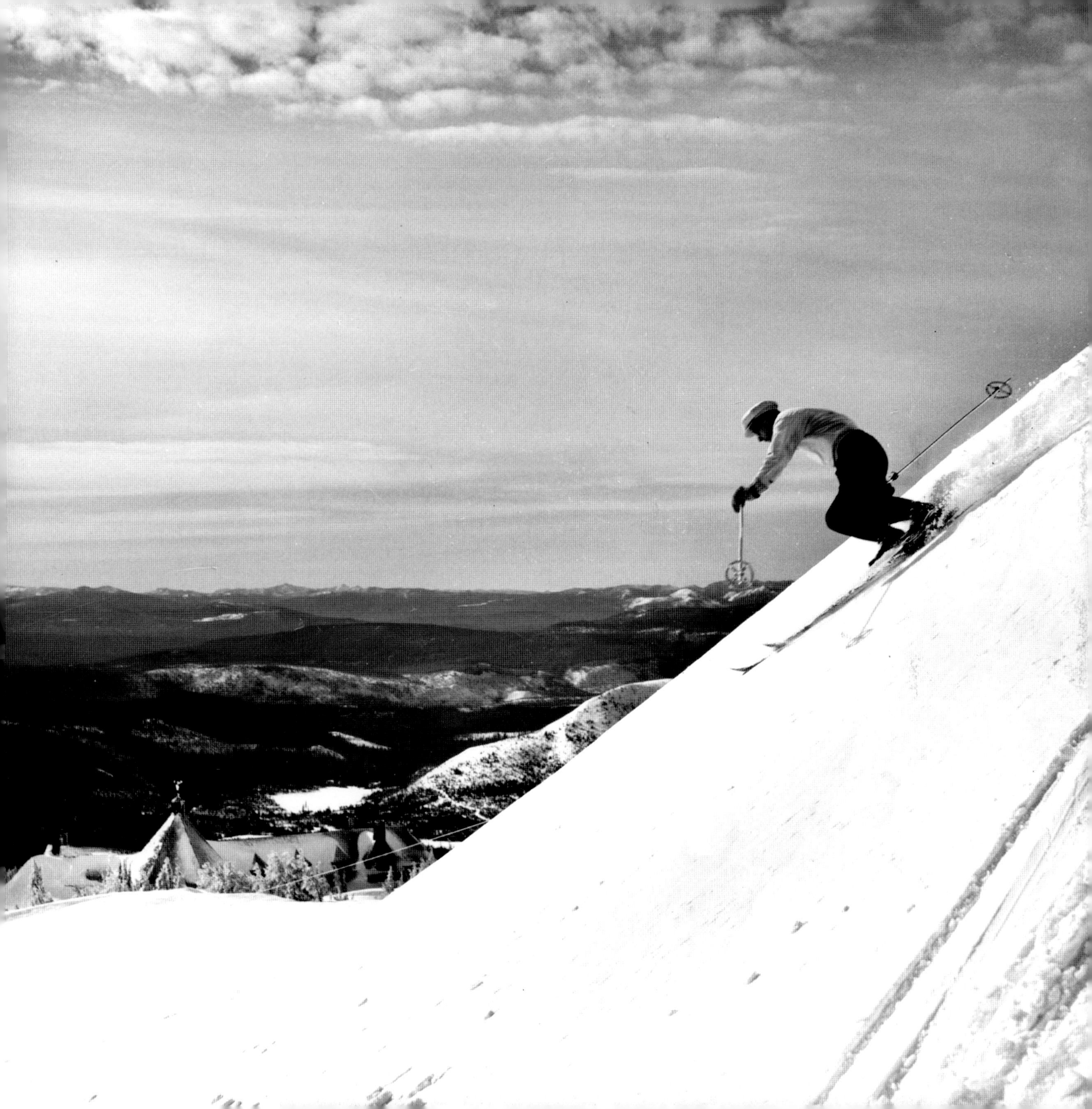

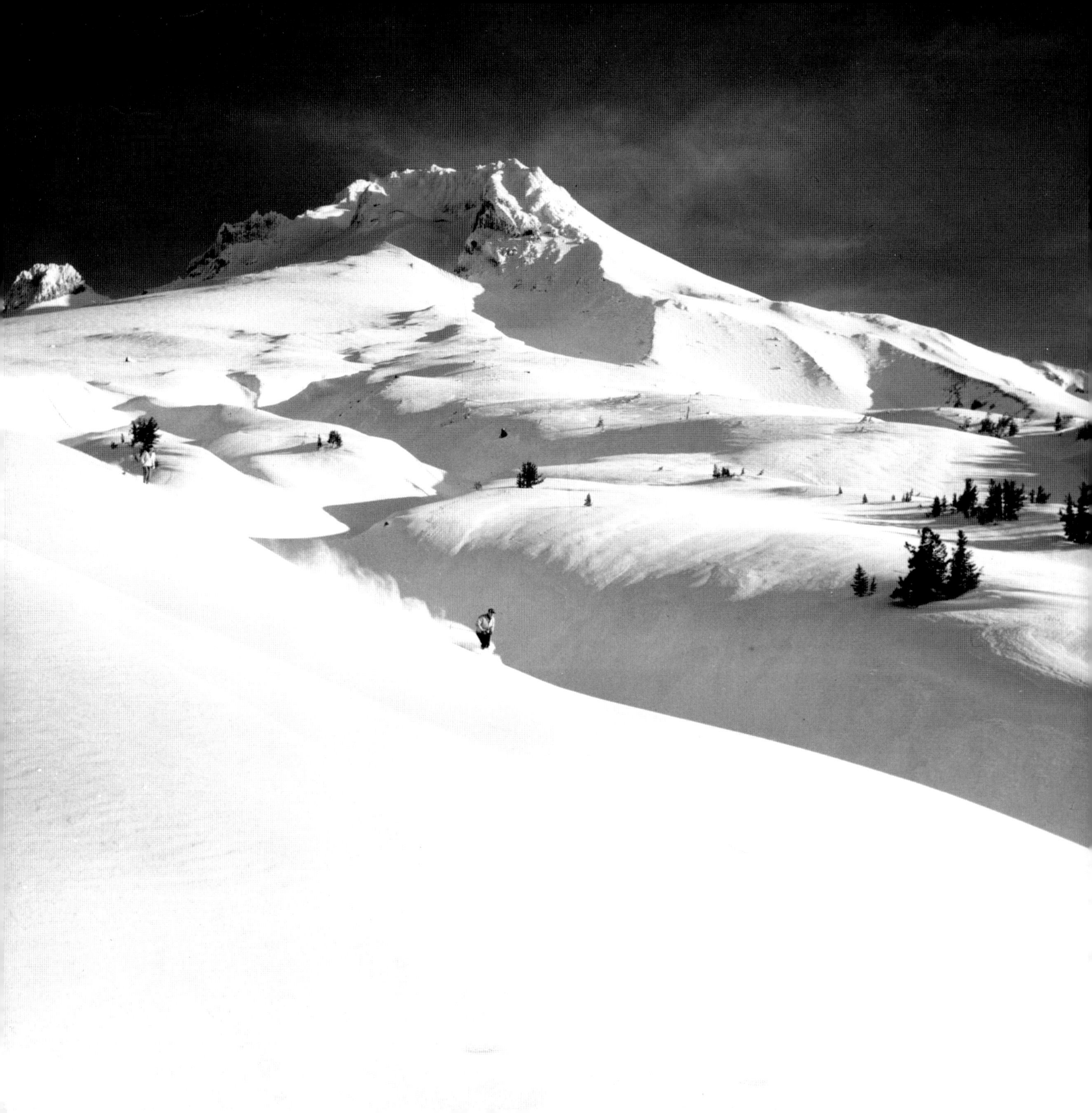

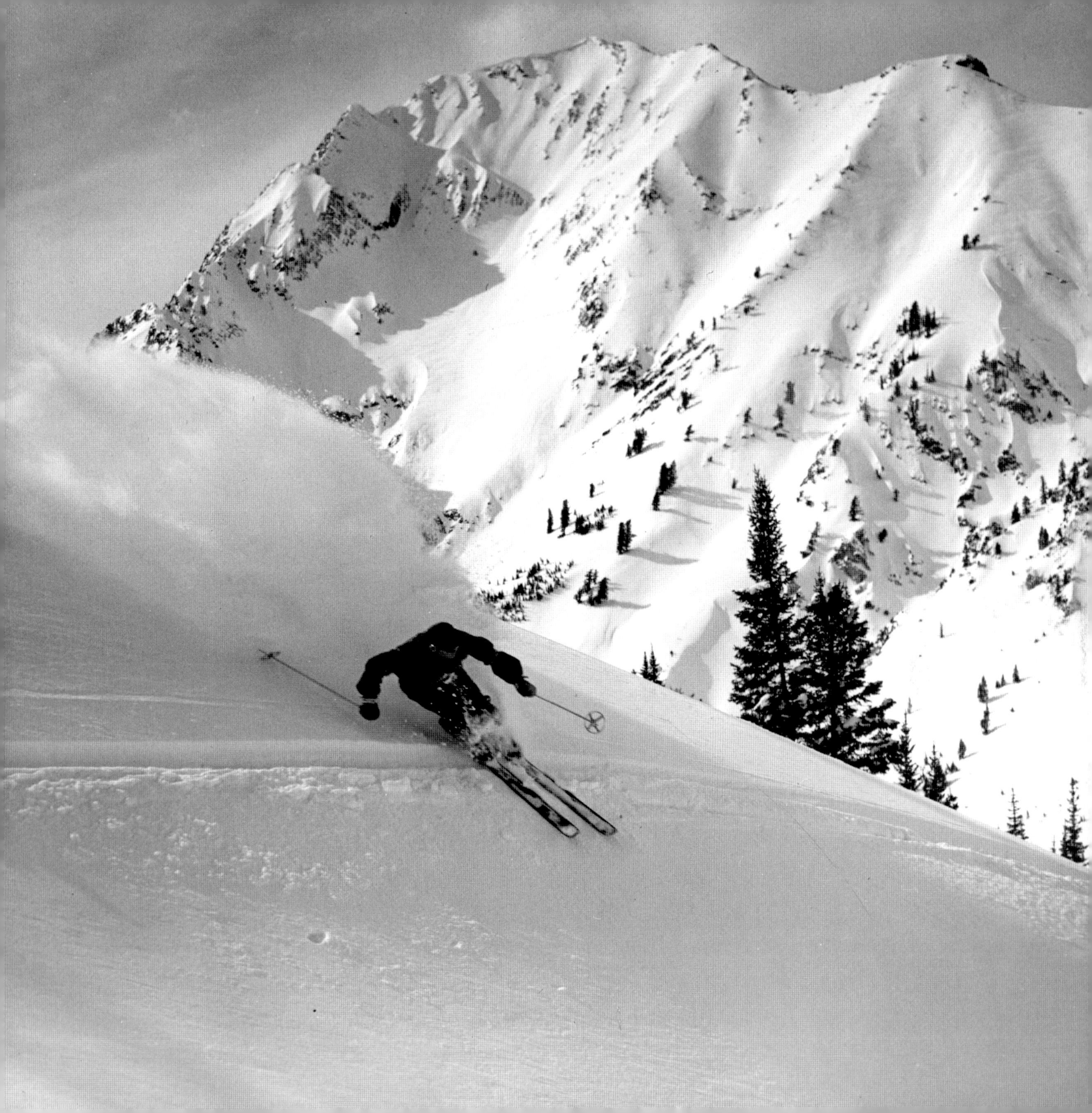

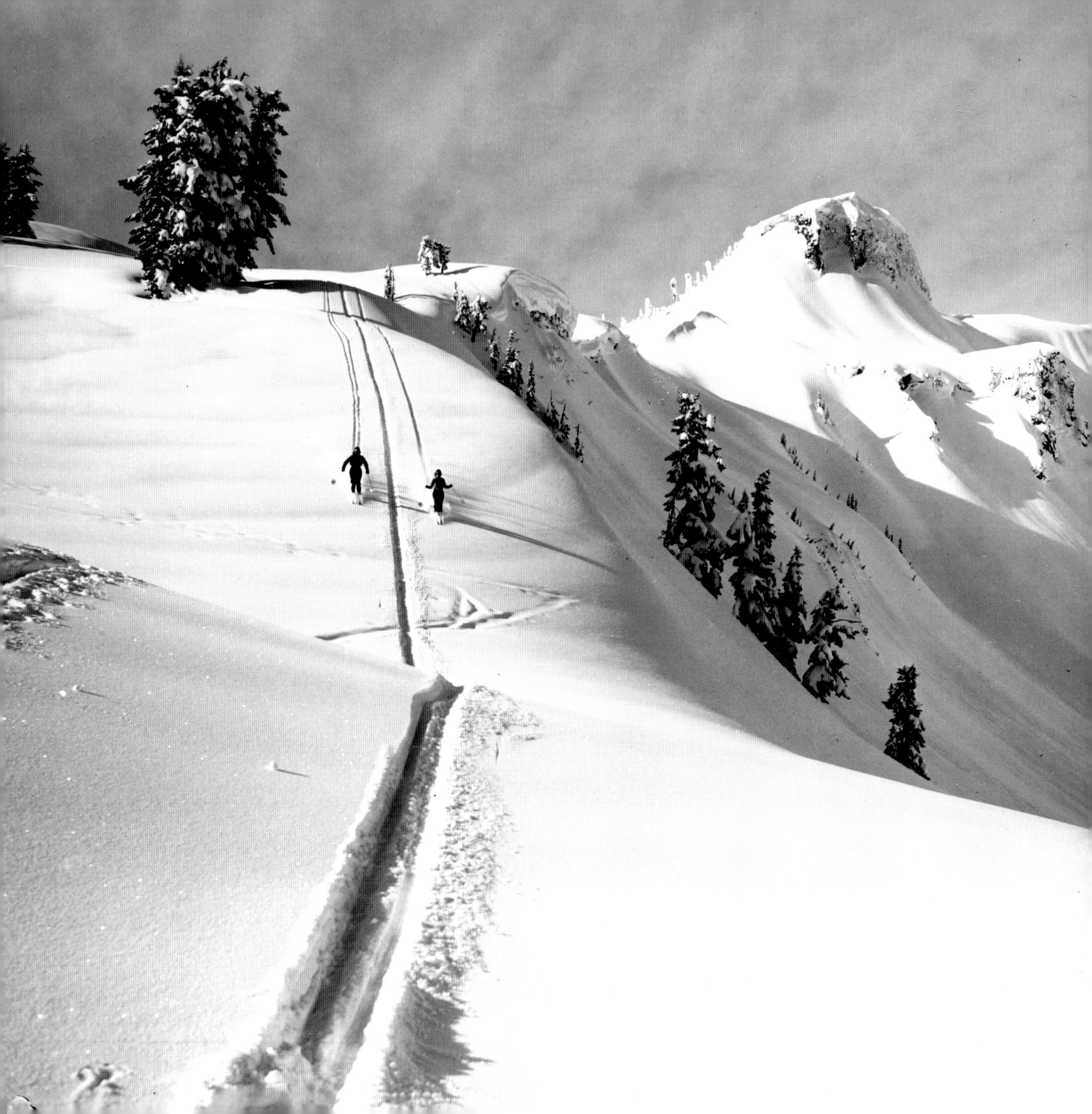

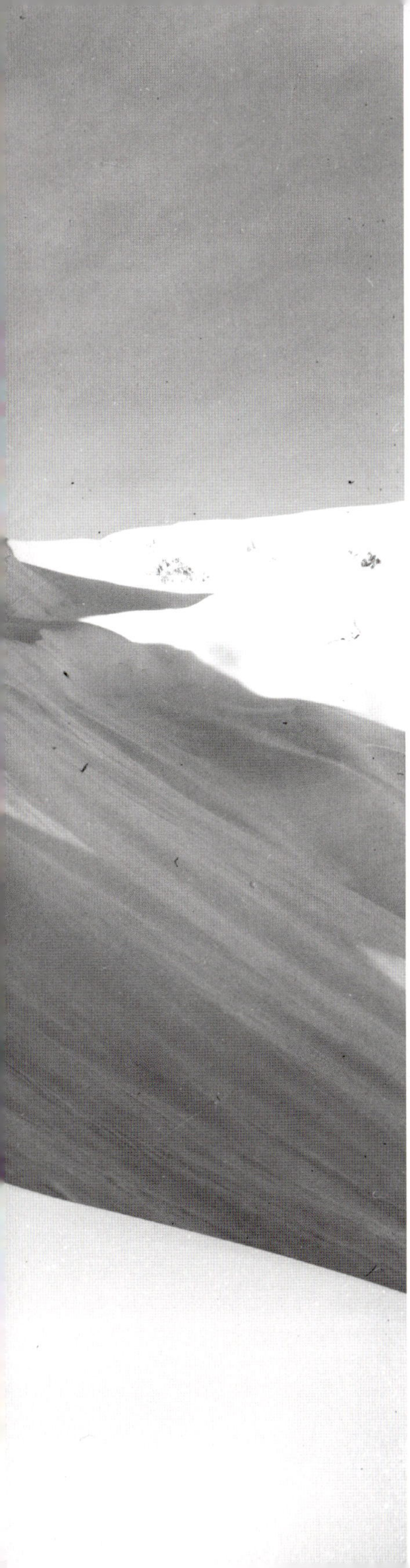

A pair of skis are the ultimate transportation to freedom.

WARREN MILLER

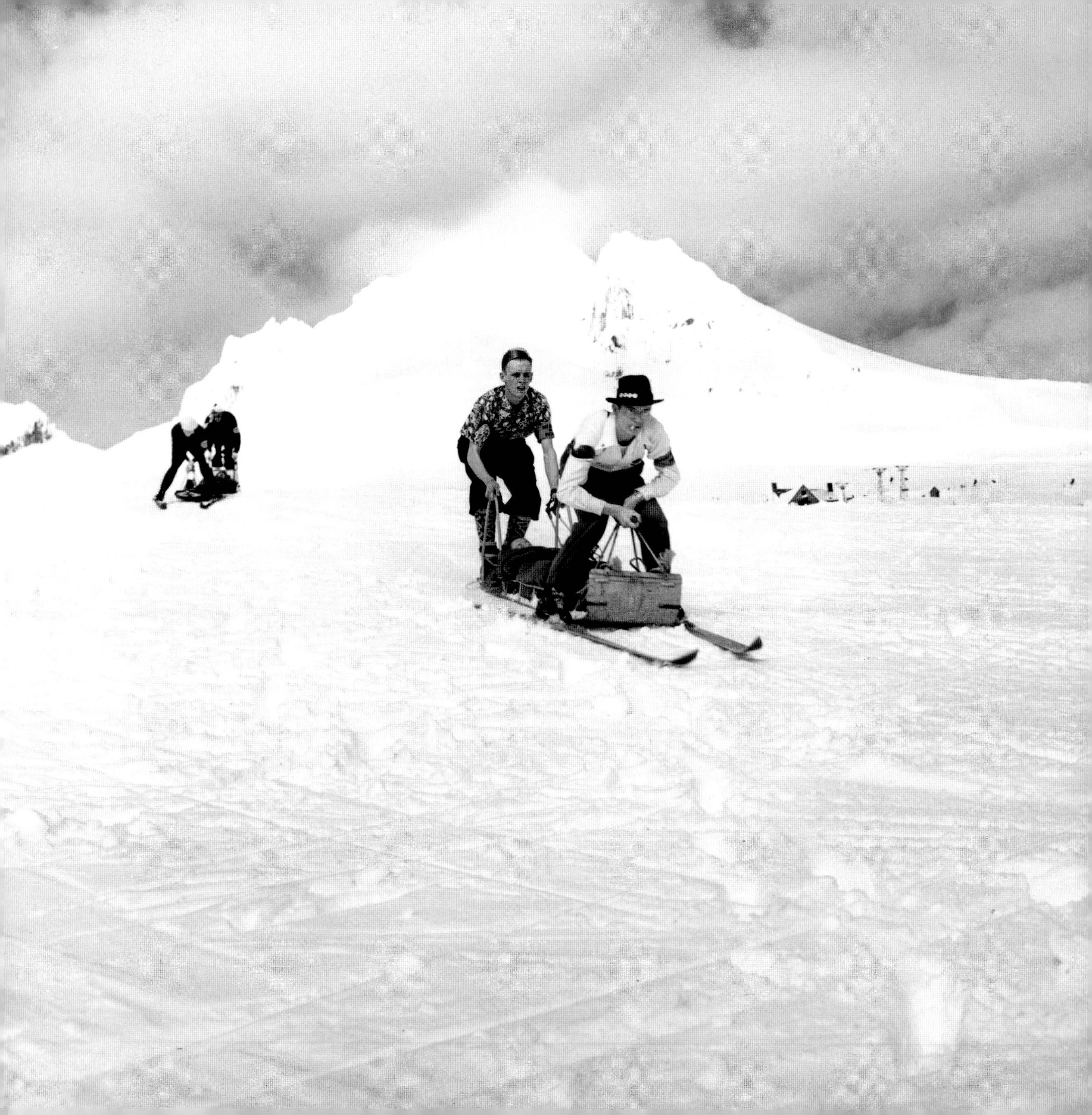

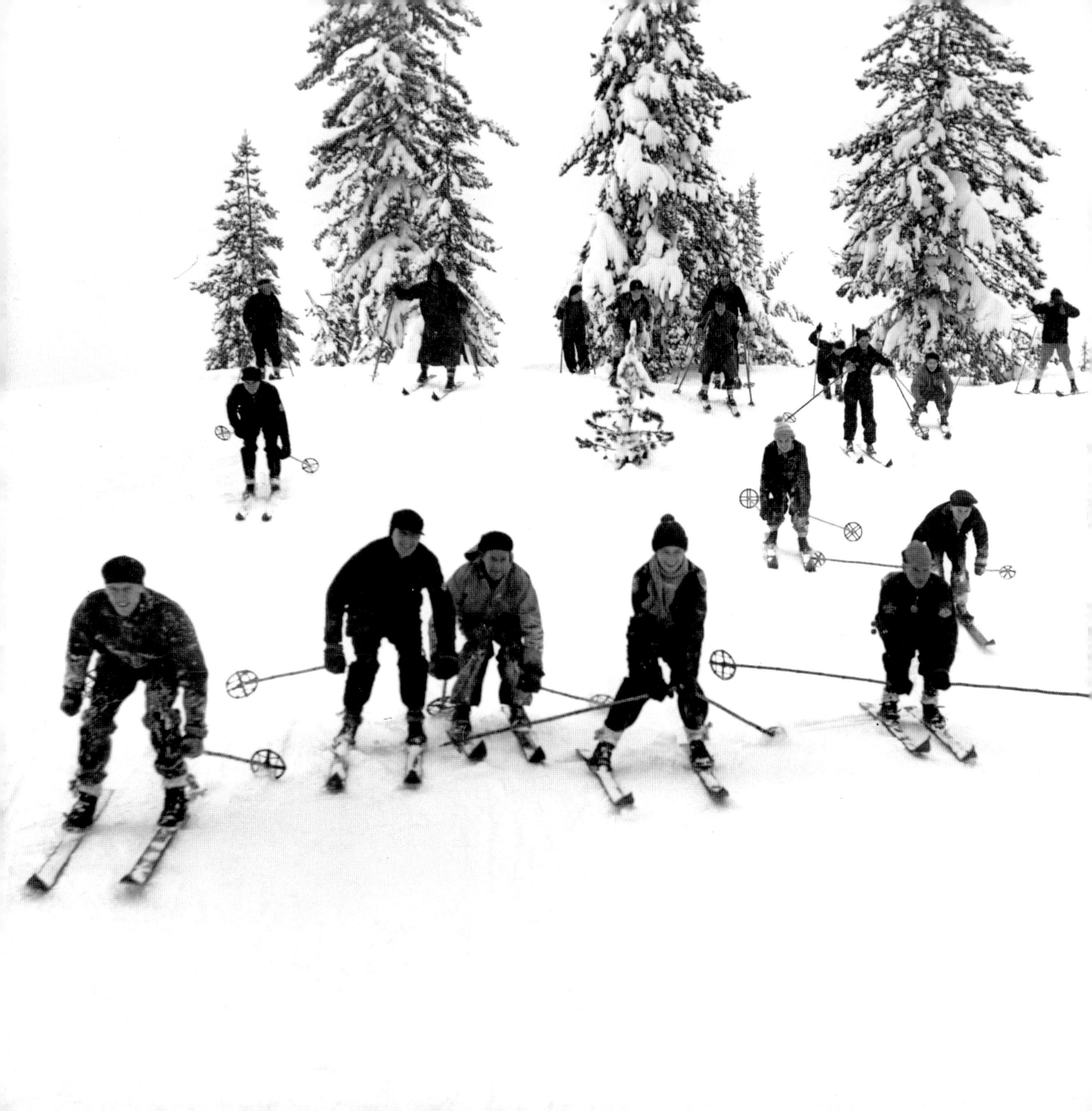

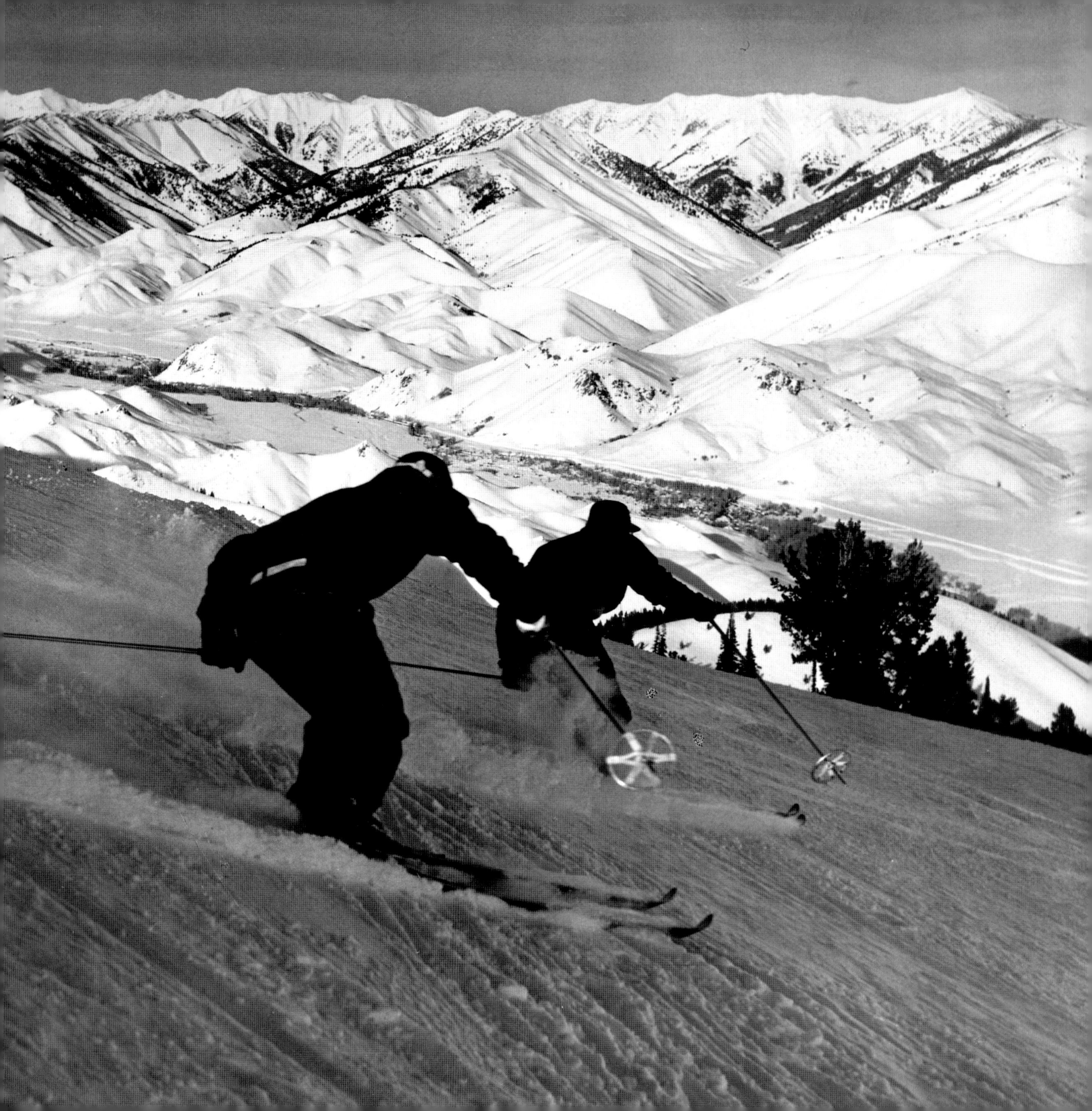

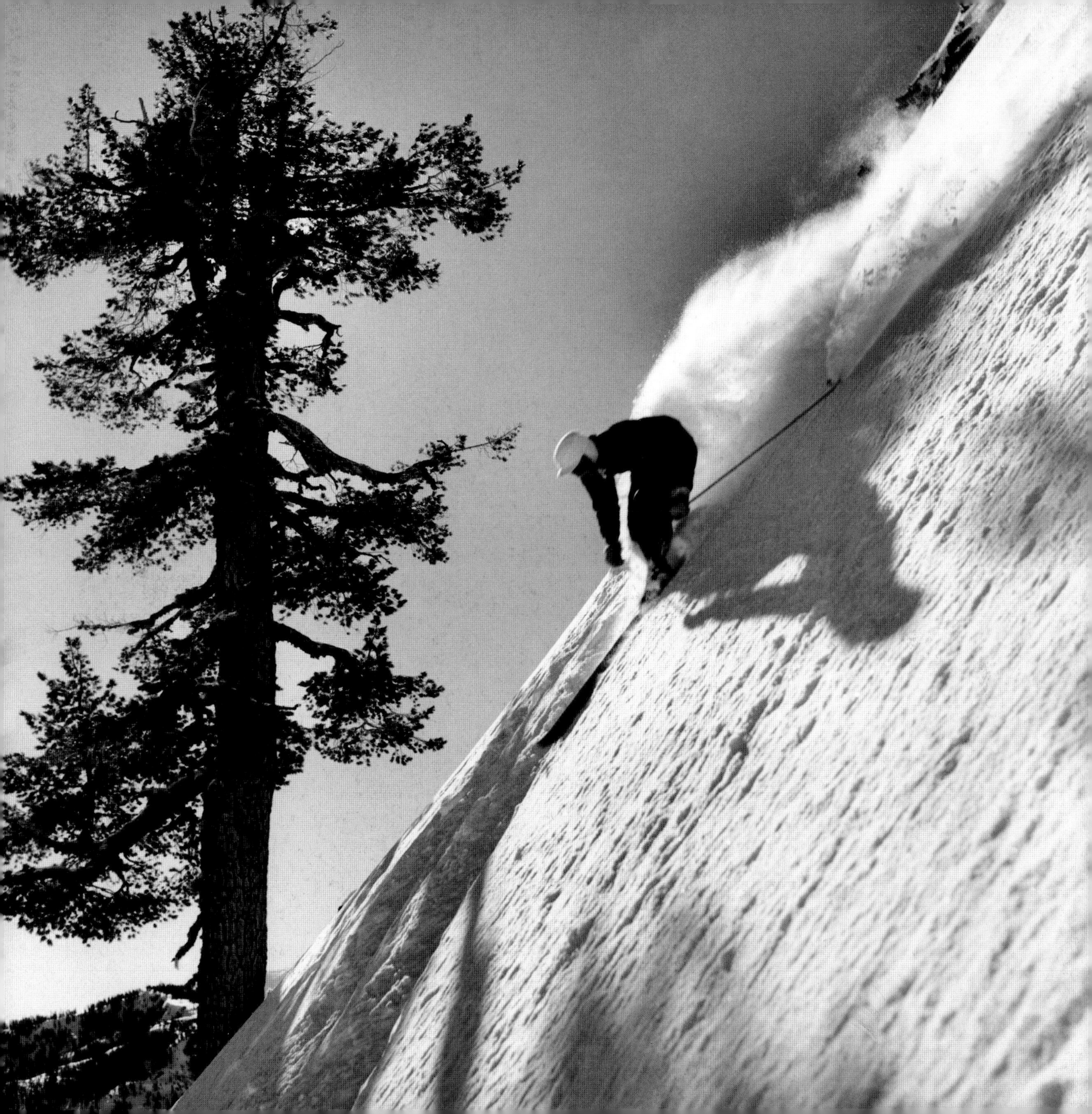

One cannot ski so softly
that the tracks cannot be seen.

FINNISH PROVERB

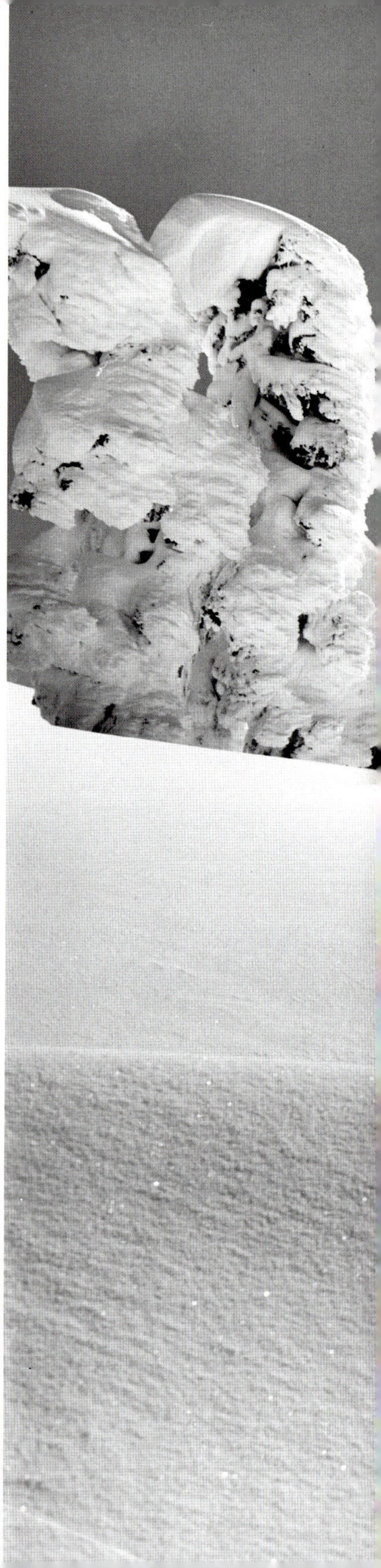

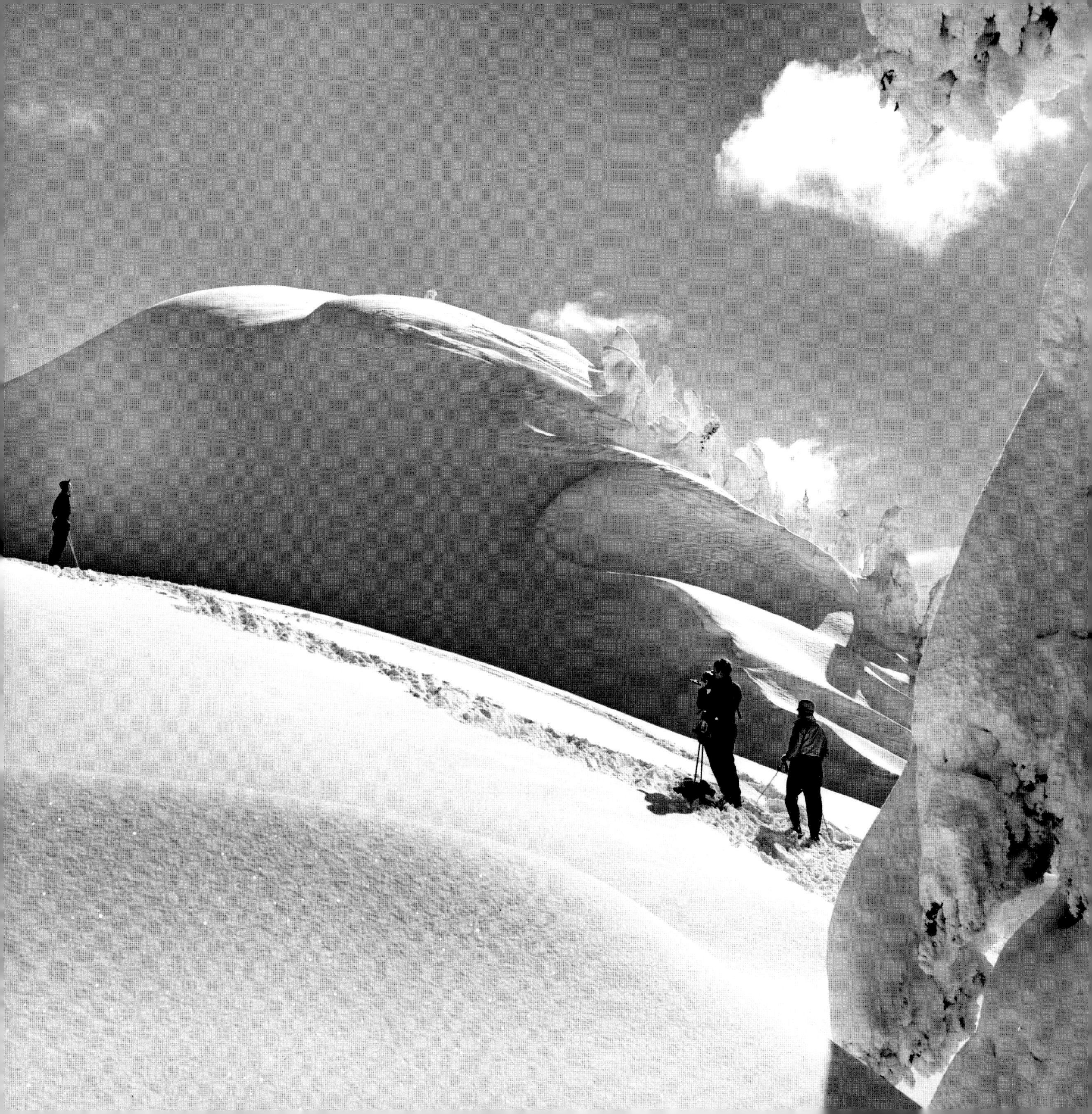

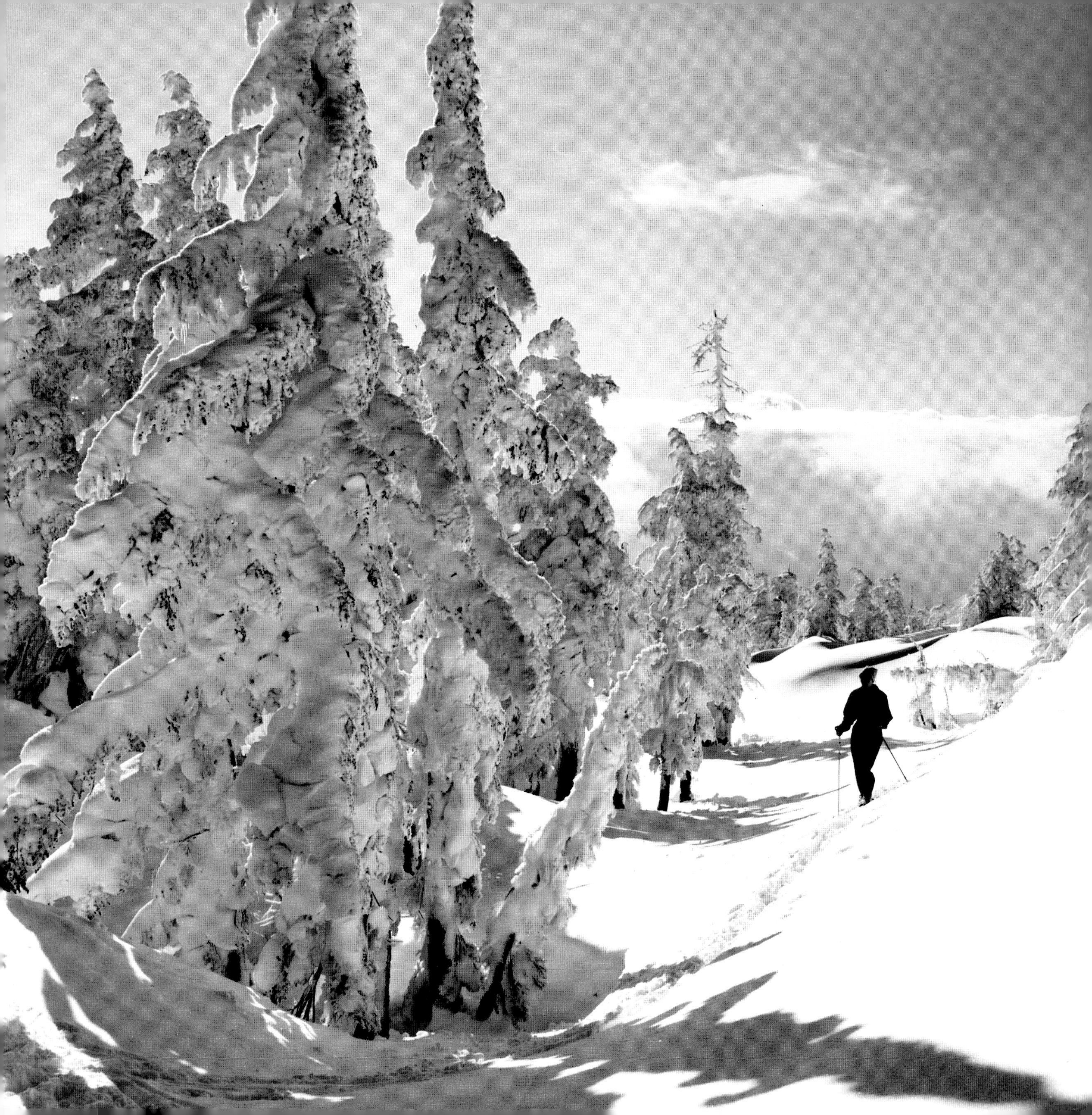

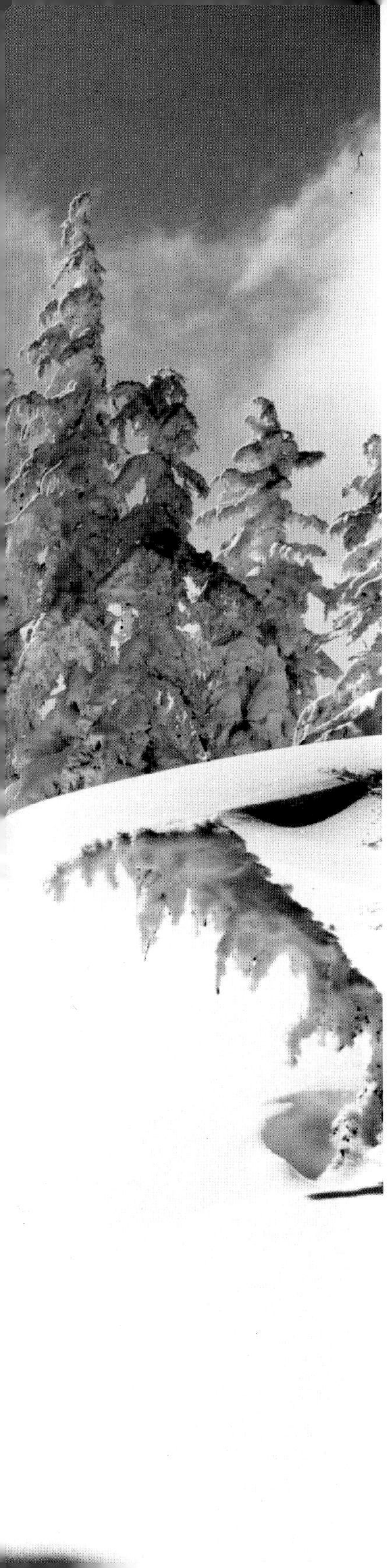

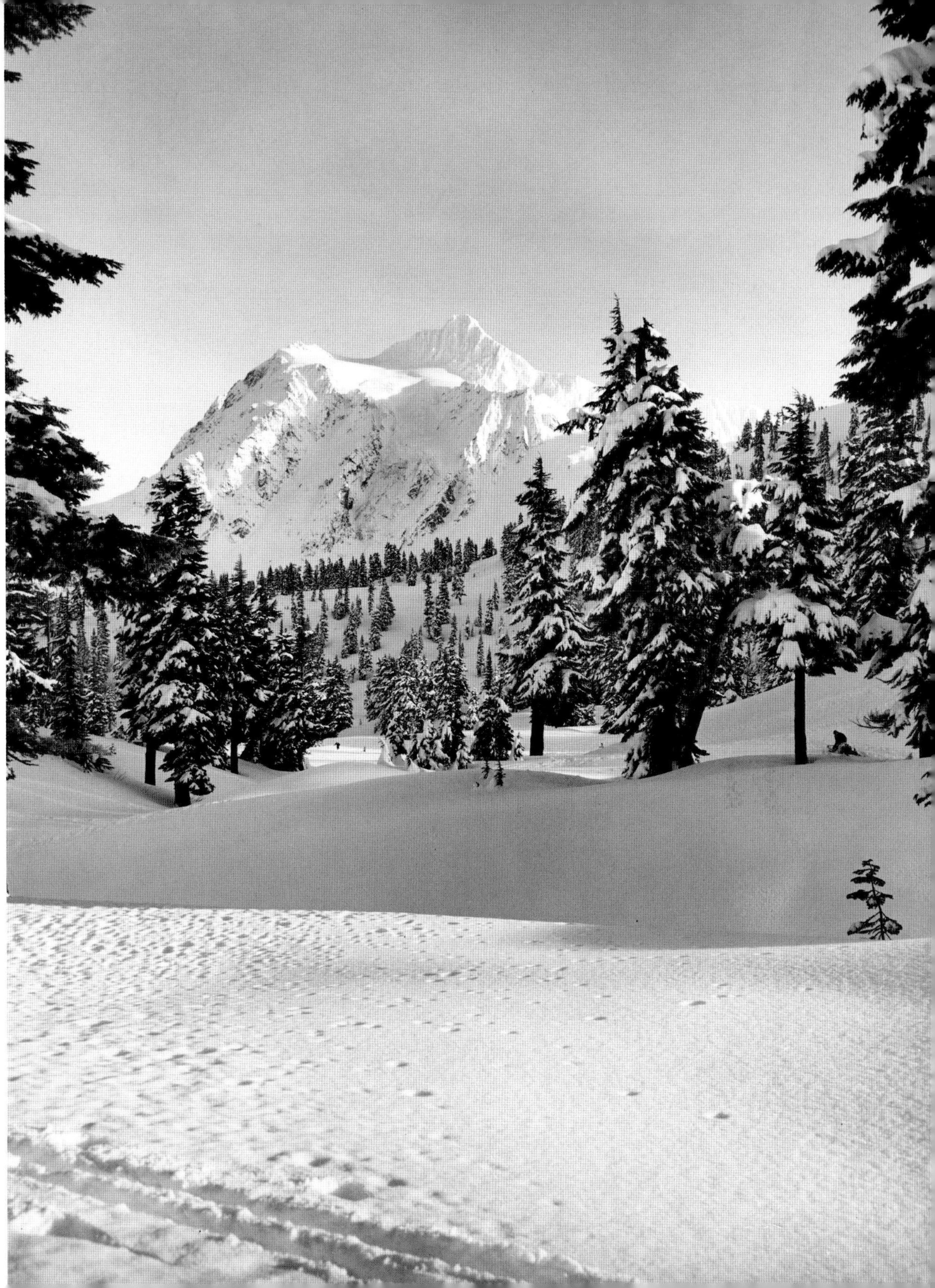

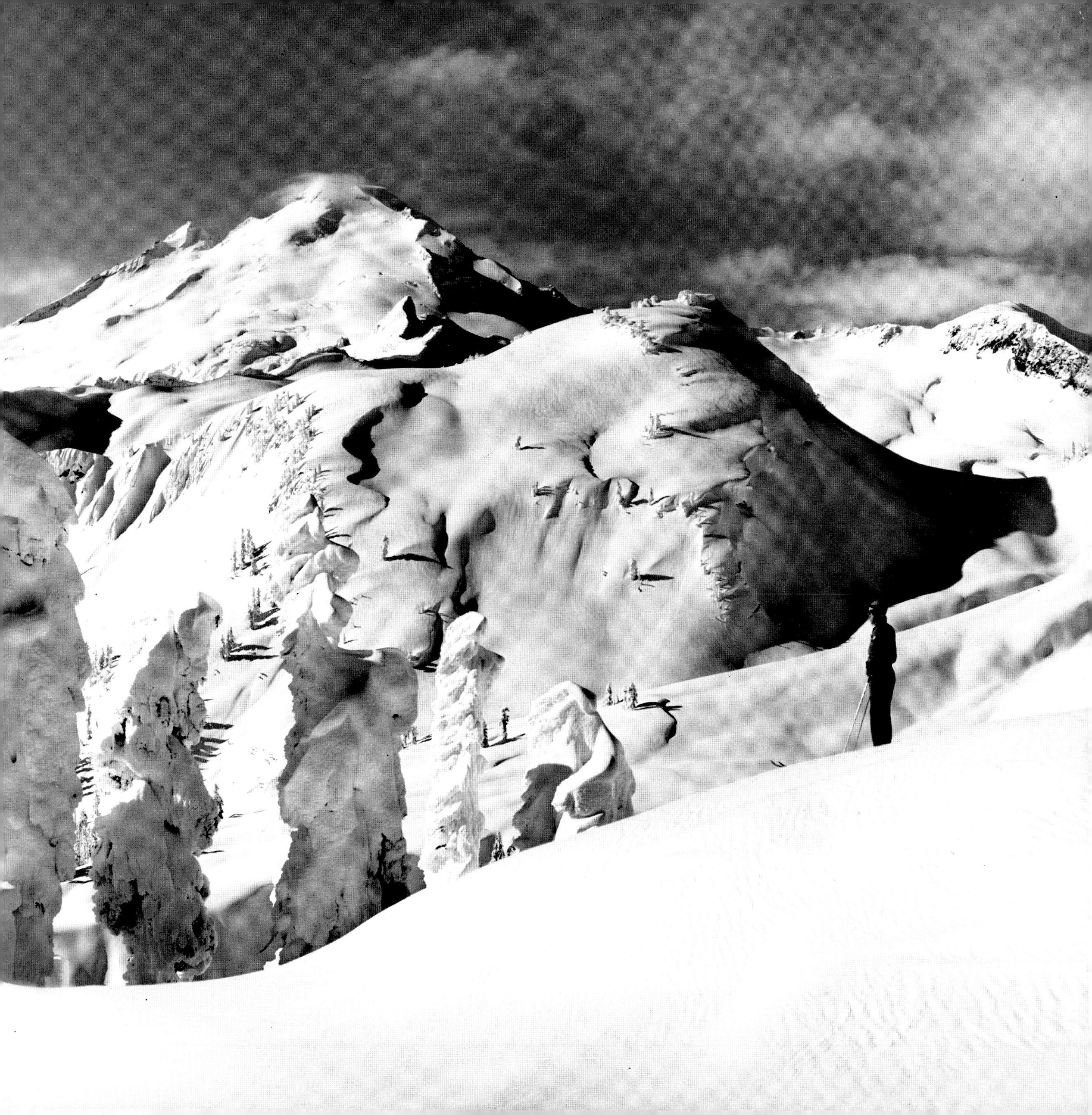

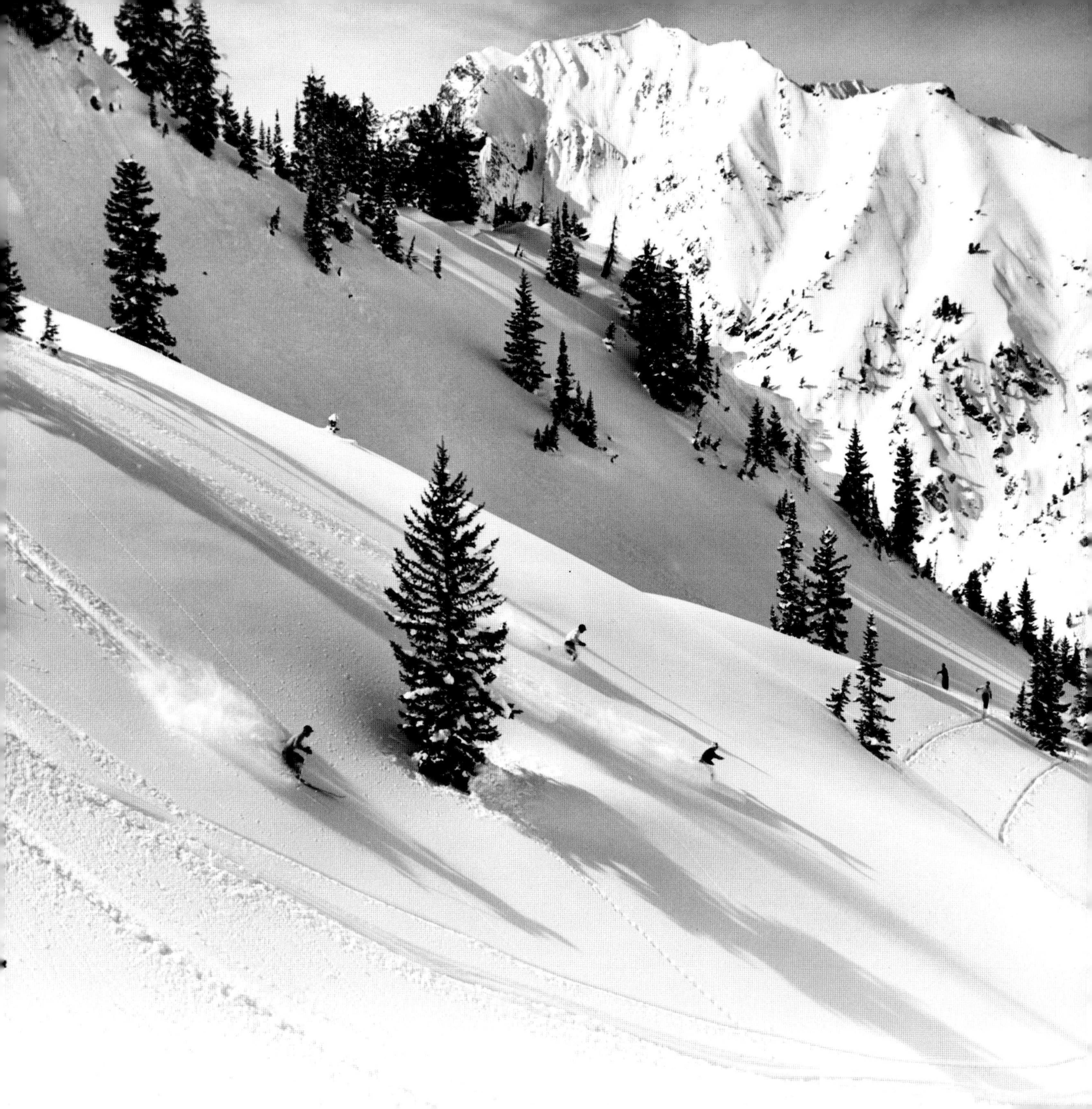

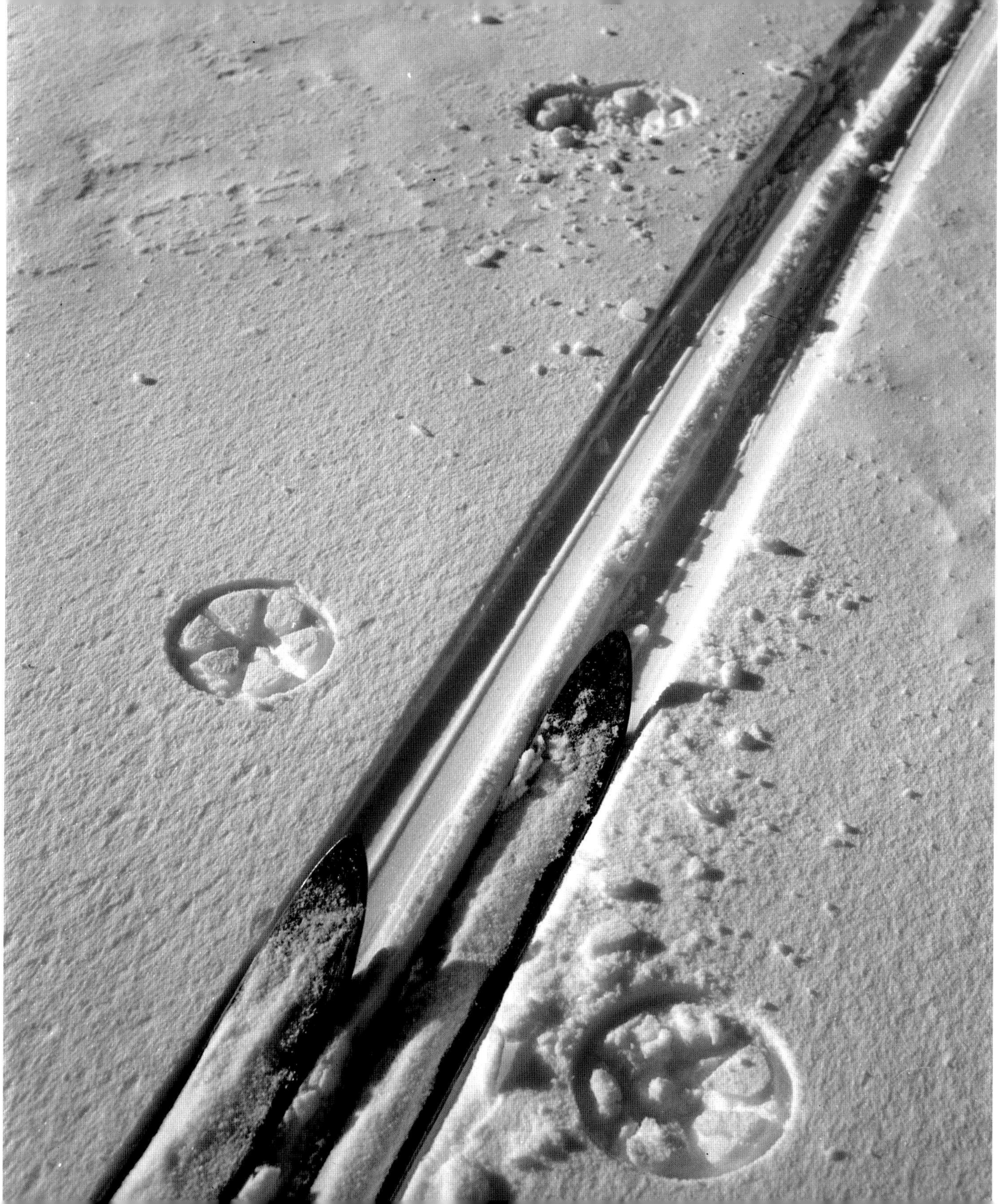

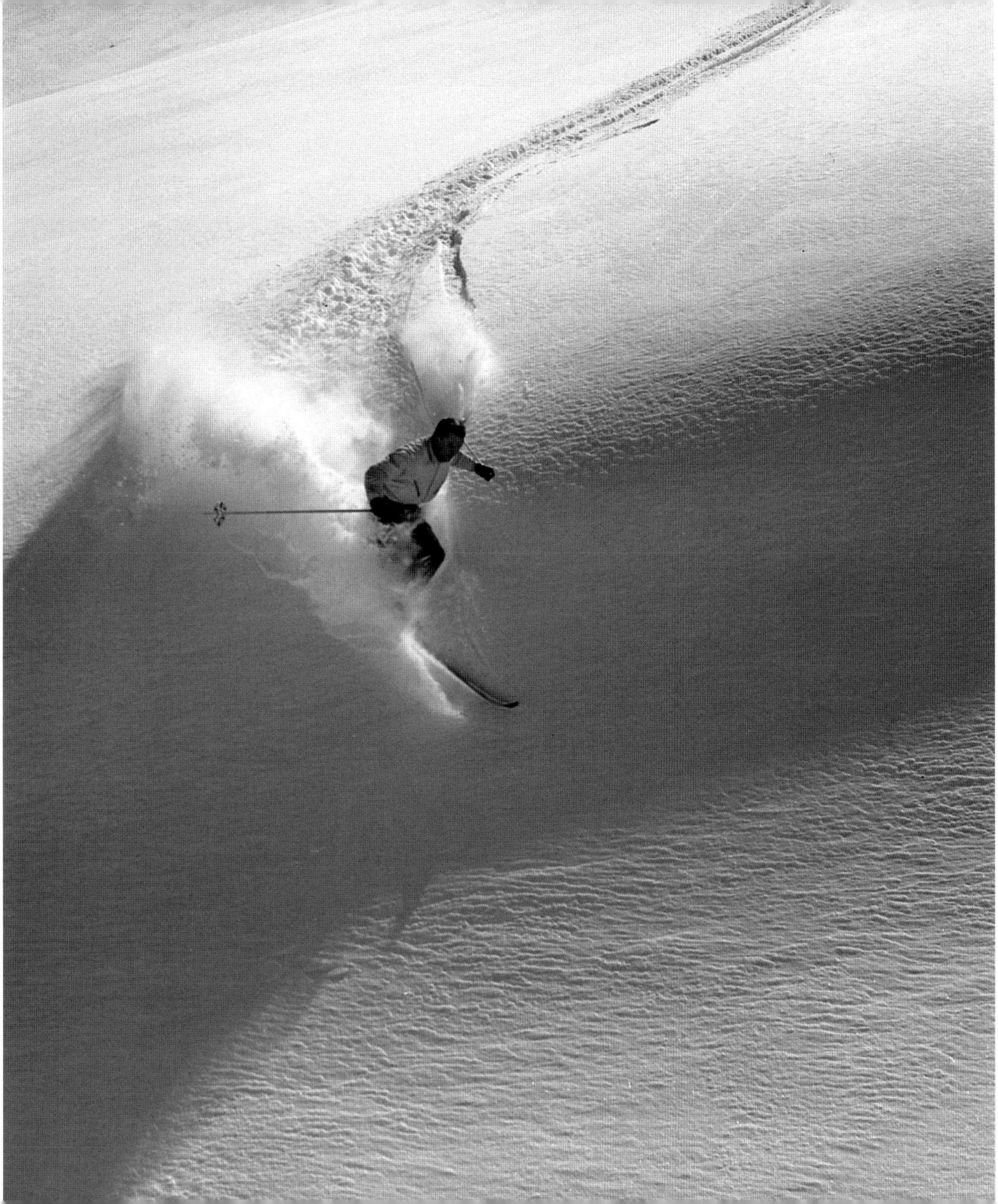

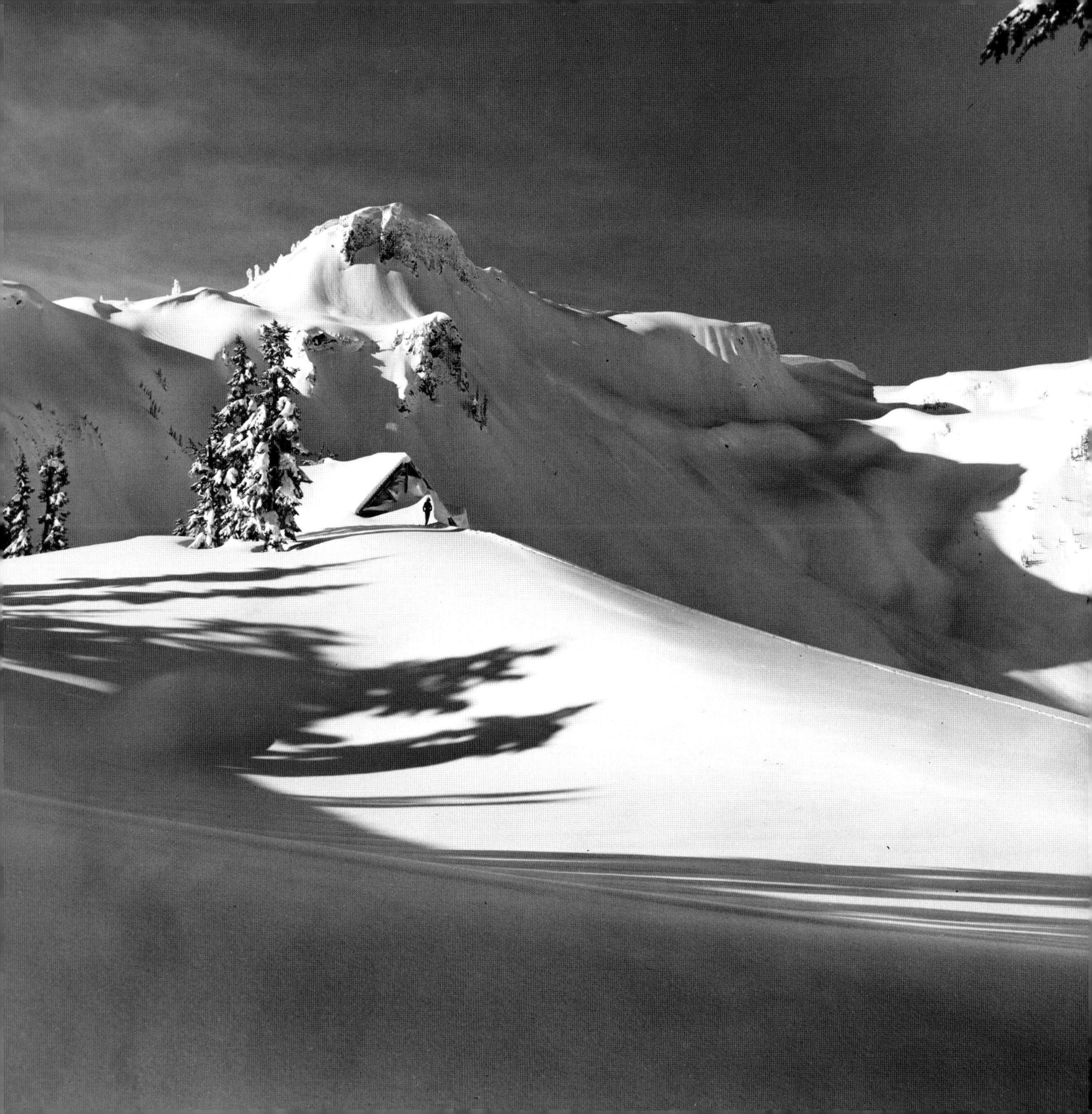

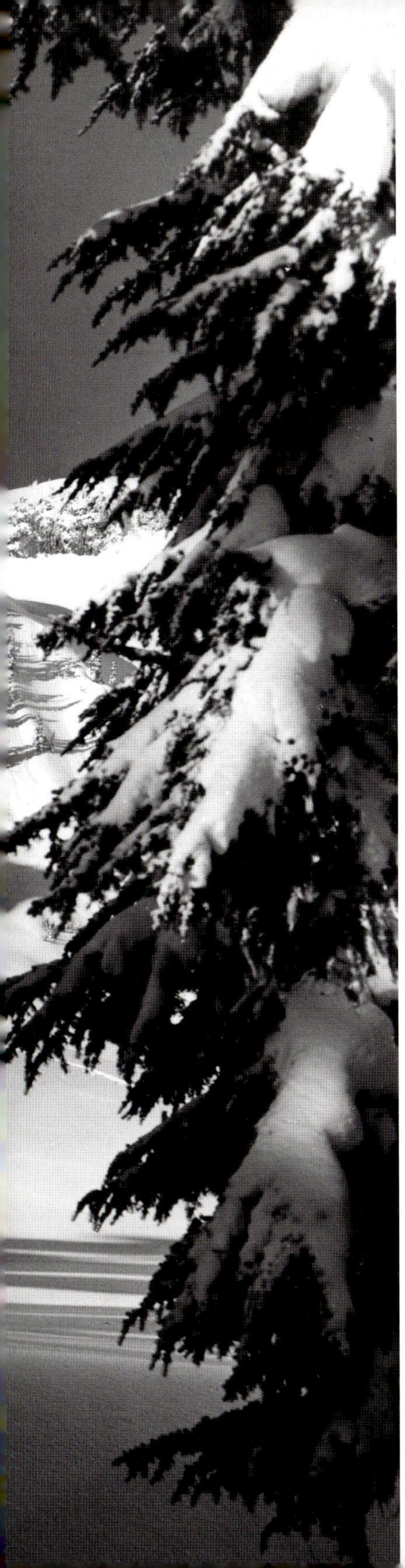

You are one with your skis and nature.
This is something that develops not only the body
but the soul as well, and it has a deeper meaning
for people than most of us perceive.

FRIDTJOF NANSEN

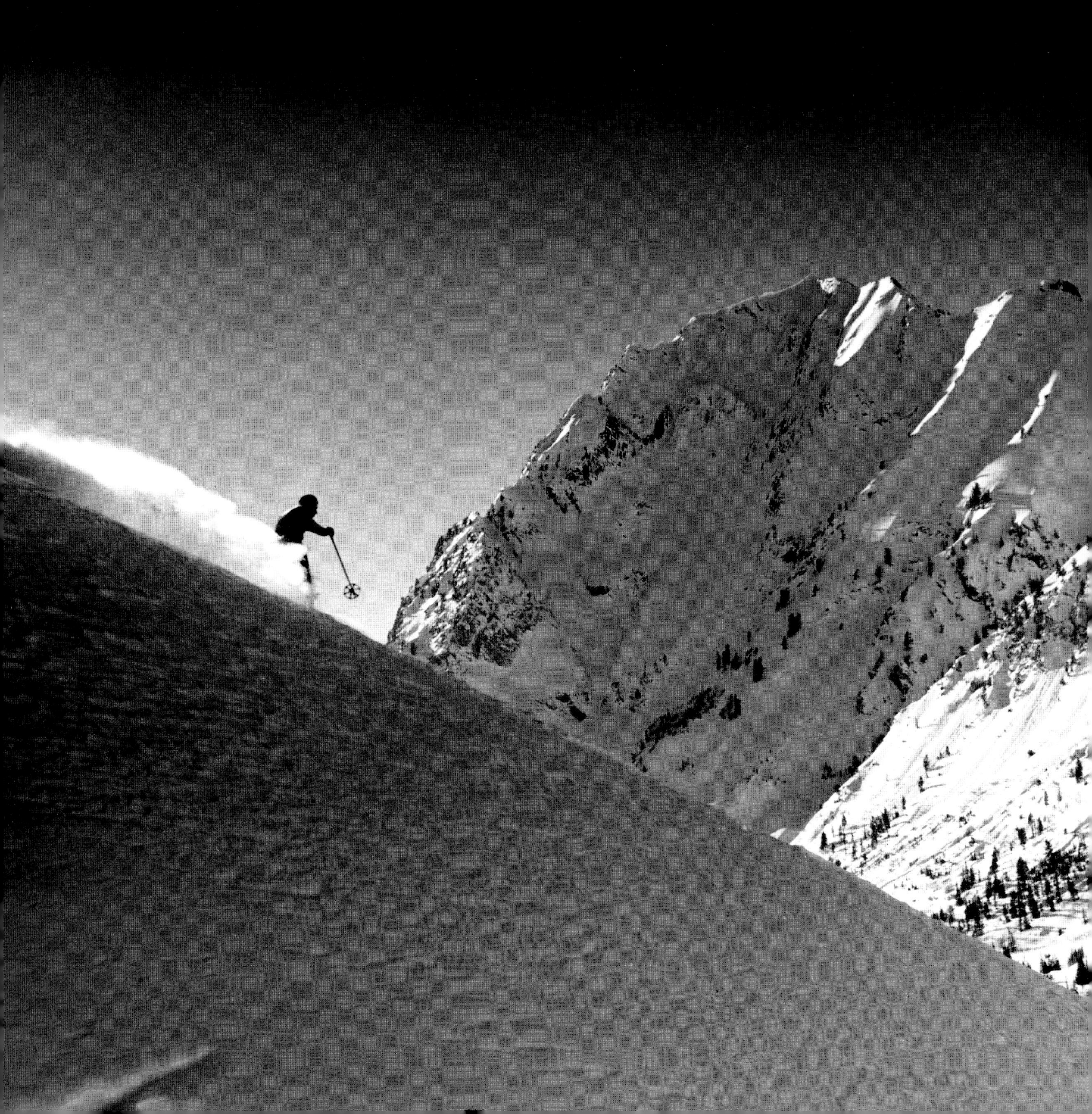

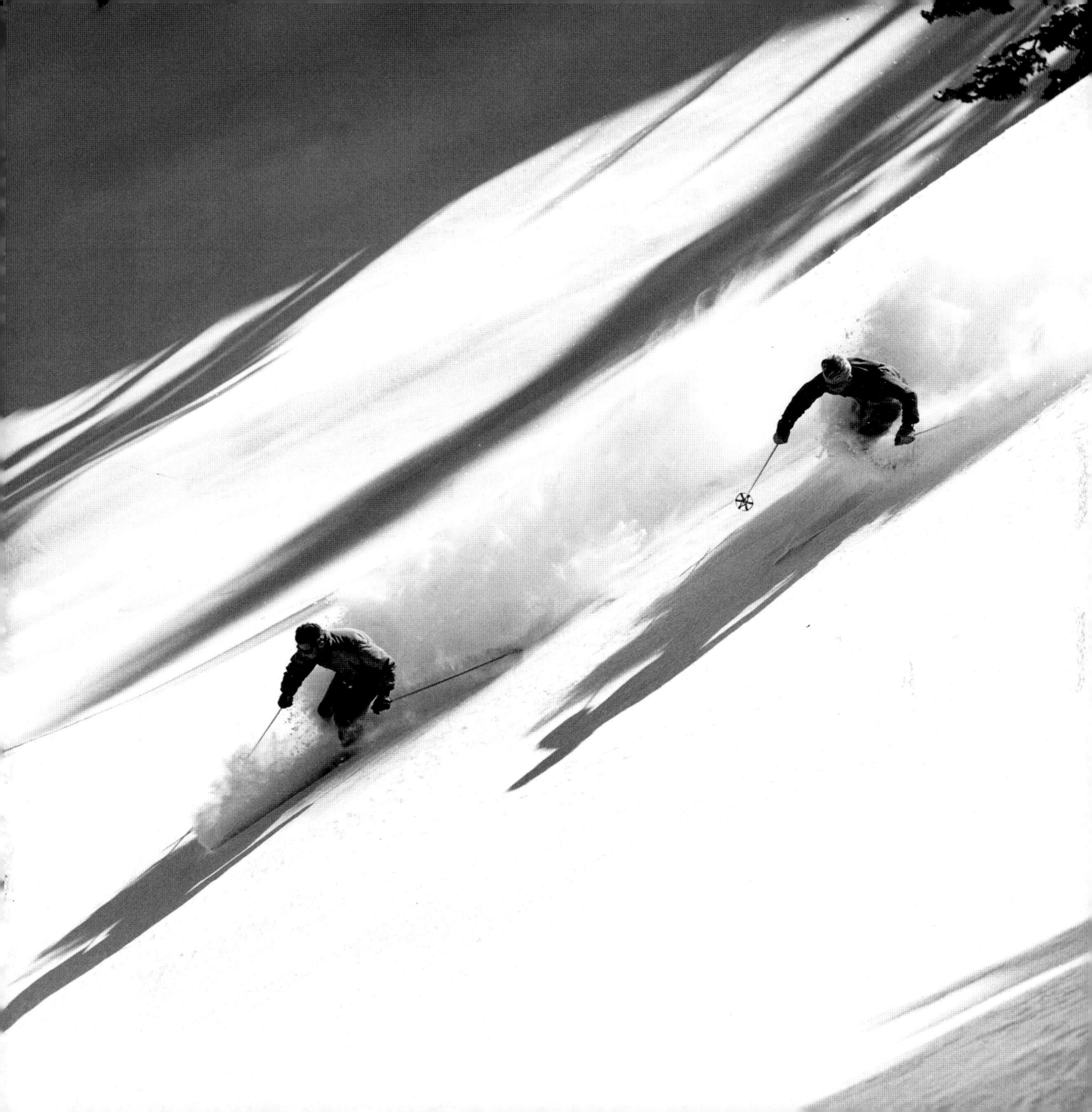

Skiing: the art of
catching cold and going broke
while rapidly heading nowhere
at great personal risk.

AUTHOR UNKNOWN

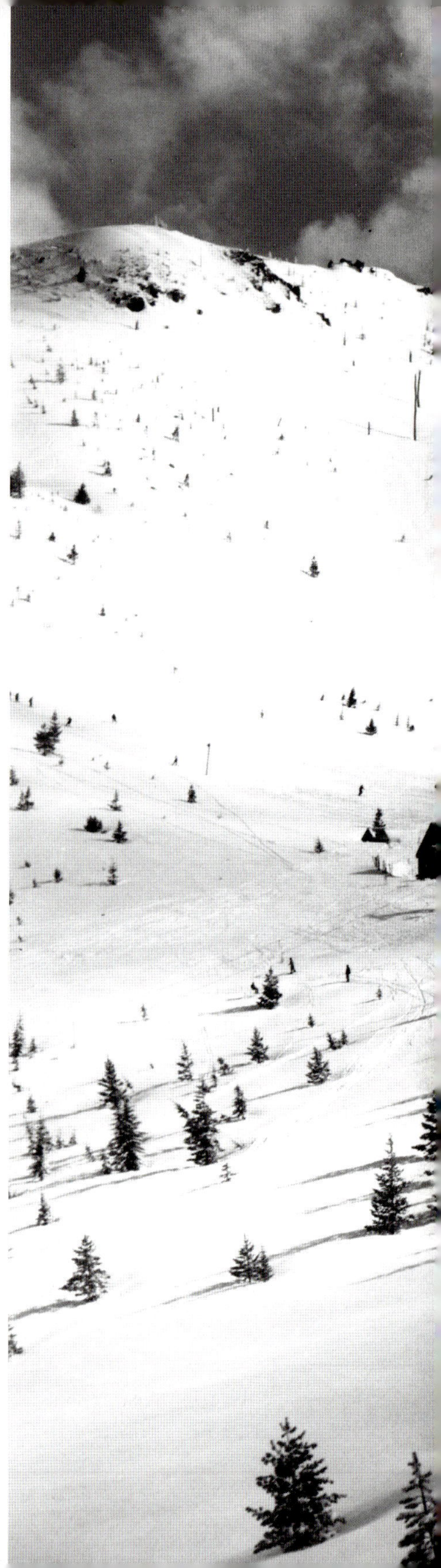

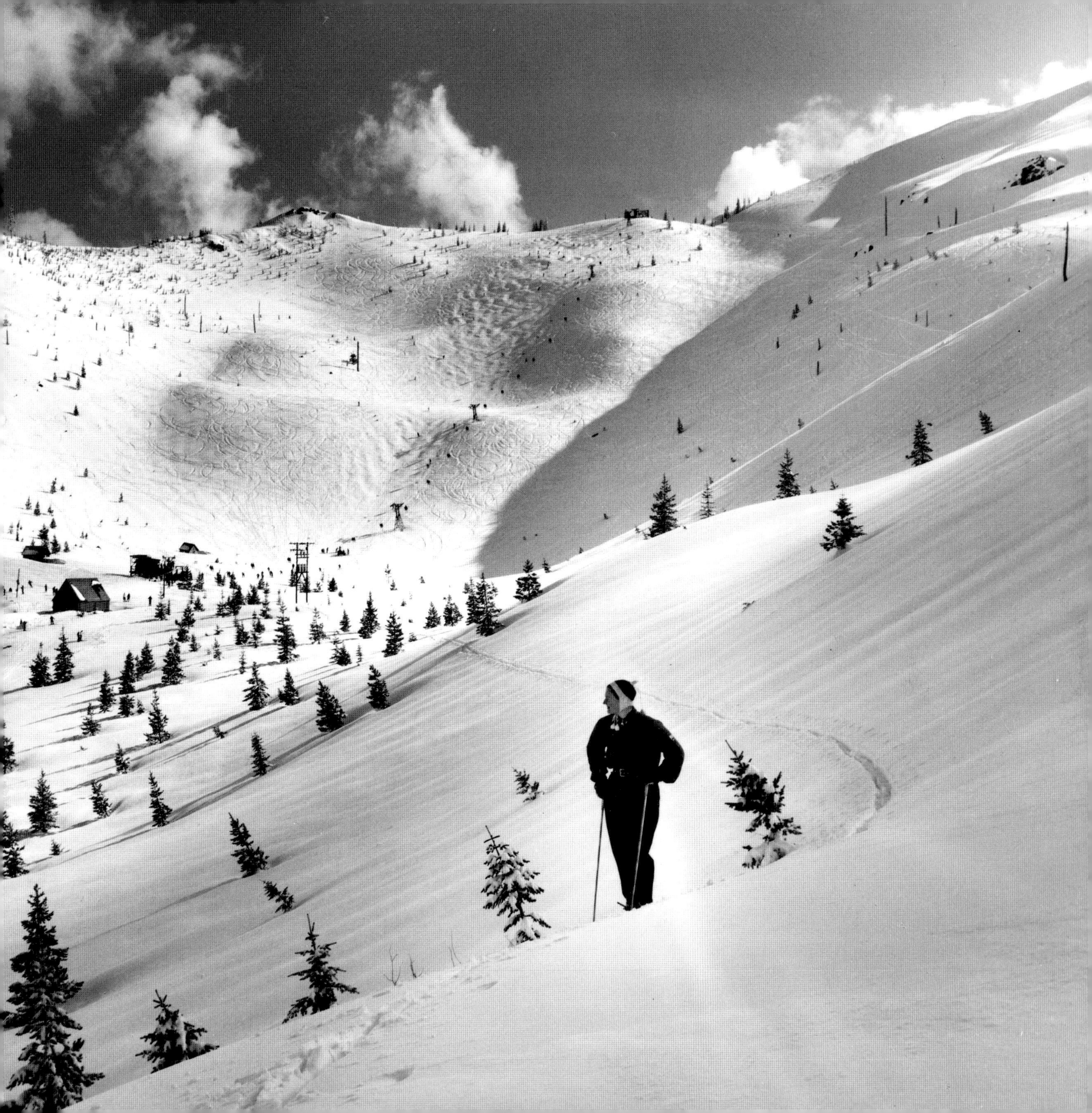

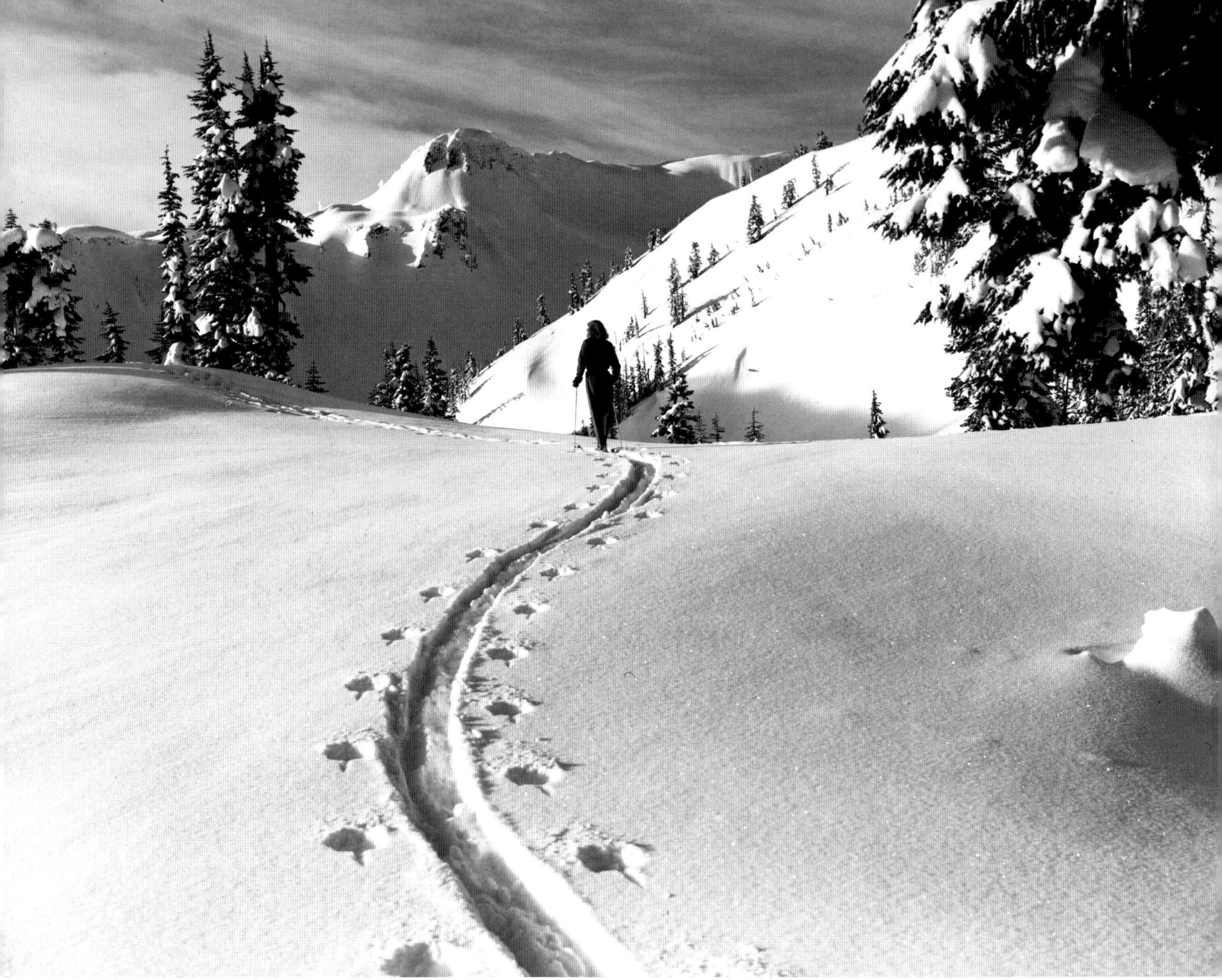

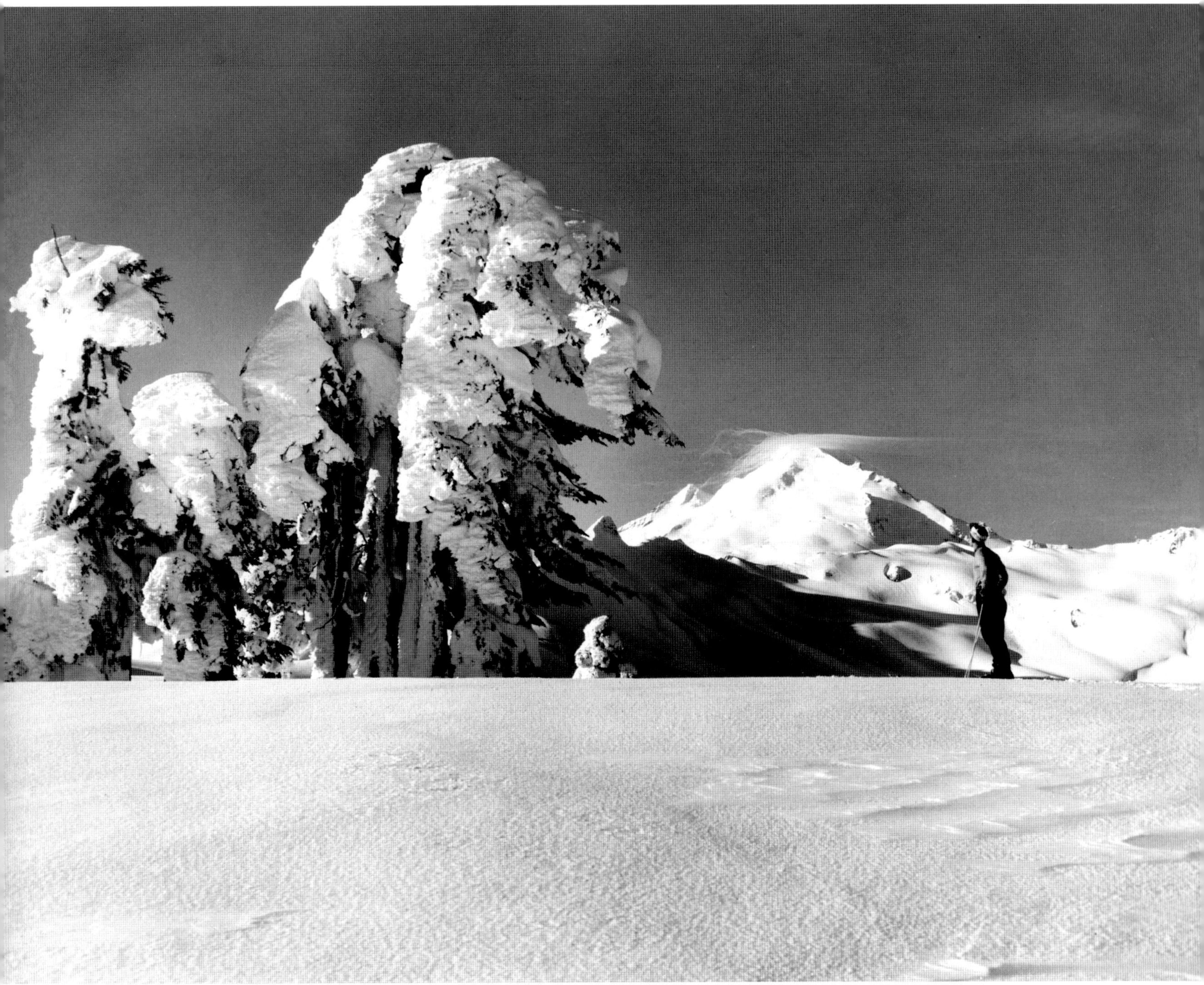

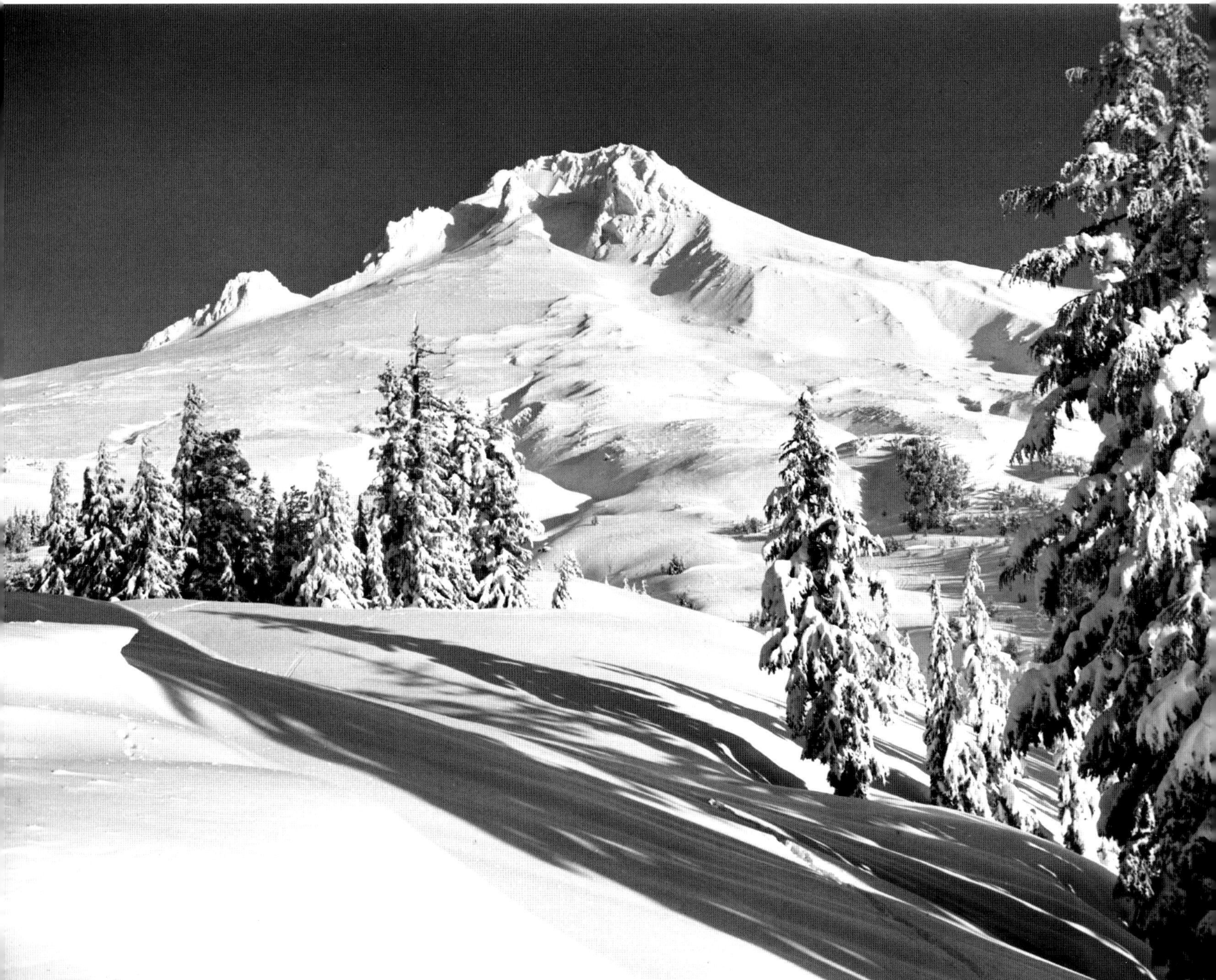

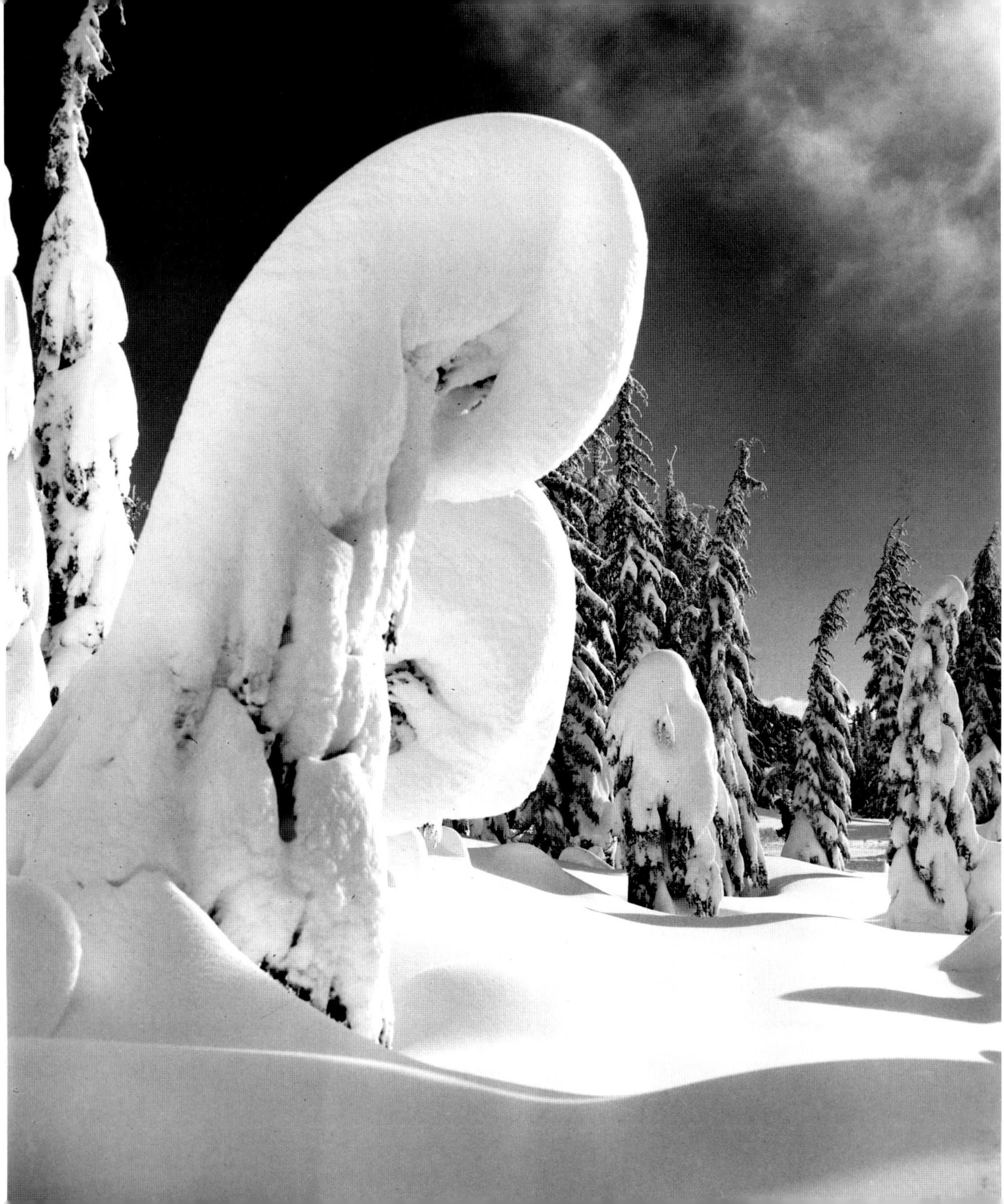

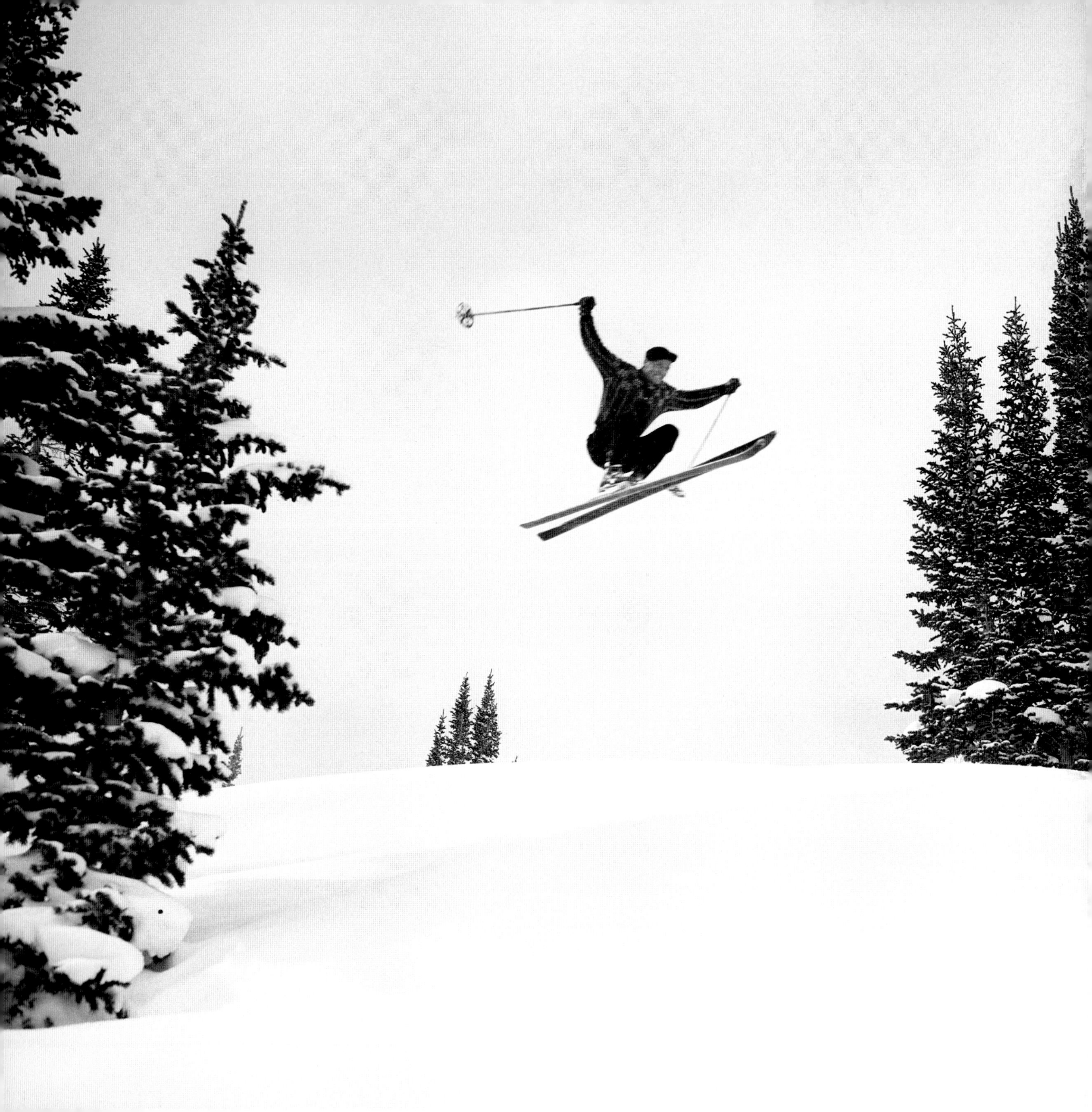

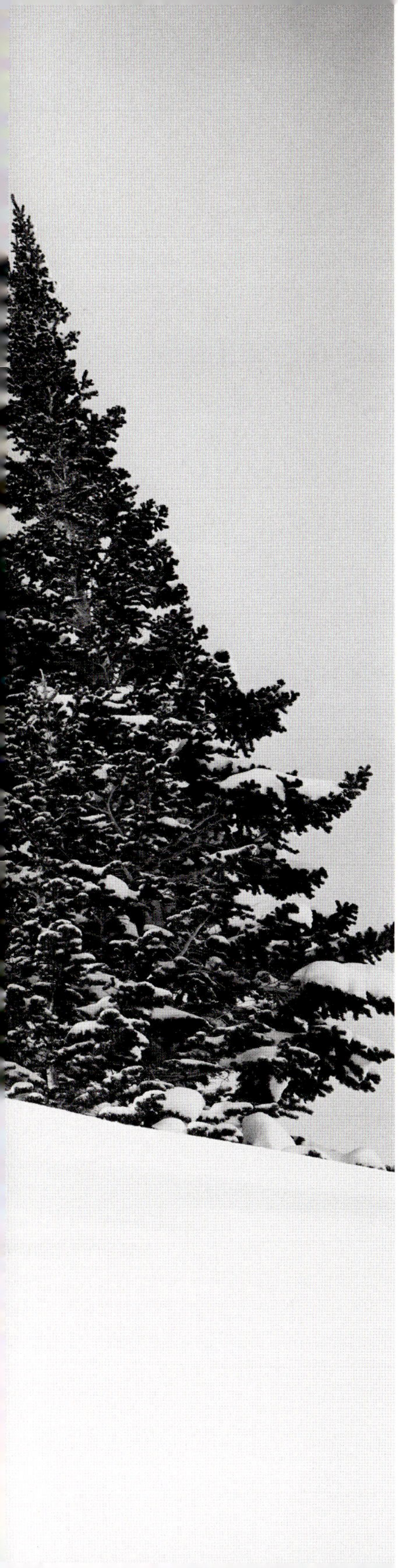

*For me, skiing is a physical necessity.
I have a need for risk.*

JEAN-MARIE MESSIER

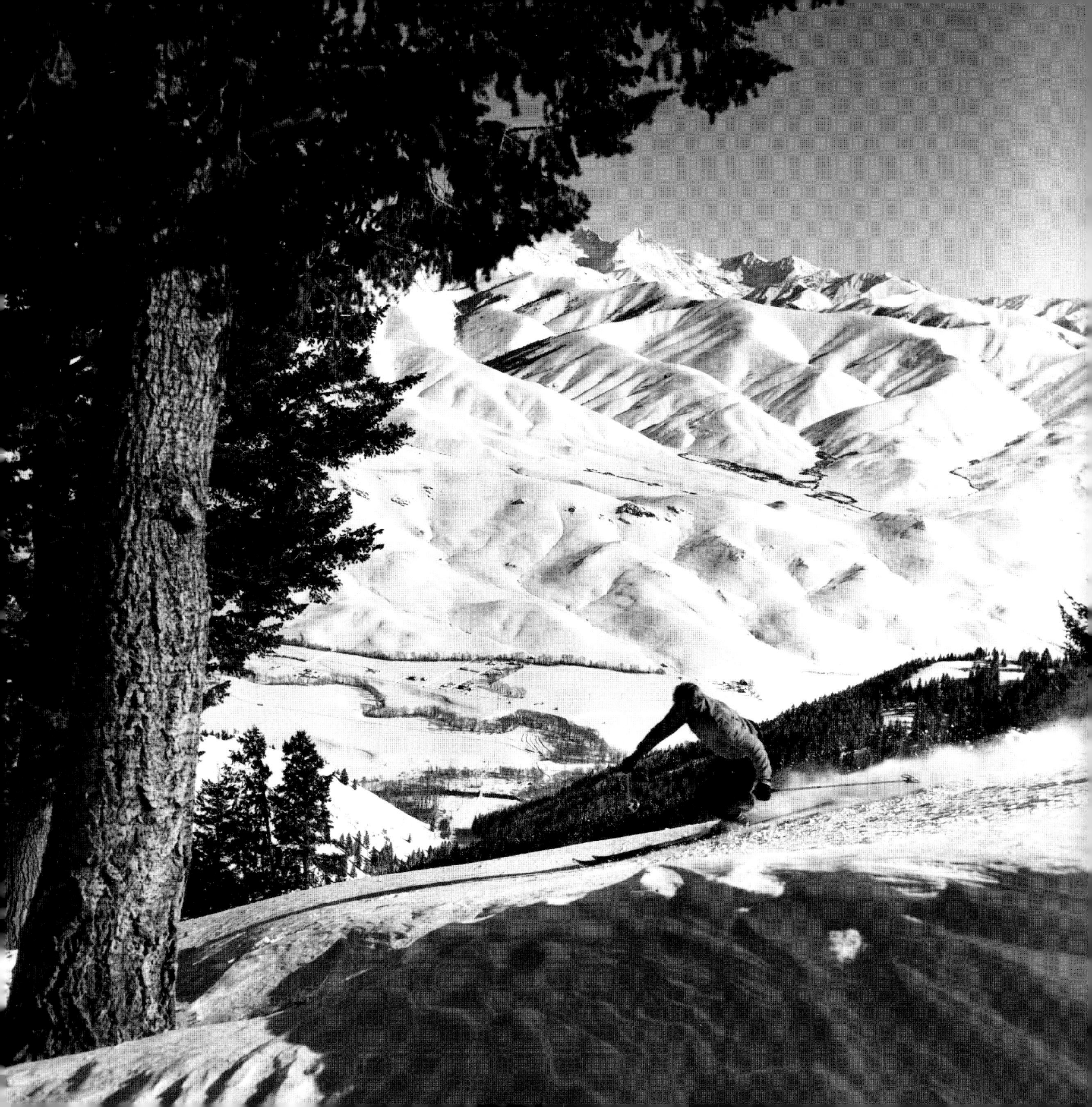

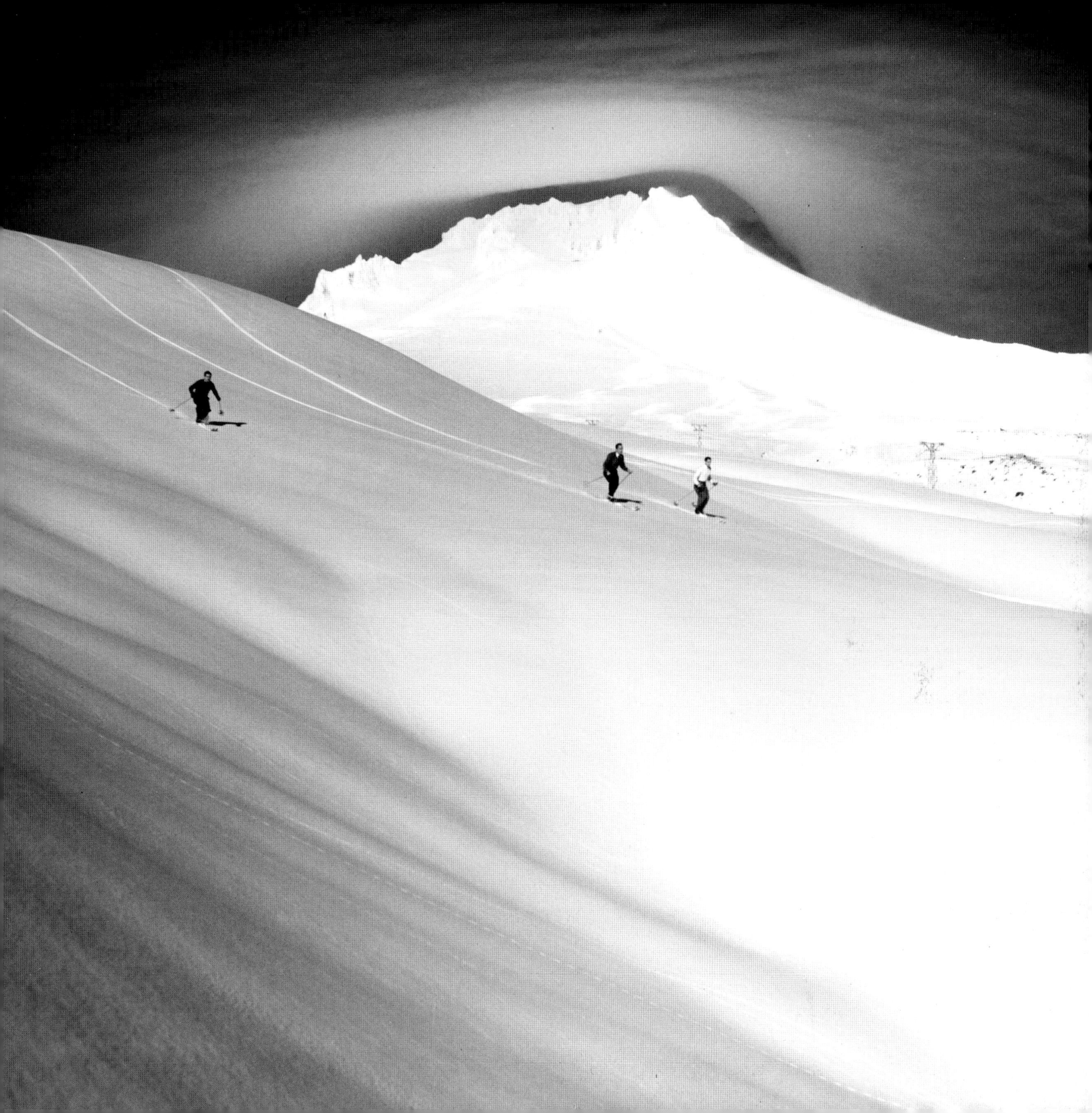

I think it's human nature to want to explore. Find your line and go beyond it. The only limit is the one you set yourself.

AMY ROBINSON

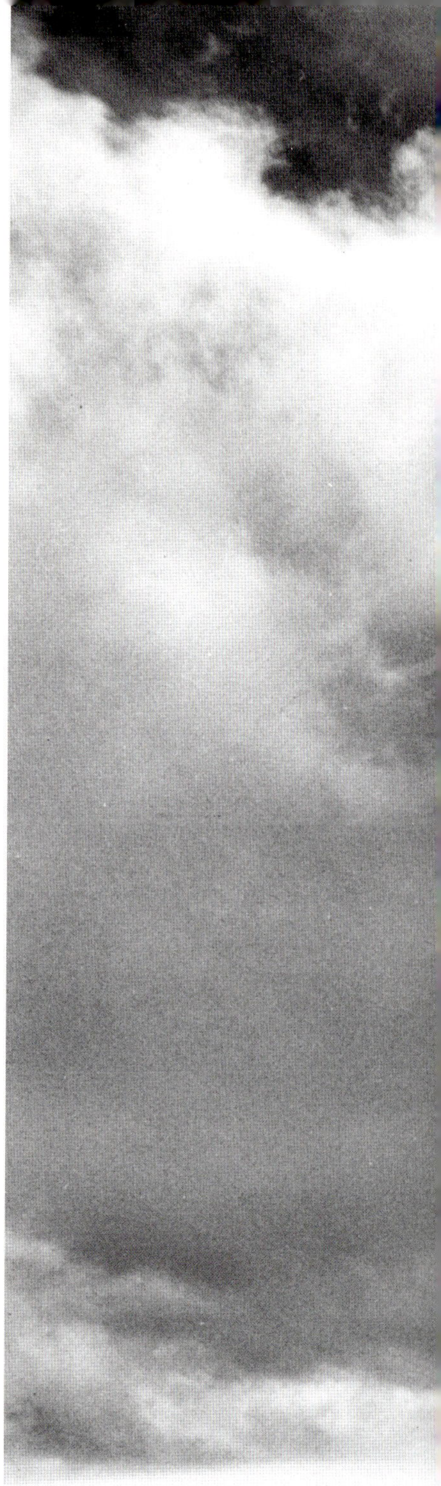

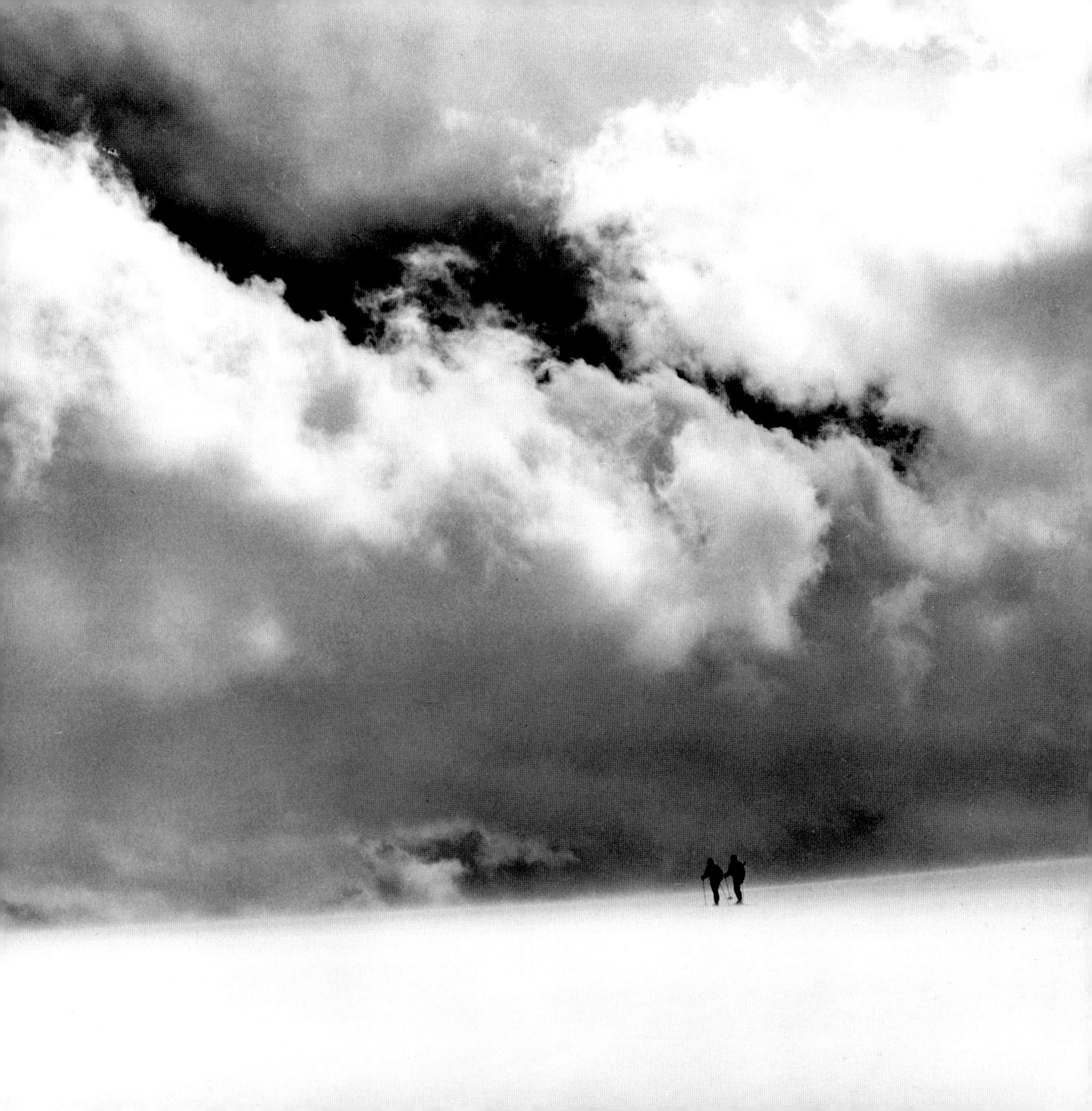

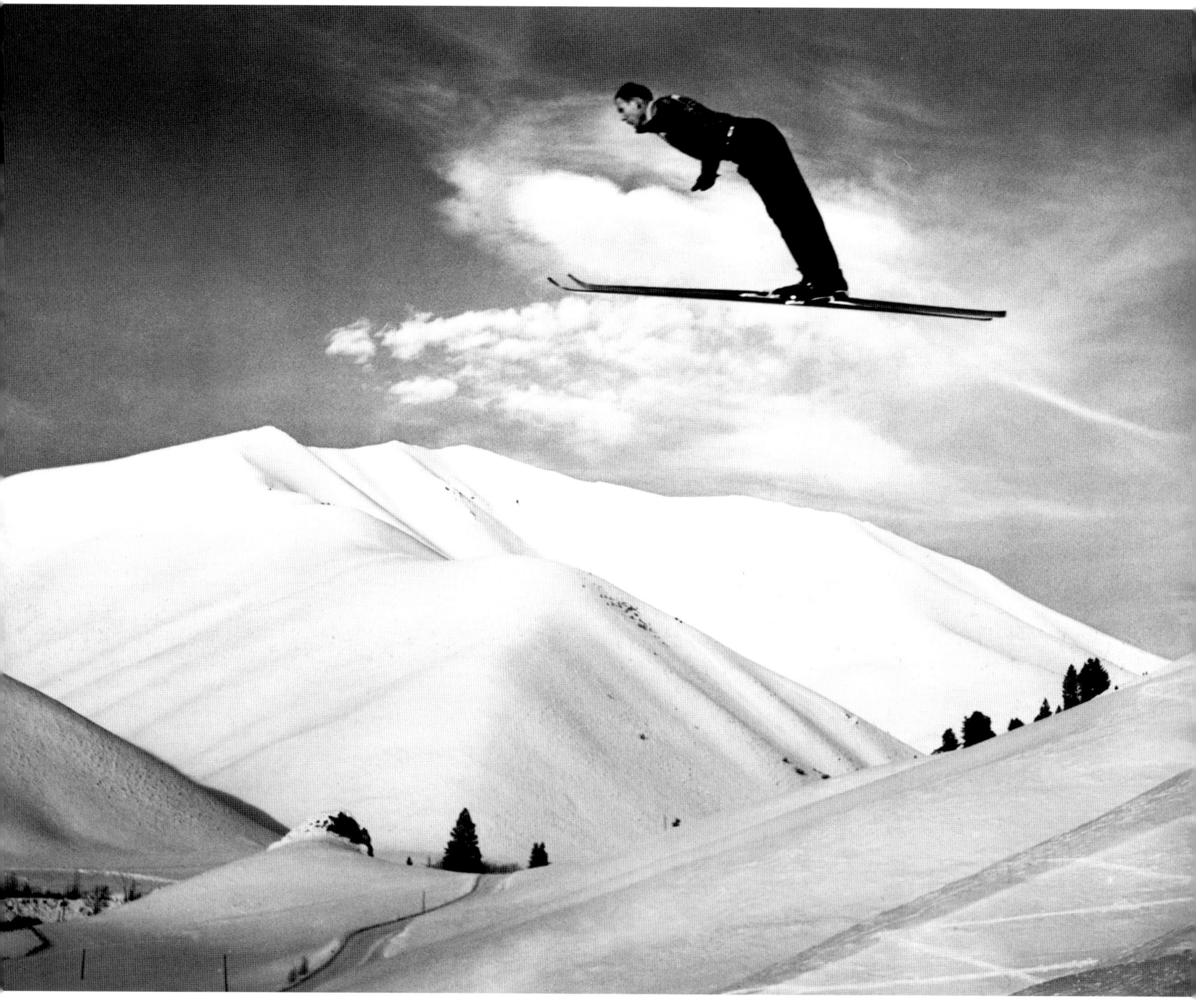

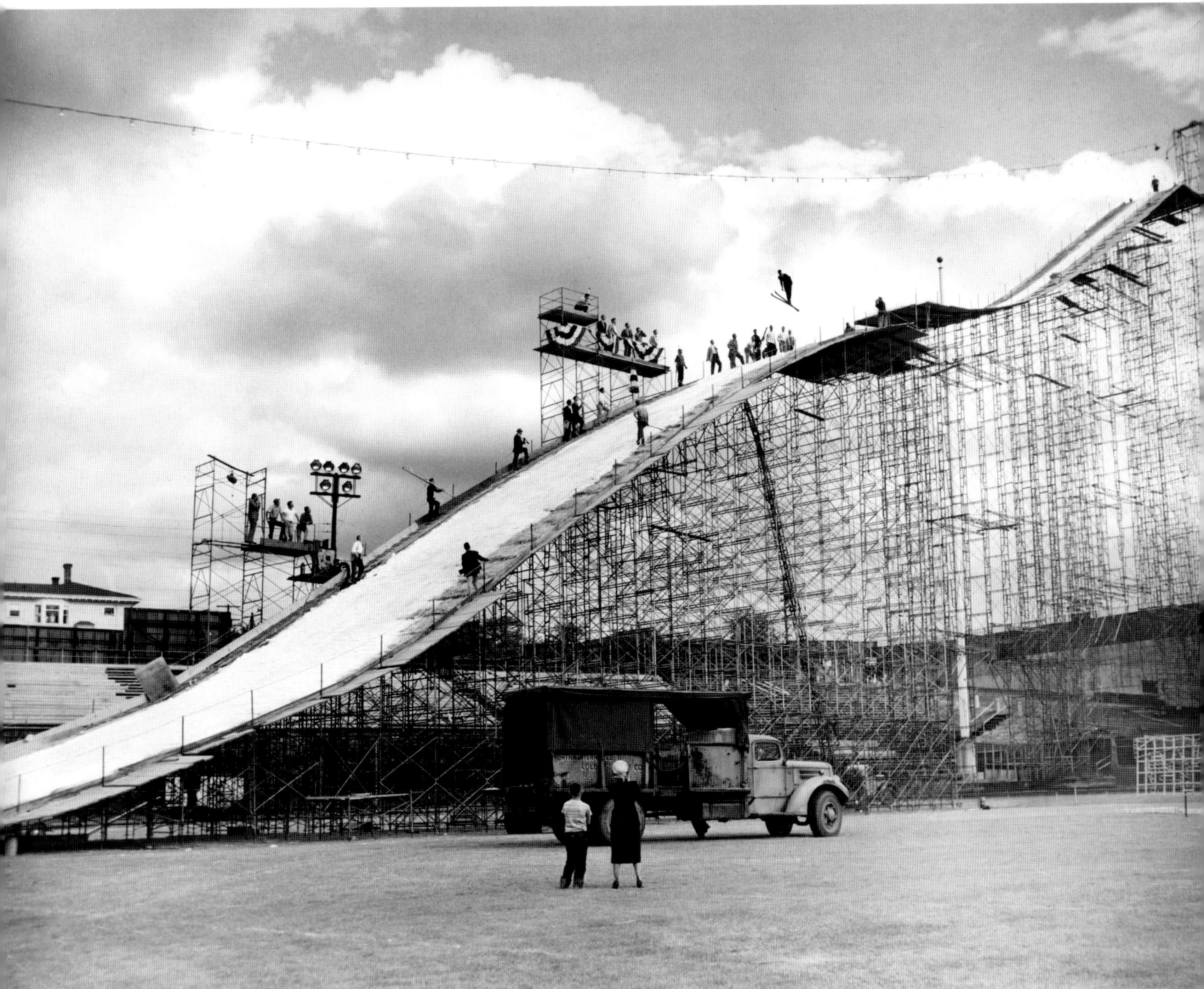

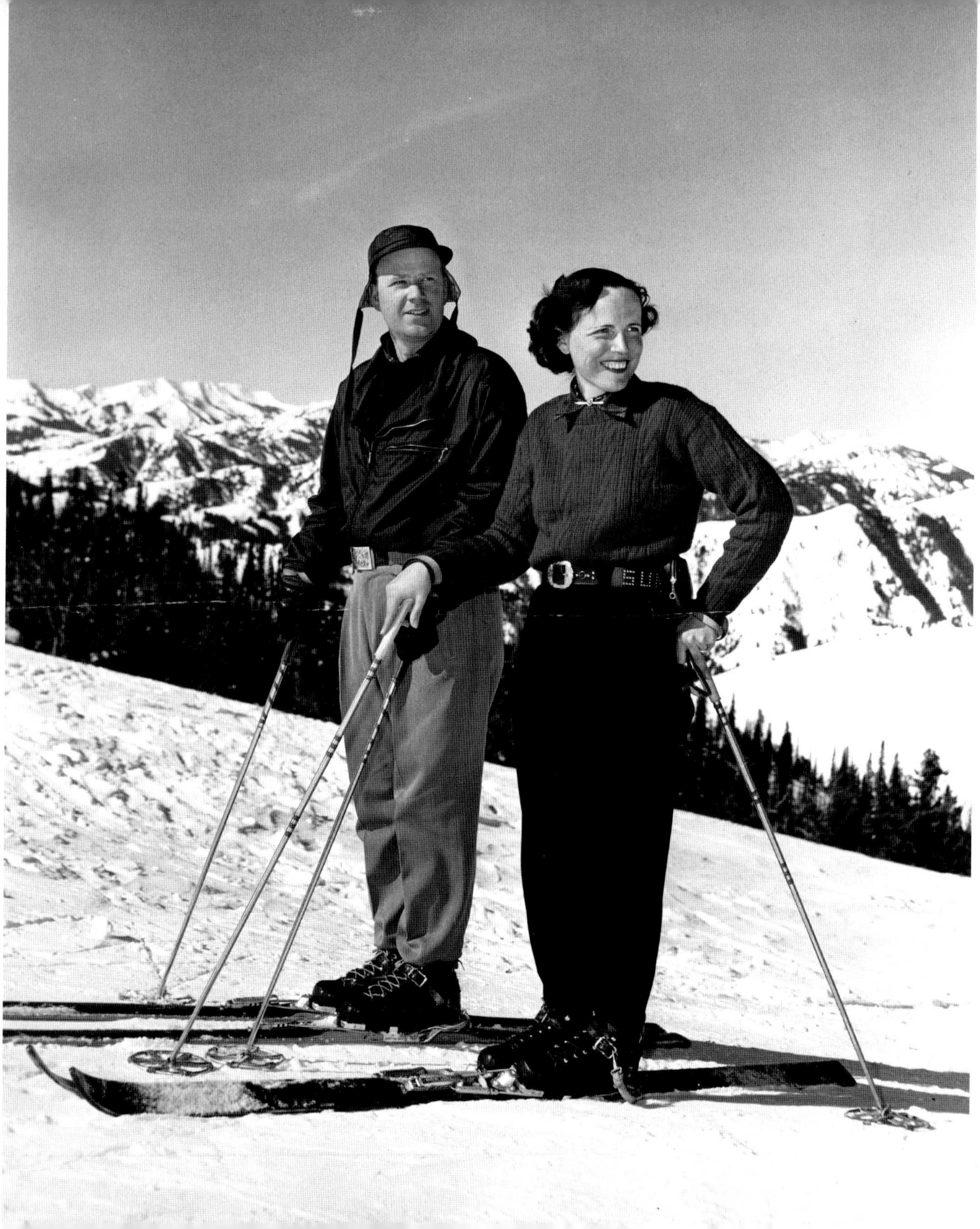

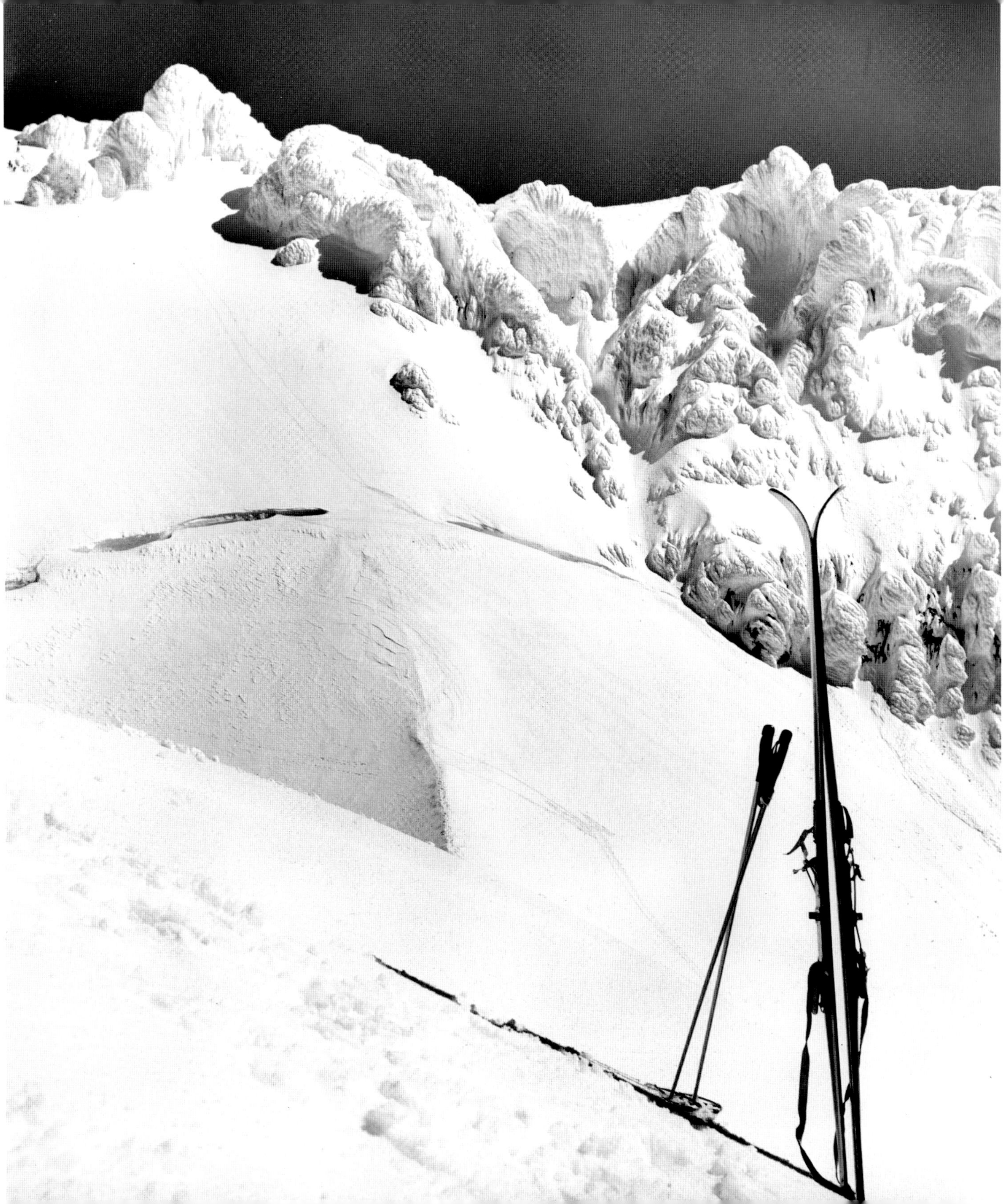

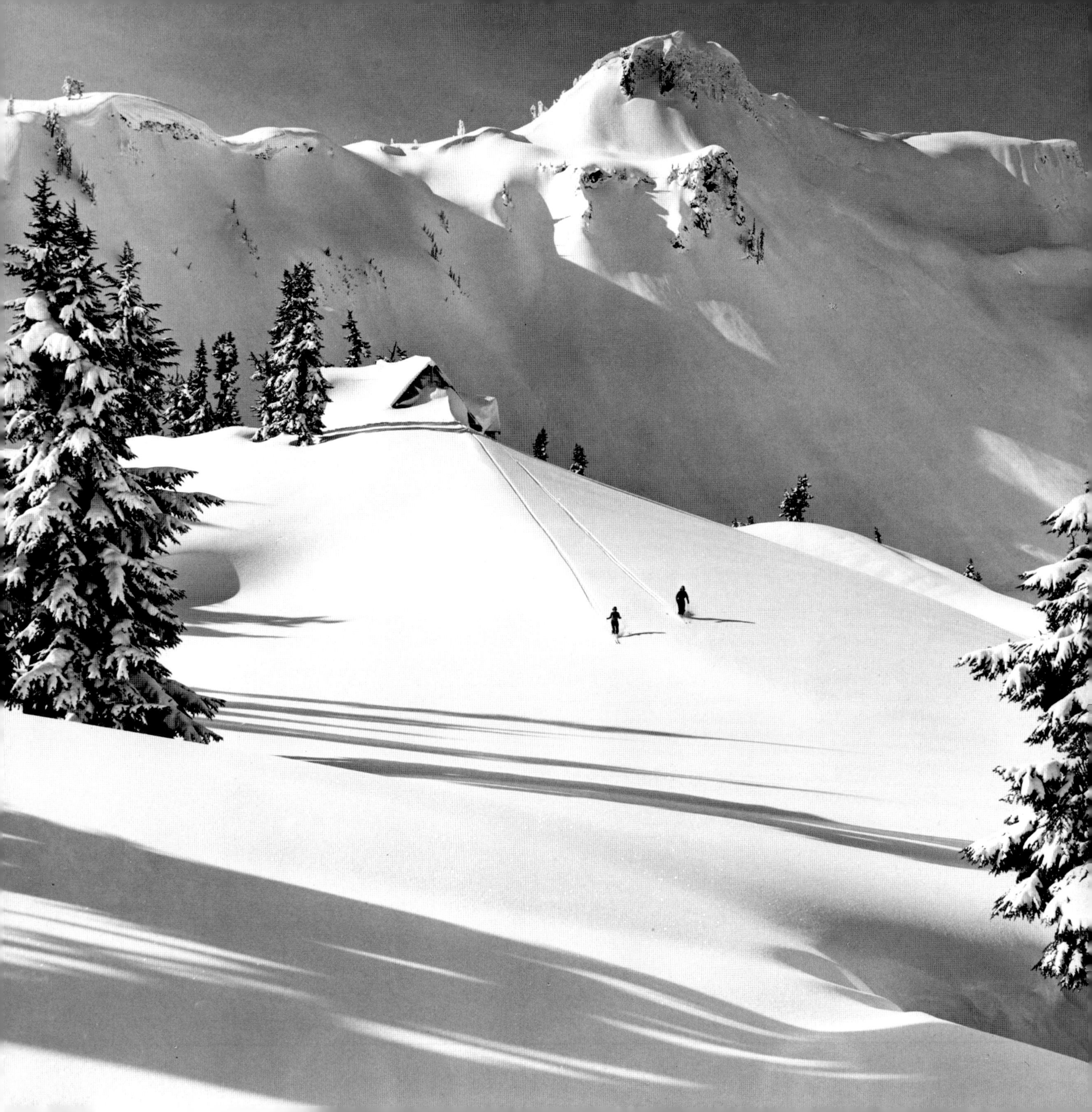

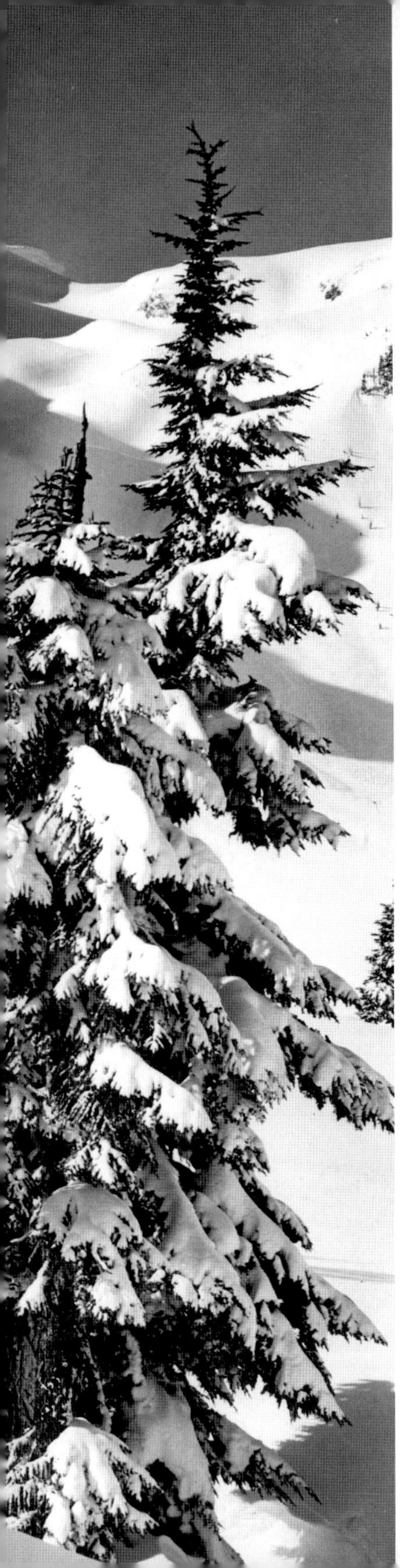
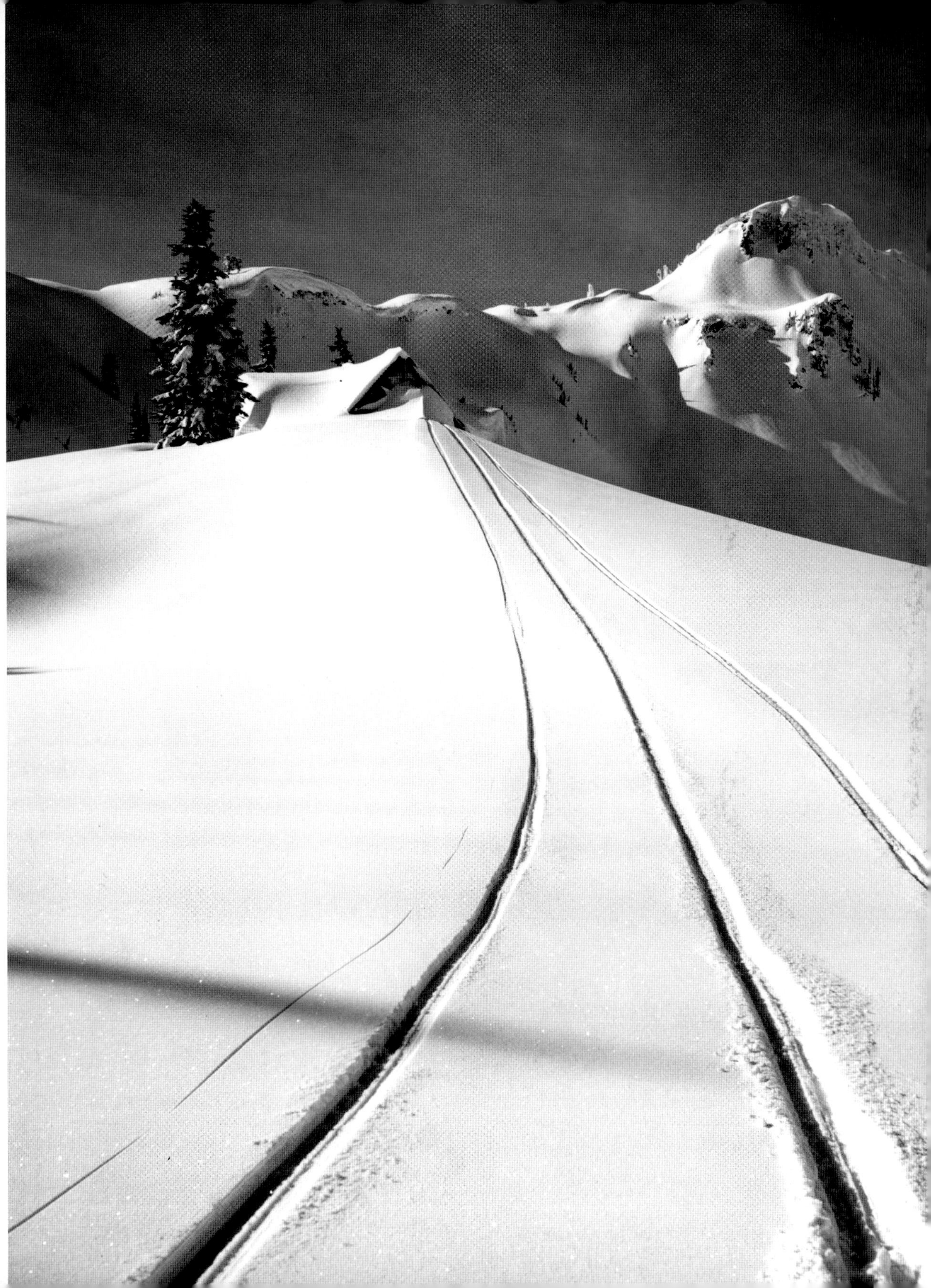

Never measure the height
of a mountain until you reach the top.
Then you will see how low it was.

DAG HAMMERSKJOLD

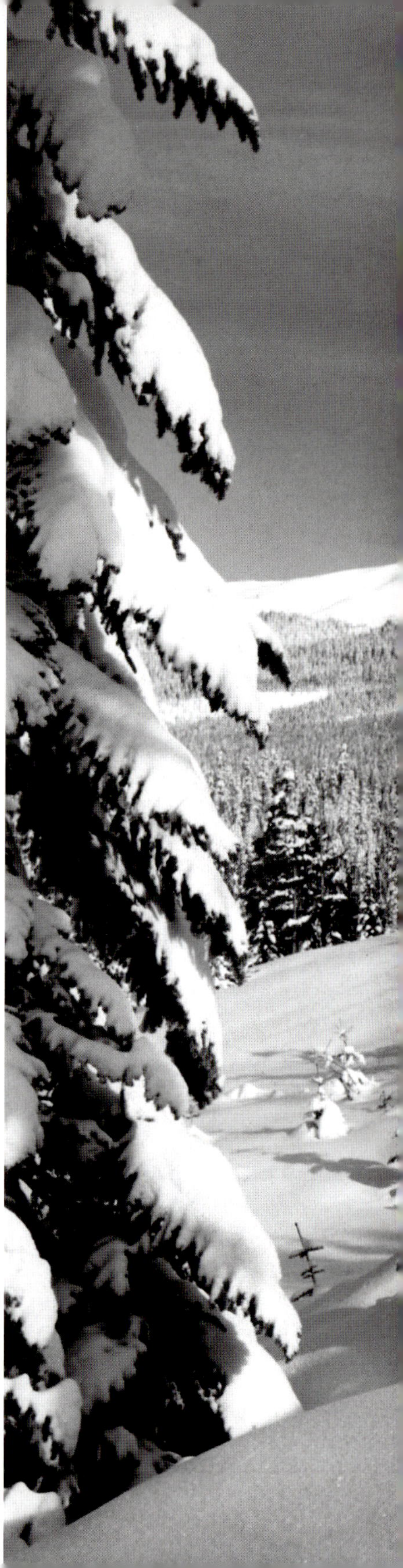

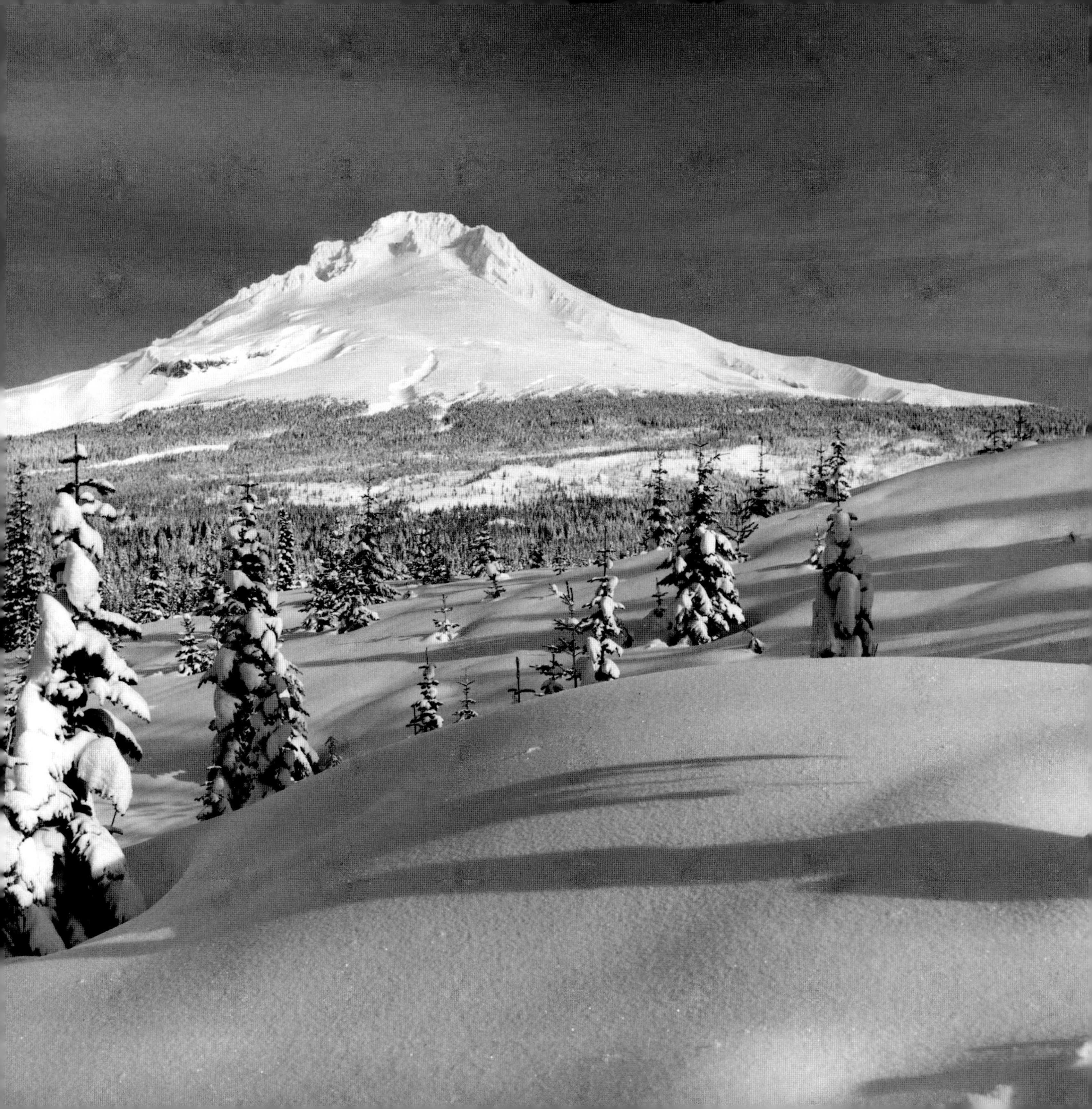

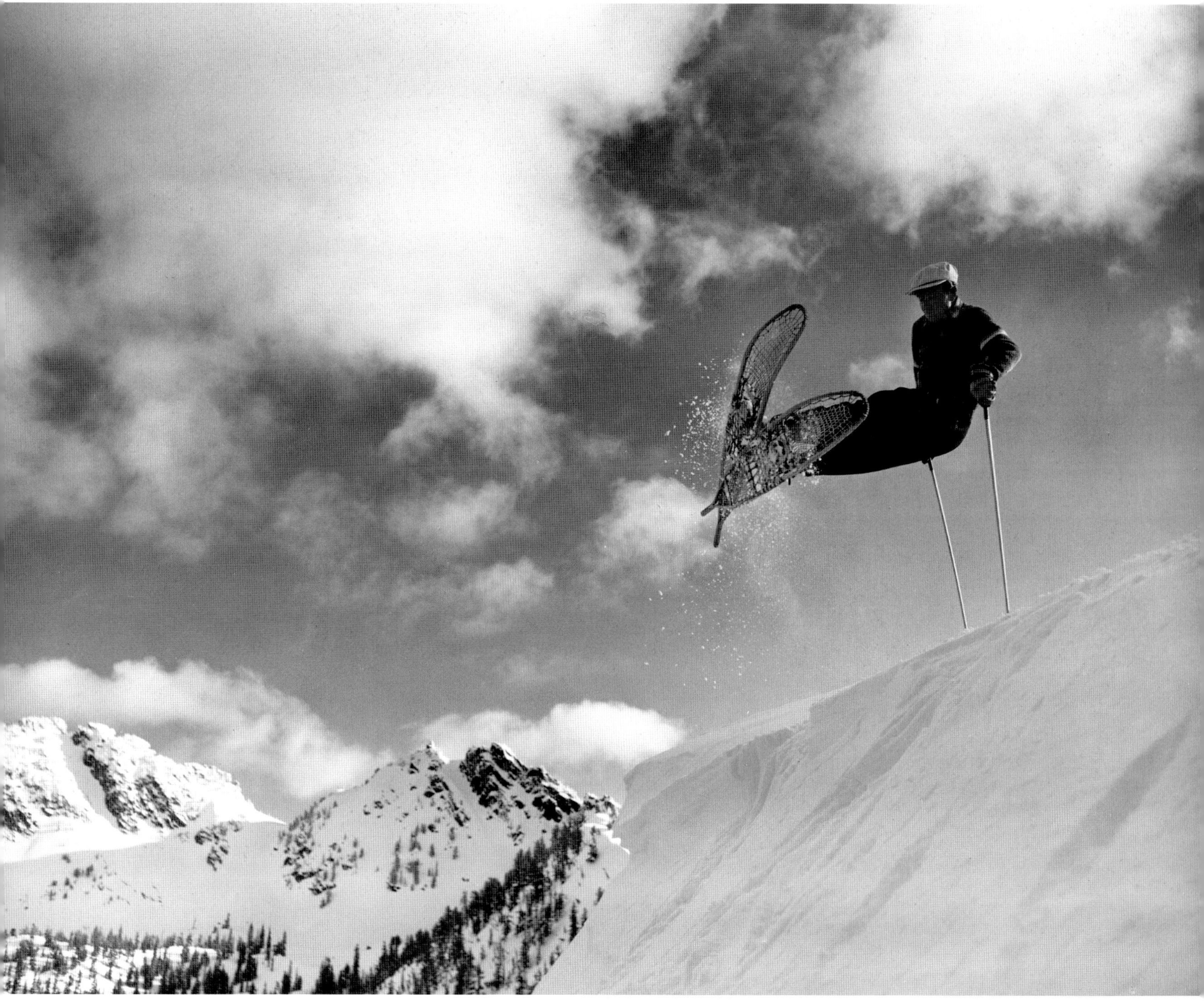

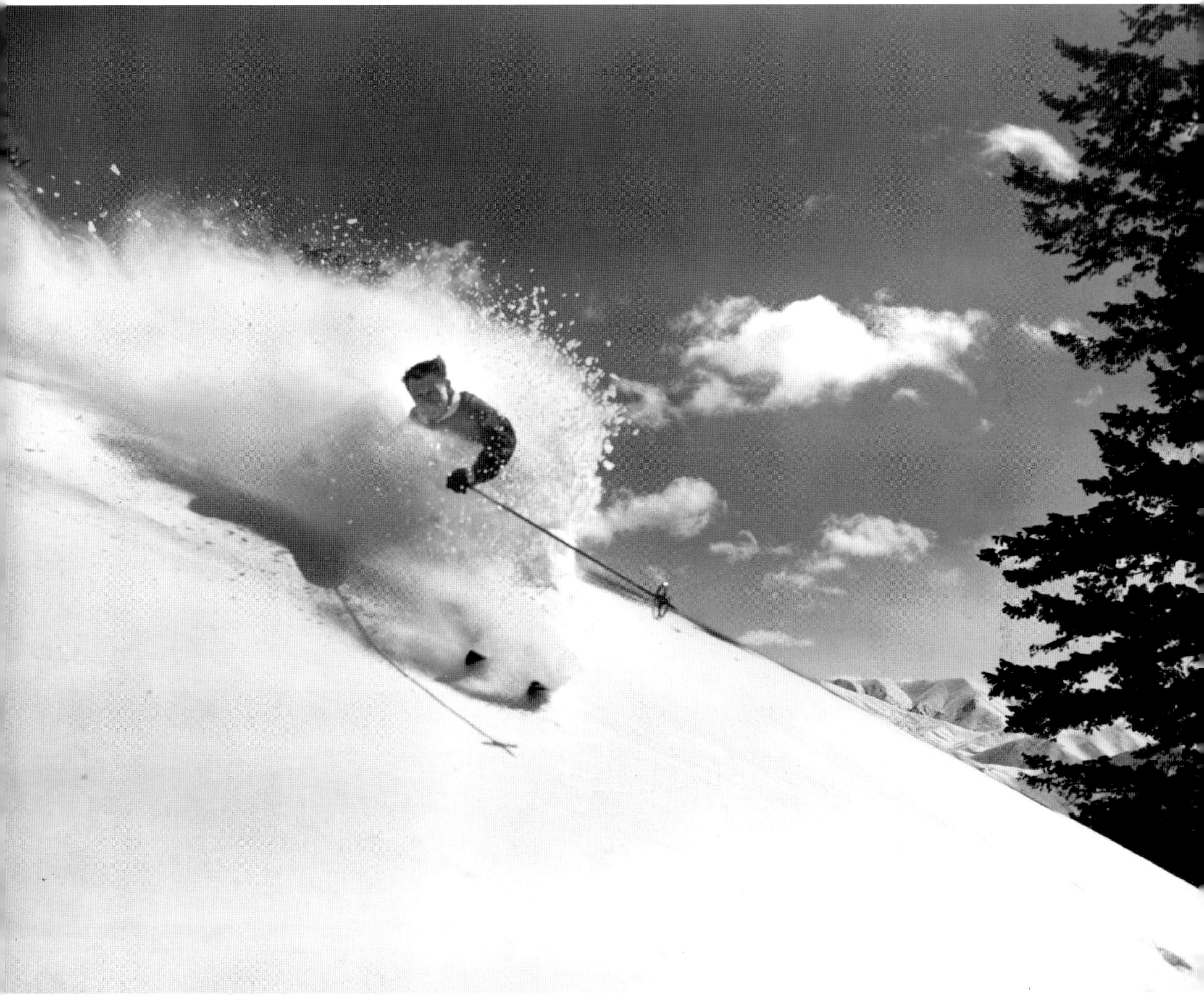

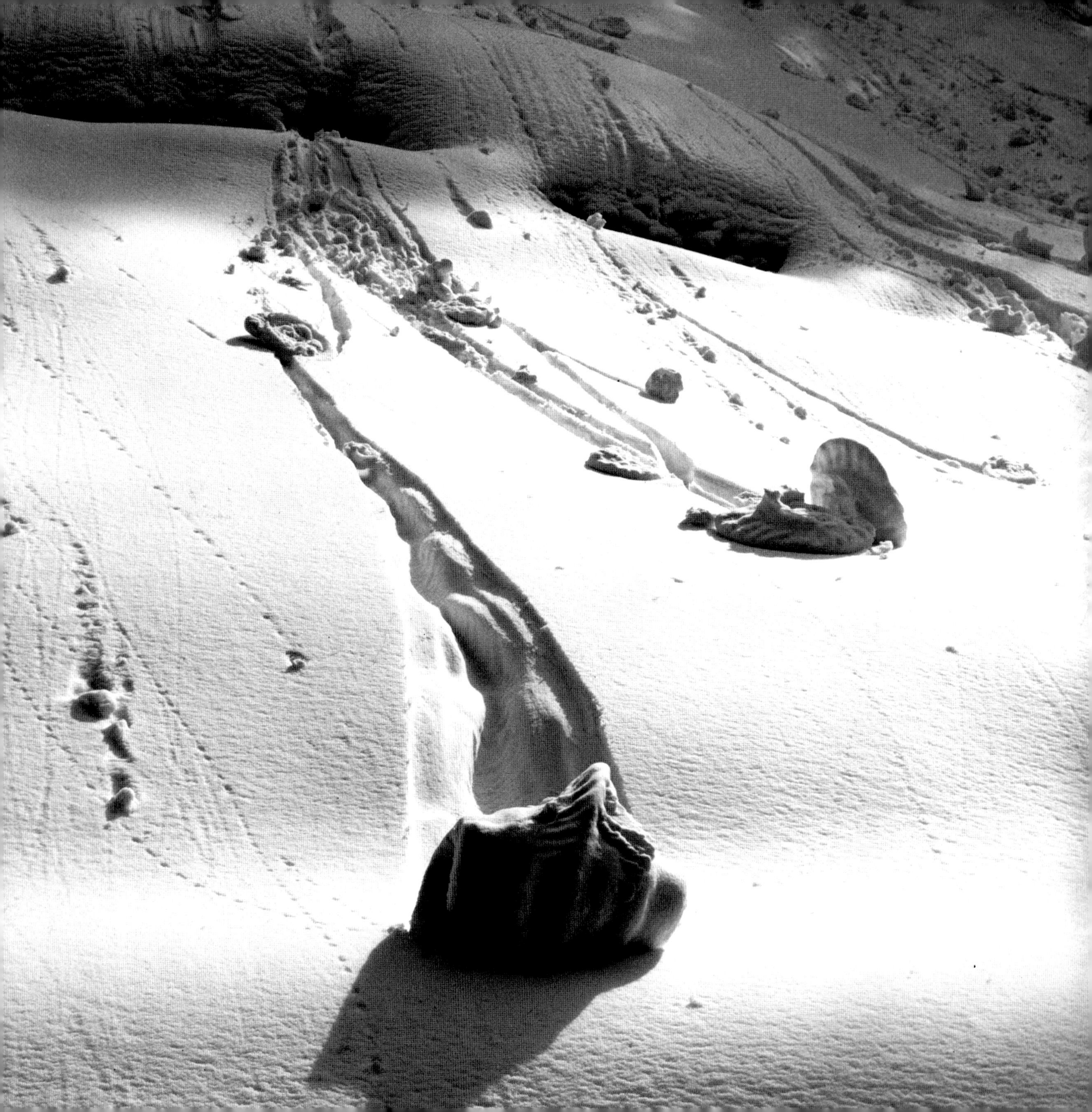

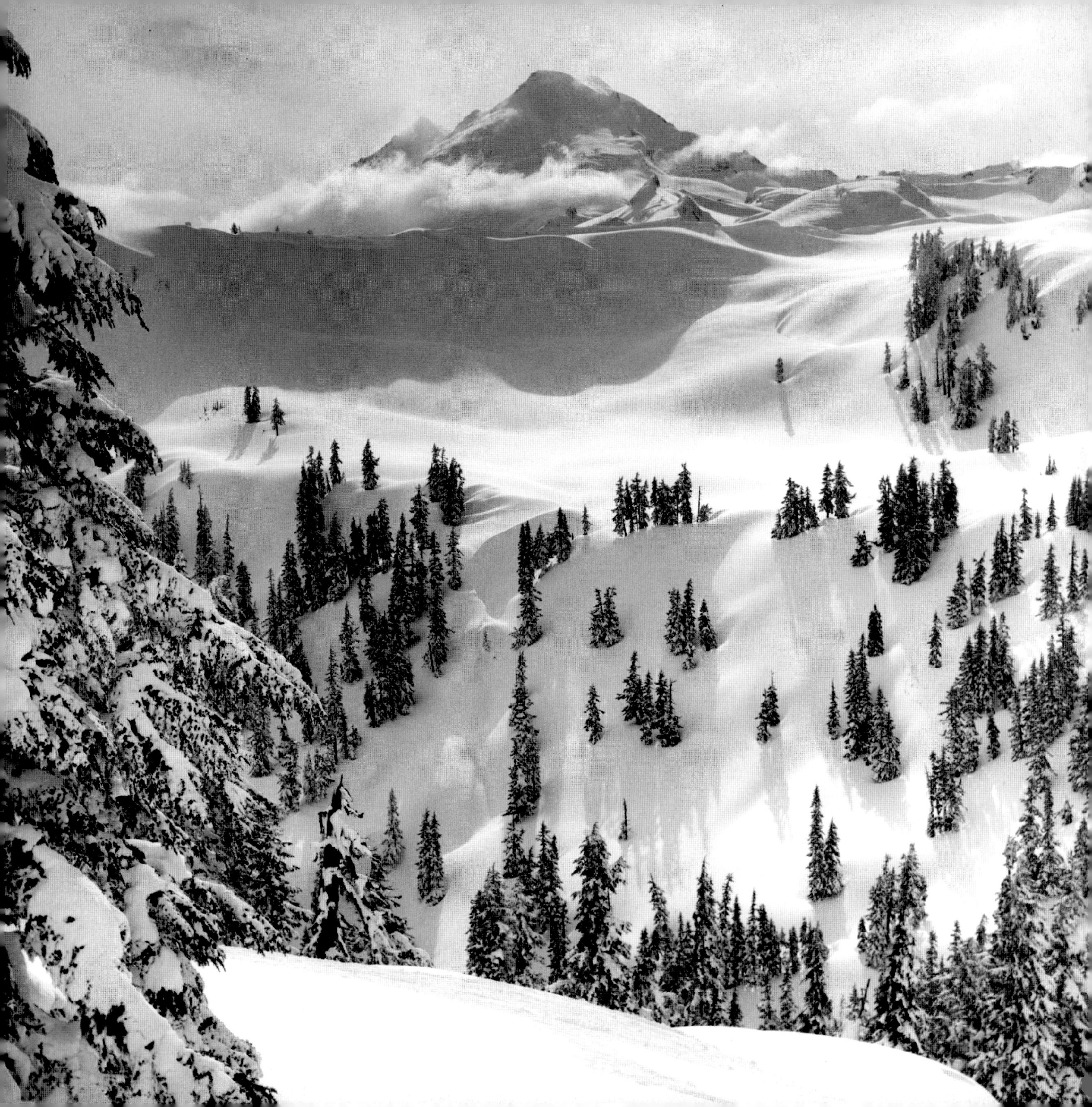

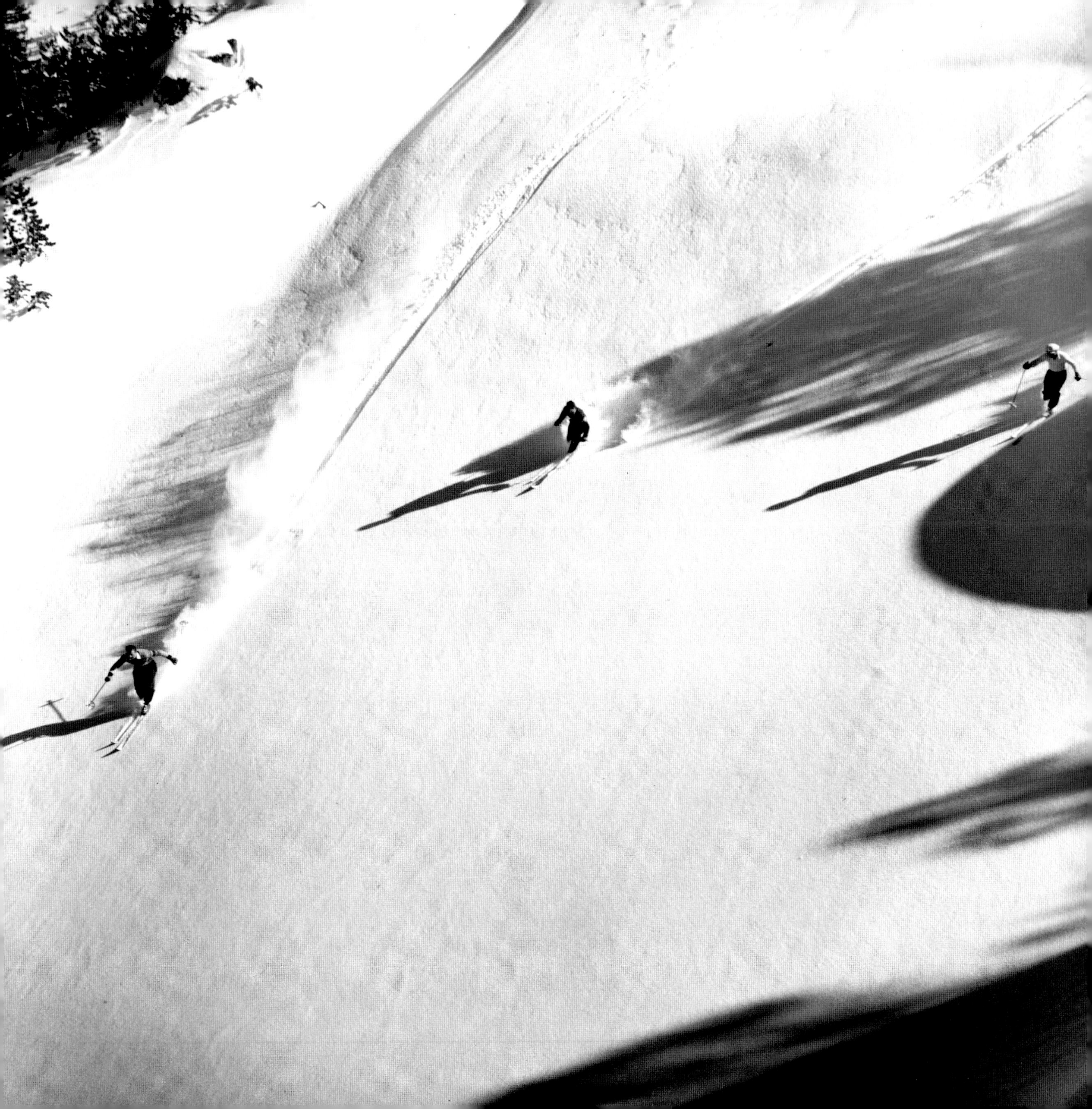

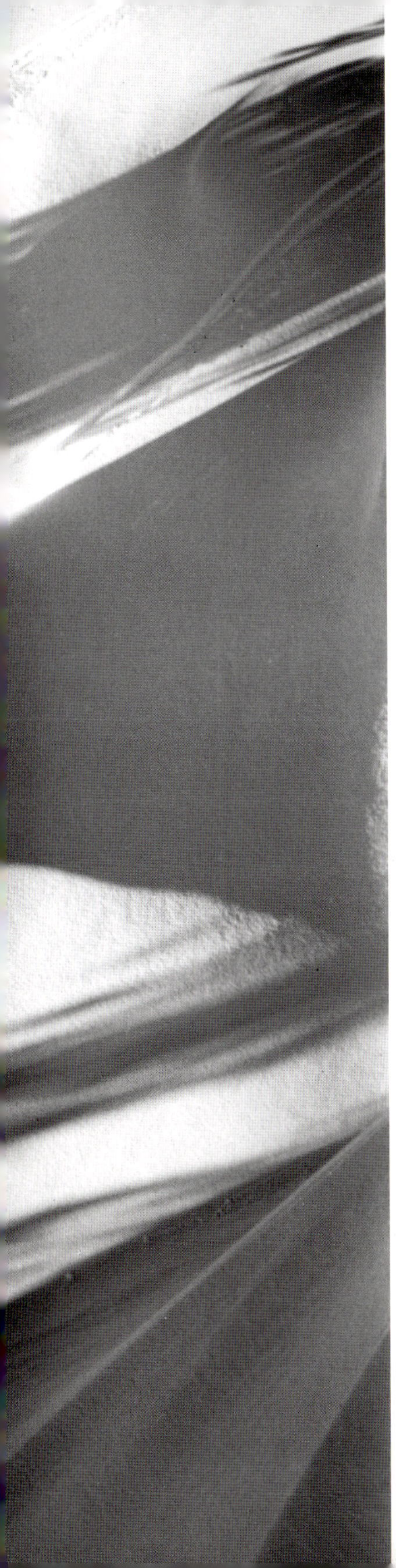

Here in the deep powder snow, you don't hear yourself ski. You don't hear your long turns or your short turns. You just float. The faster you go, the better. The less you struggle, the better. You move through the deep, light snow, through the deep snow with some crust on it, through the deep snow with some wind in it.

JACQUES LABRIE

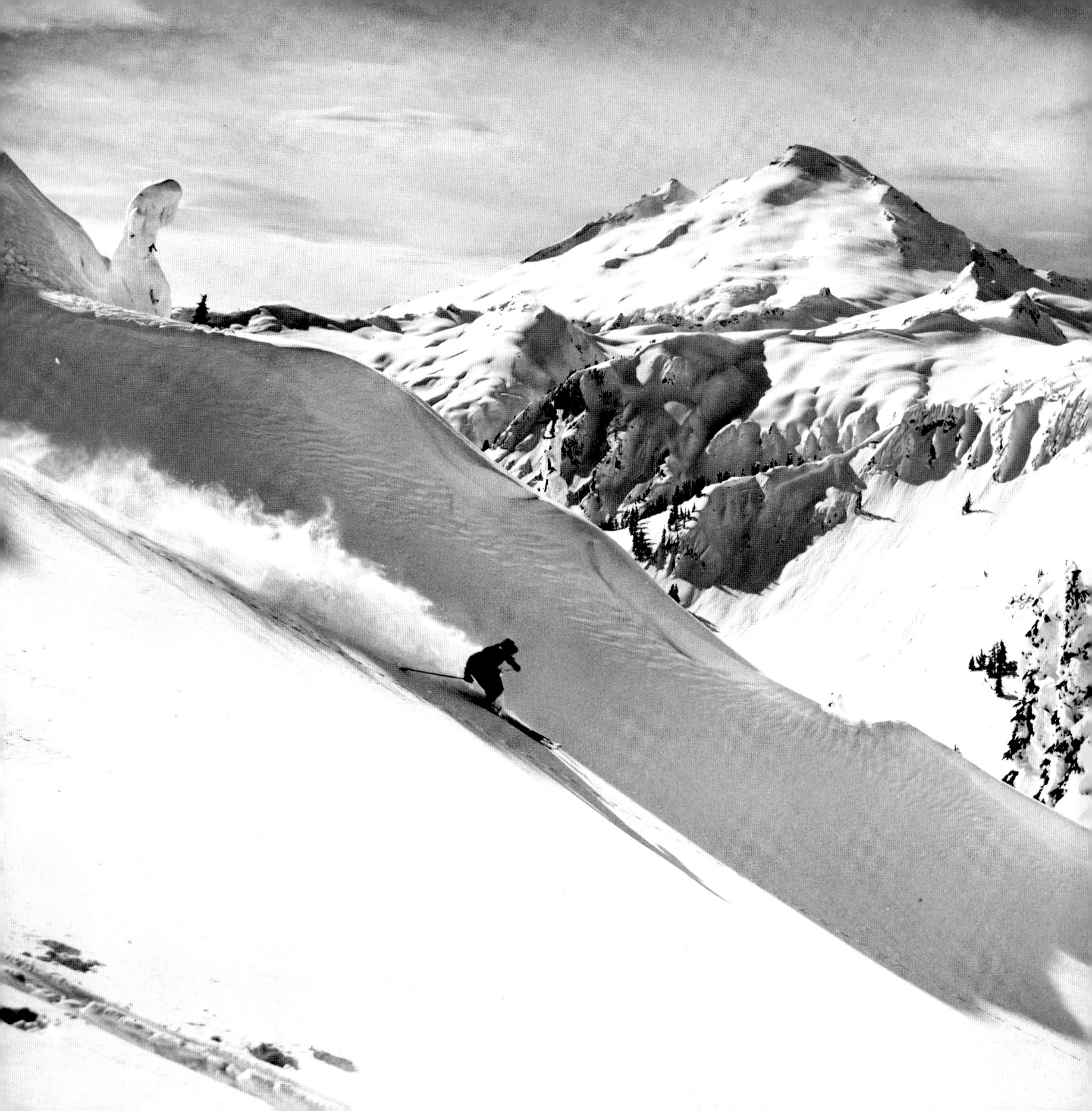

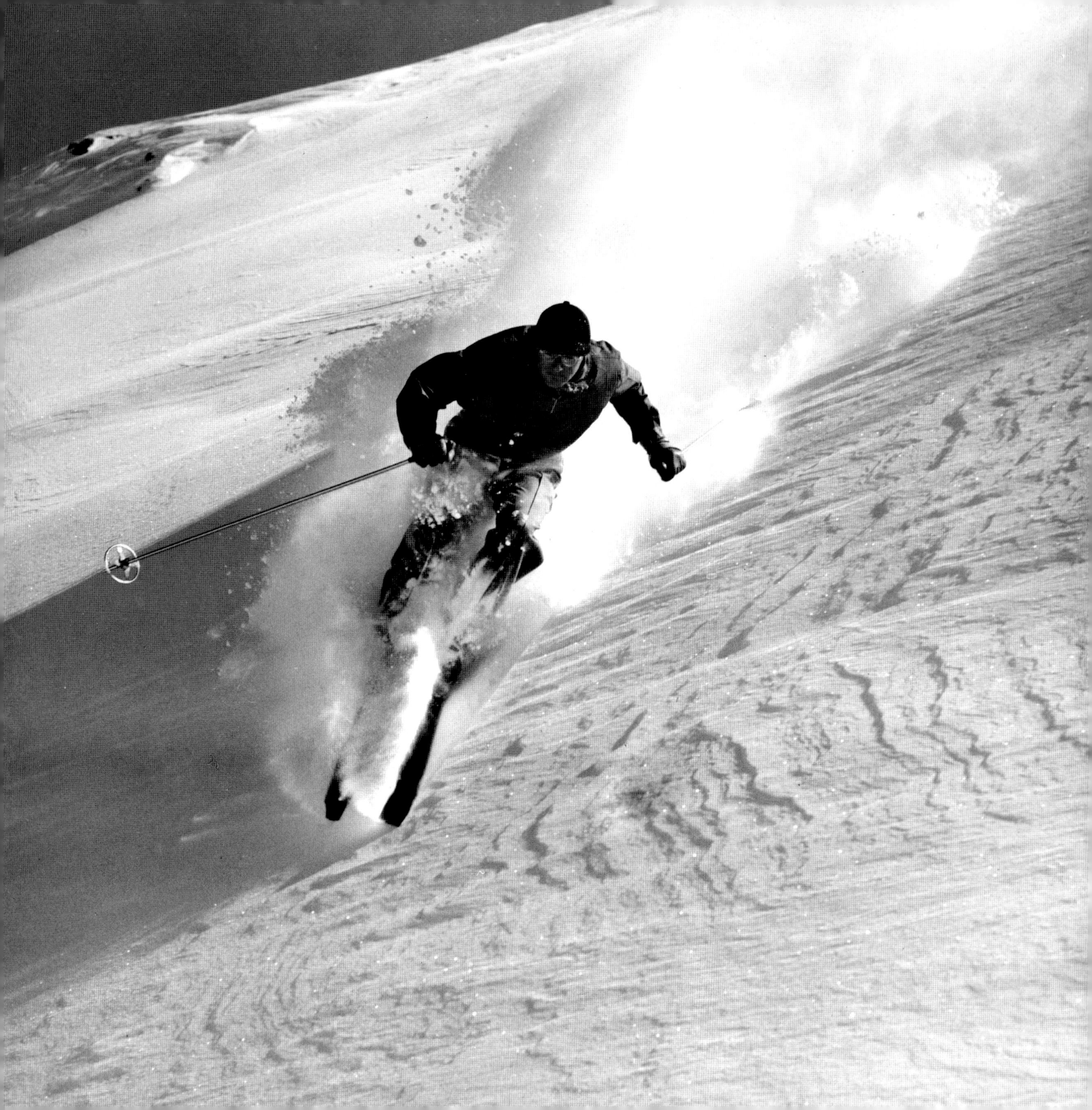

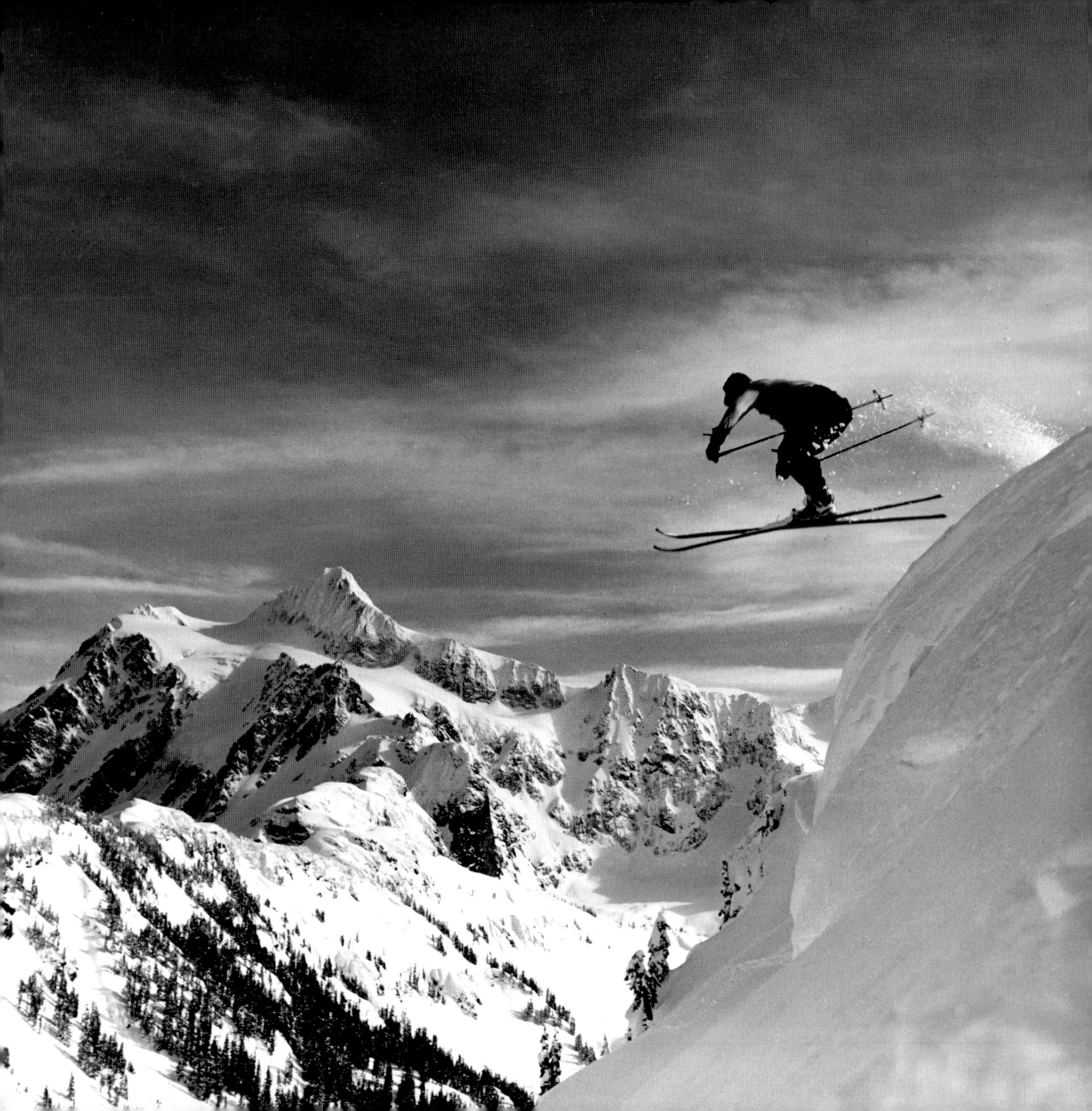

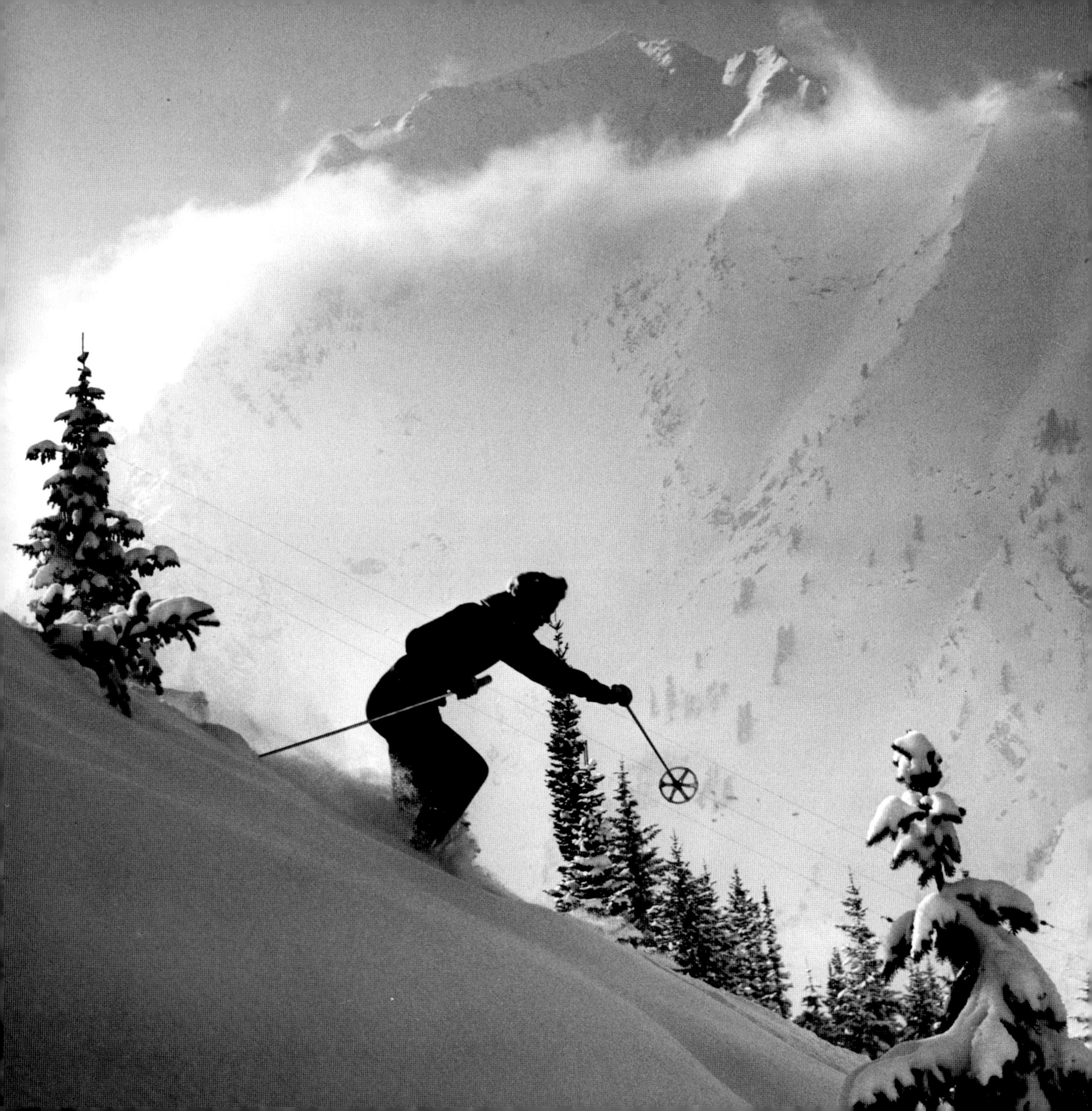

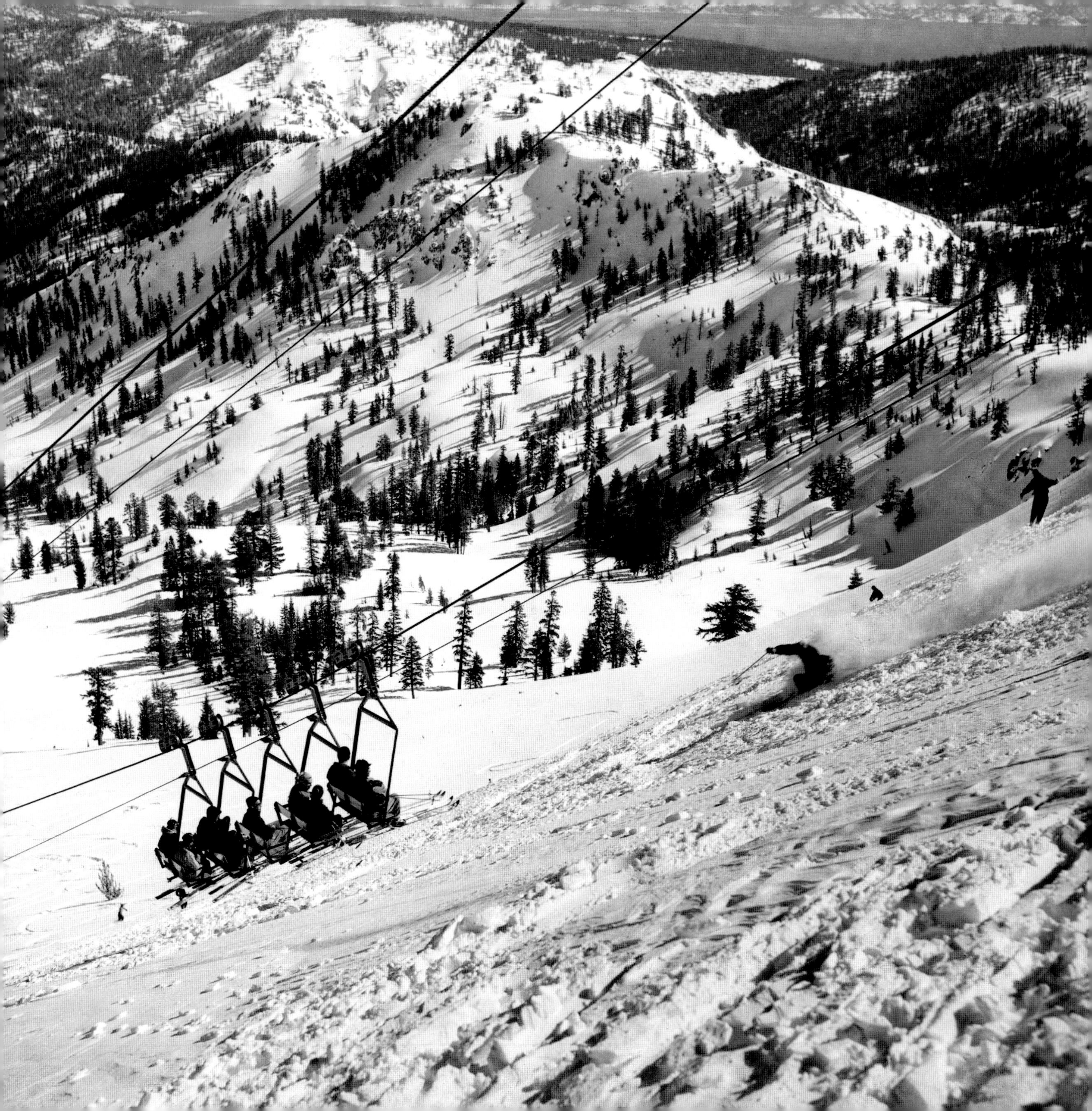

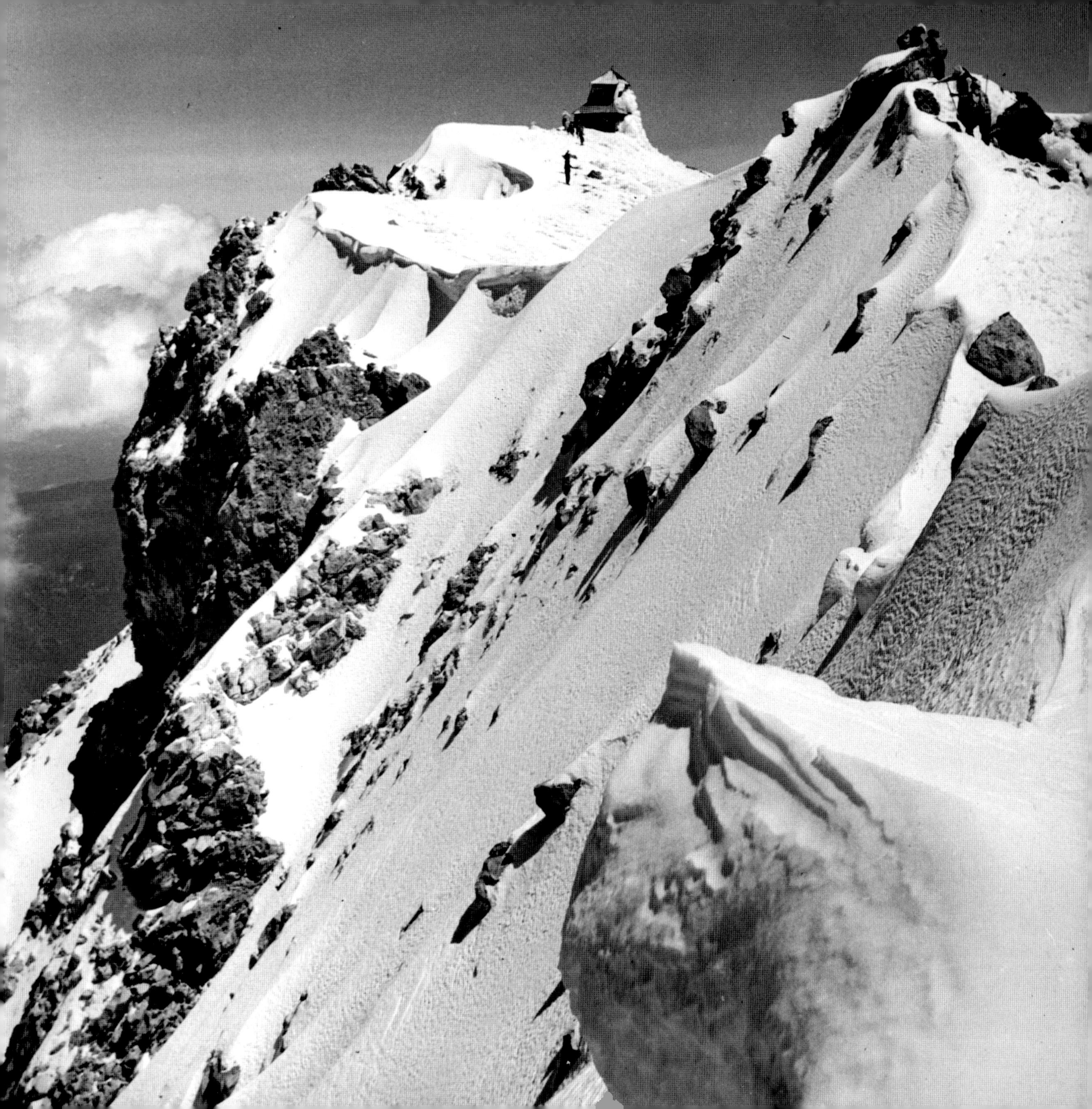

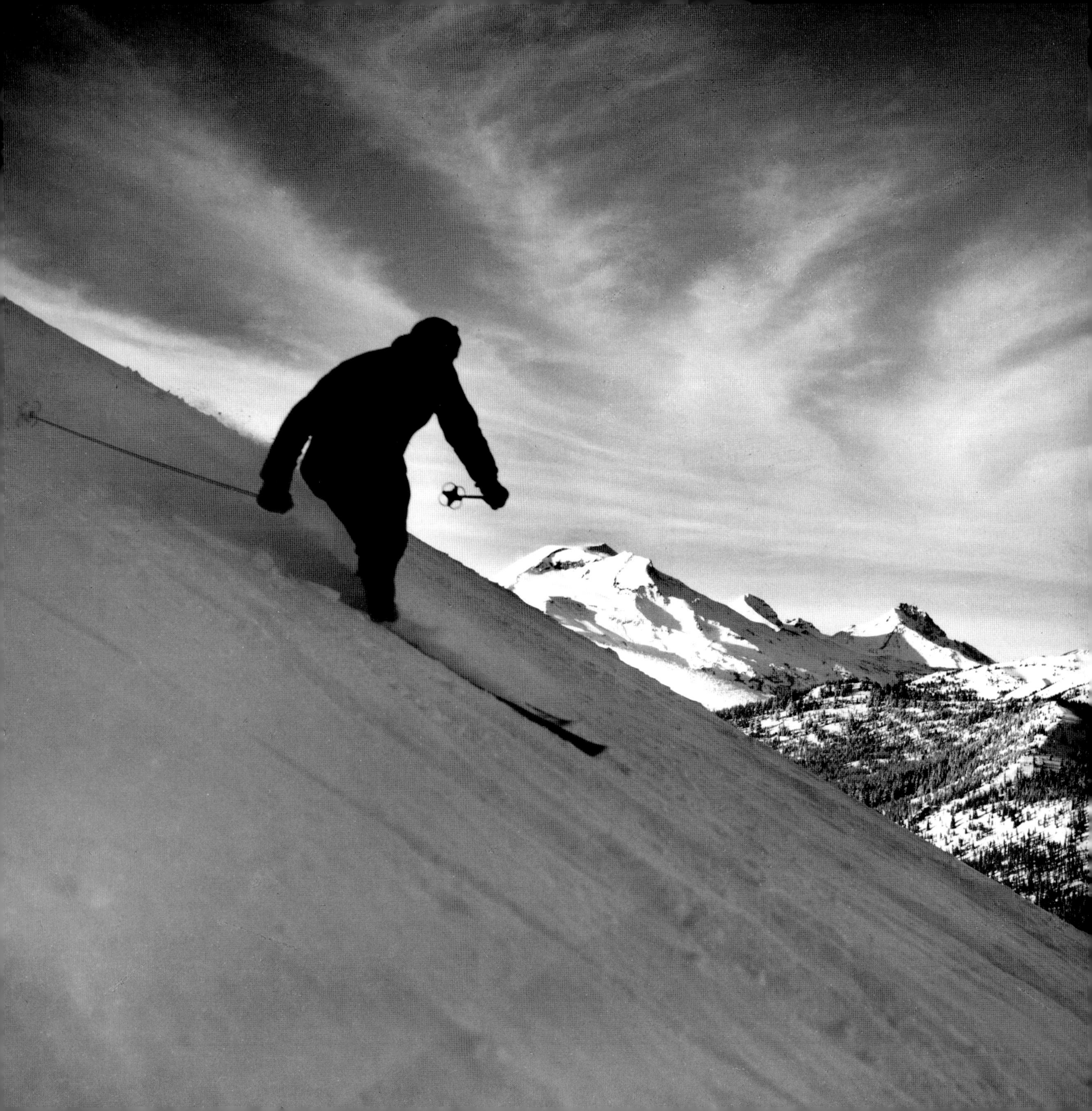

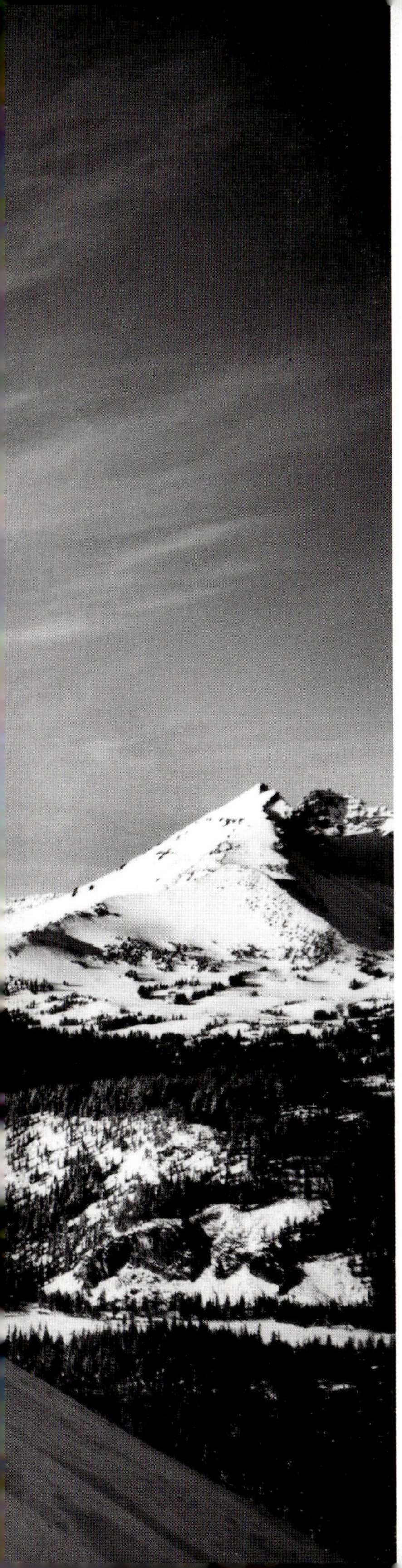

I've realized that at the top of the mountain, there's another mountain.

ANDREW GARFIELD

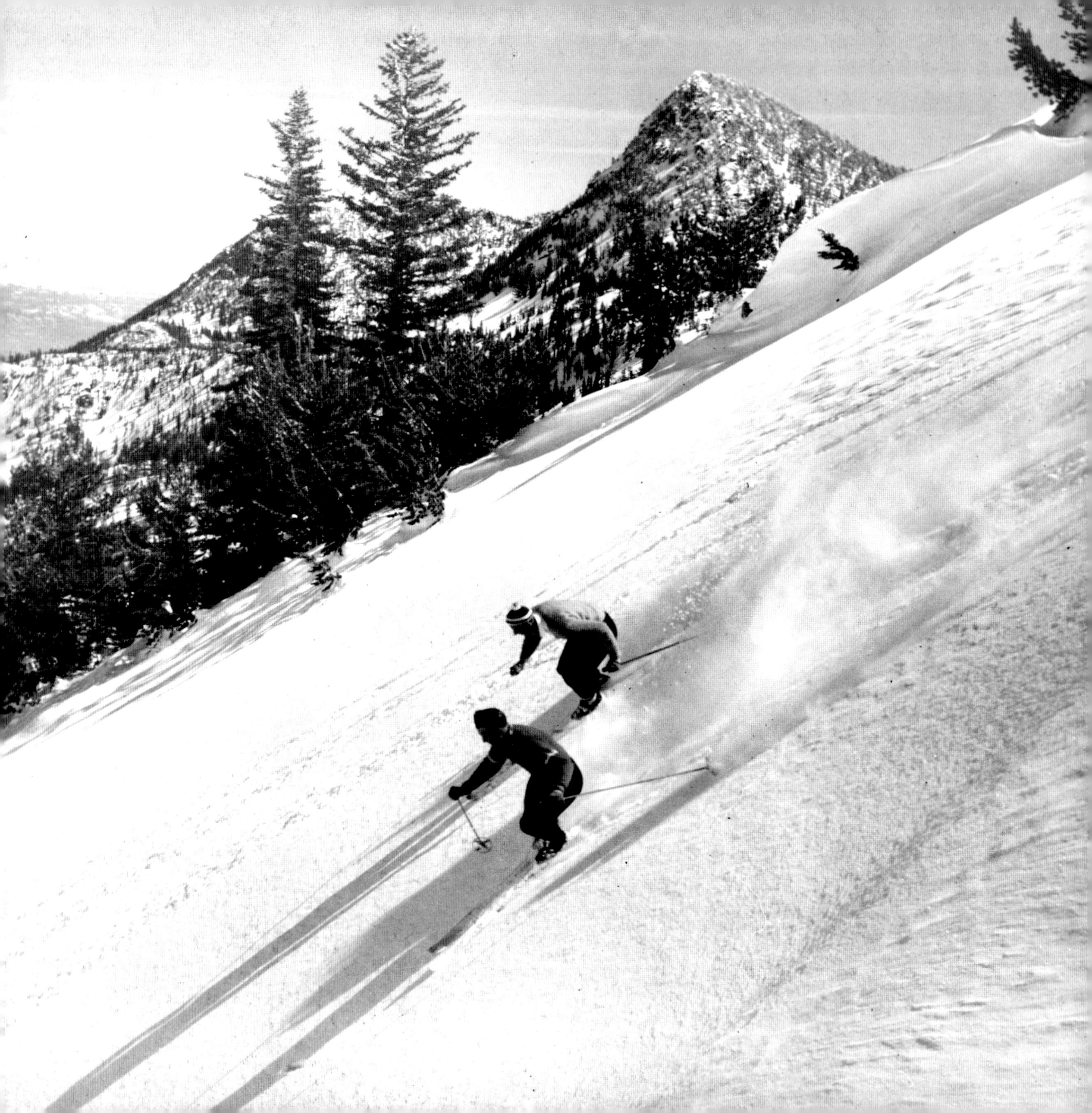

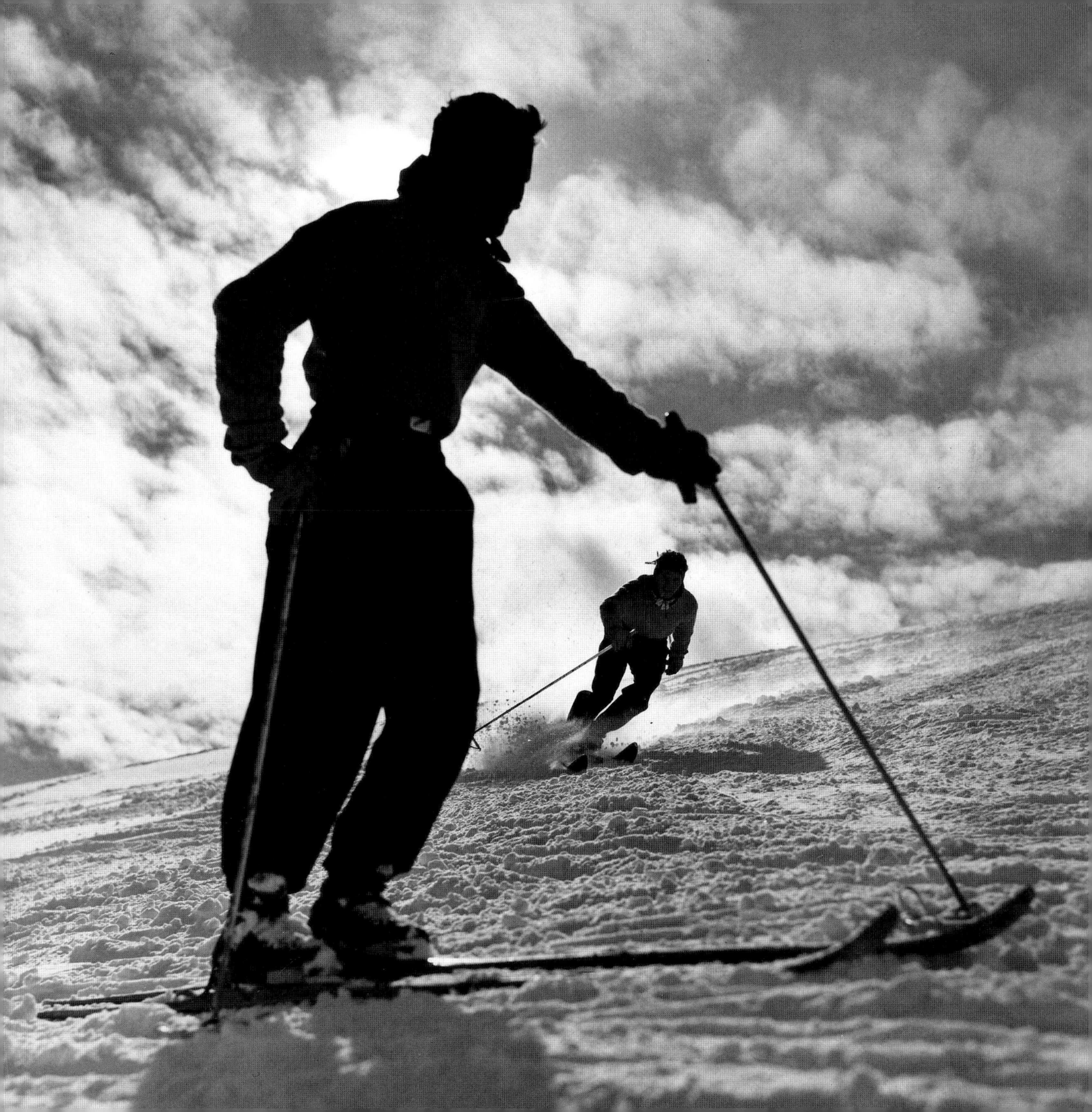

If you are faced with a mountain, you have several options. You can climb it and cross to the other side. You can go around it. You can dig under it. You can fly over it. You can blow it up. You can ignore it and pretend it's not there. You can turn around and go back the way you came. Or you can stay on the mountain and make it your home.

VERA NAZARIAN

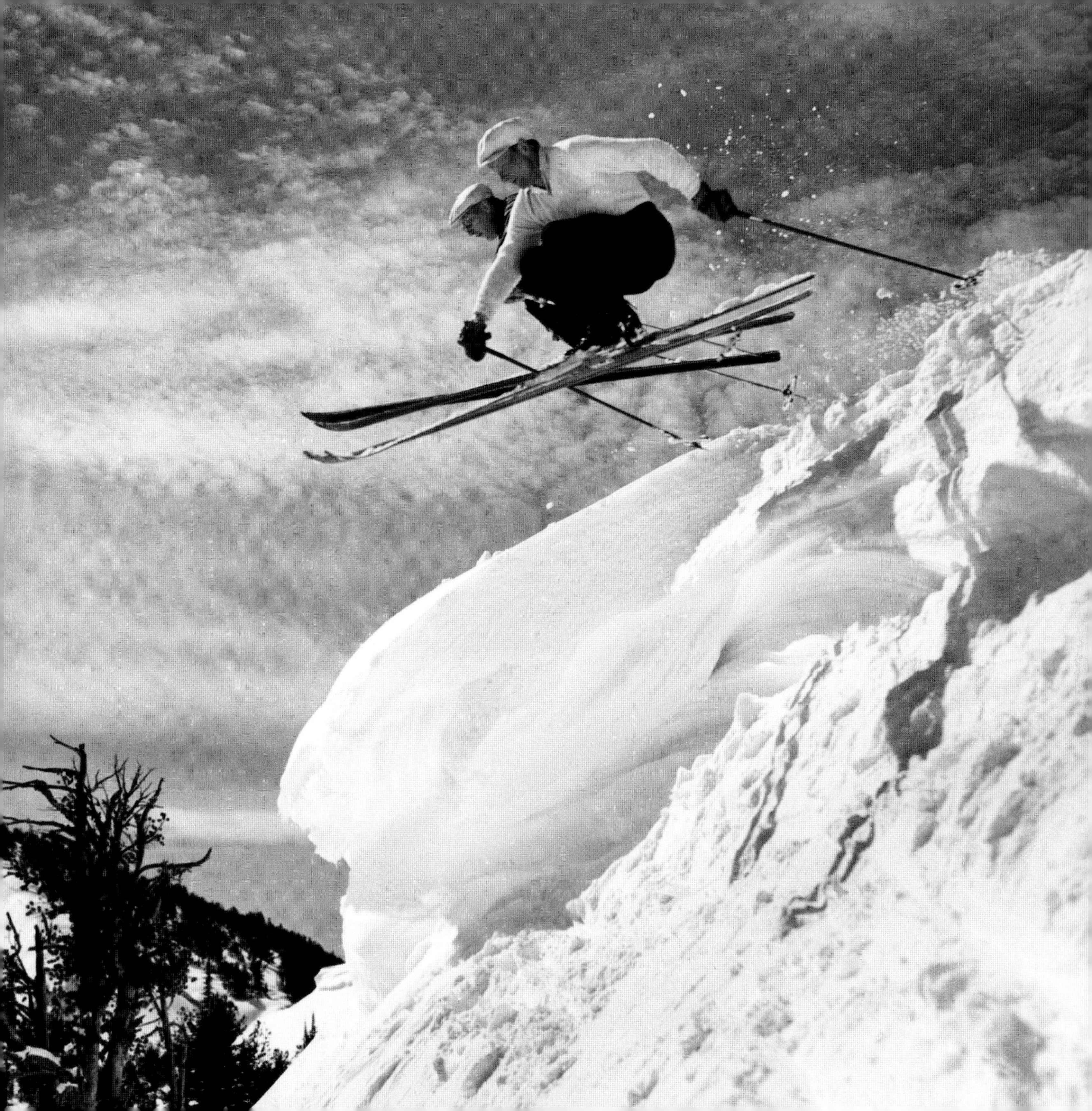

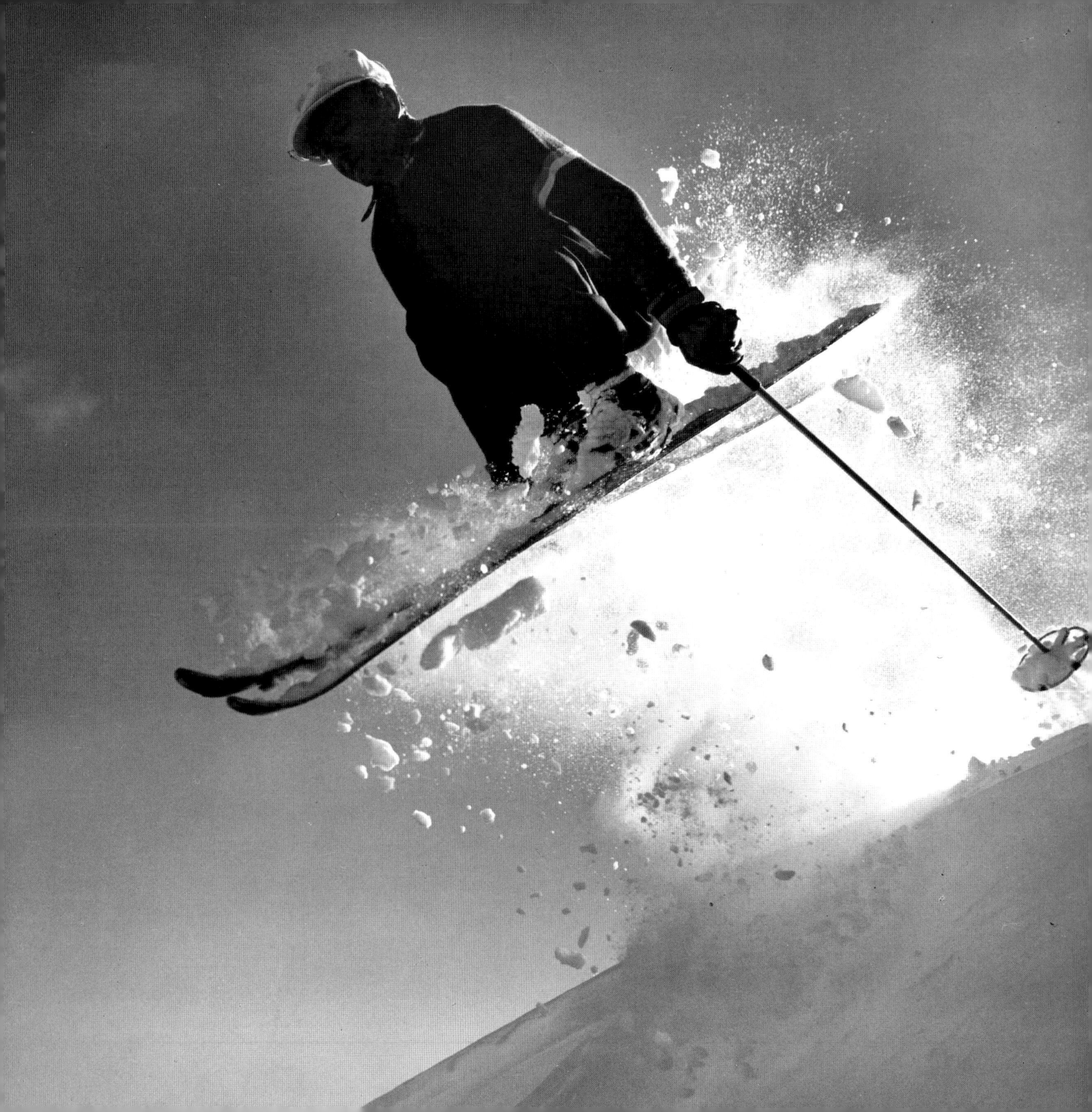

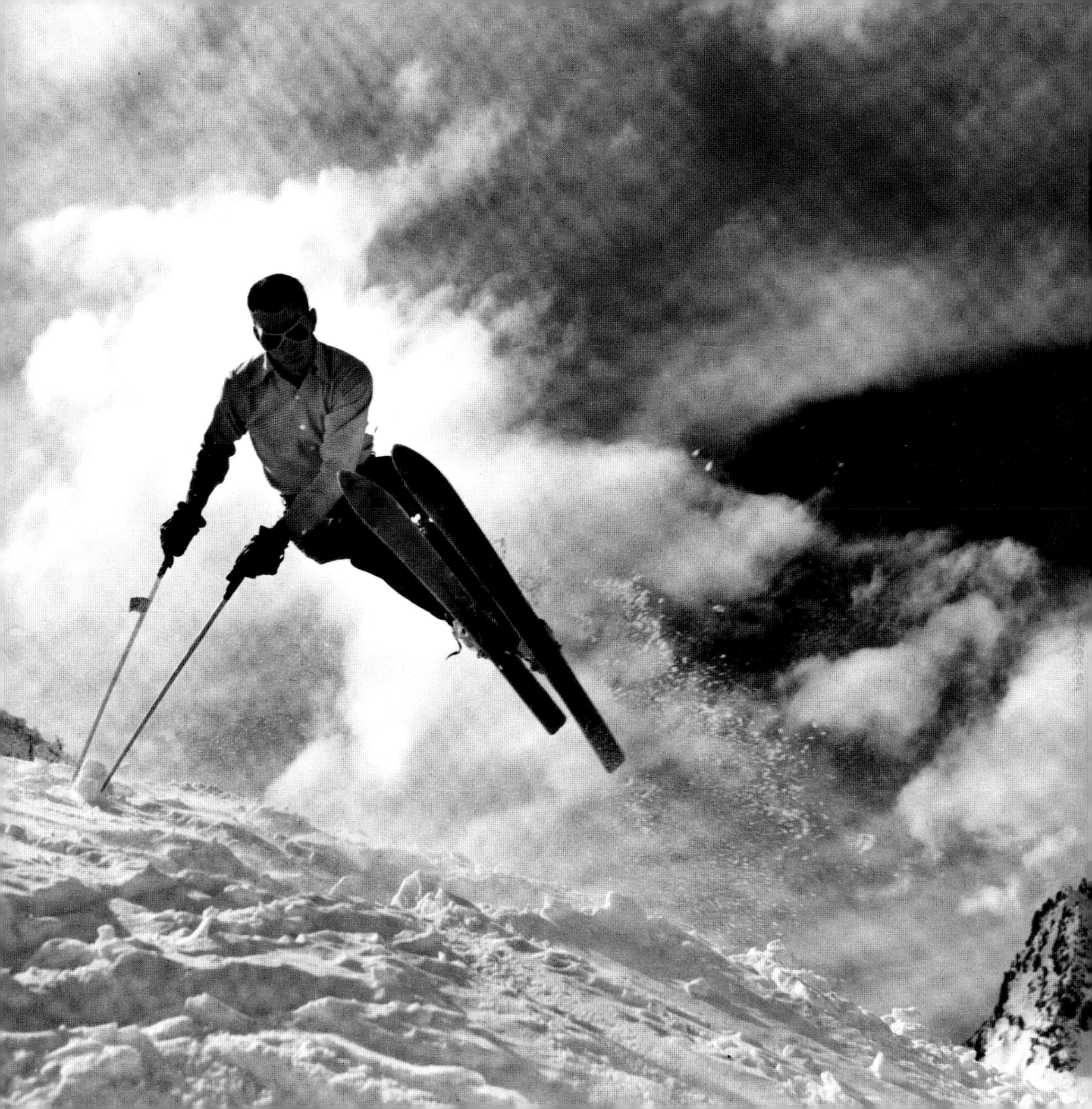

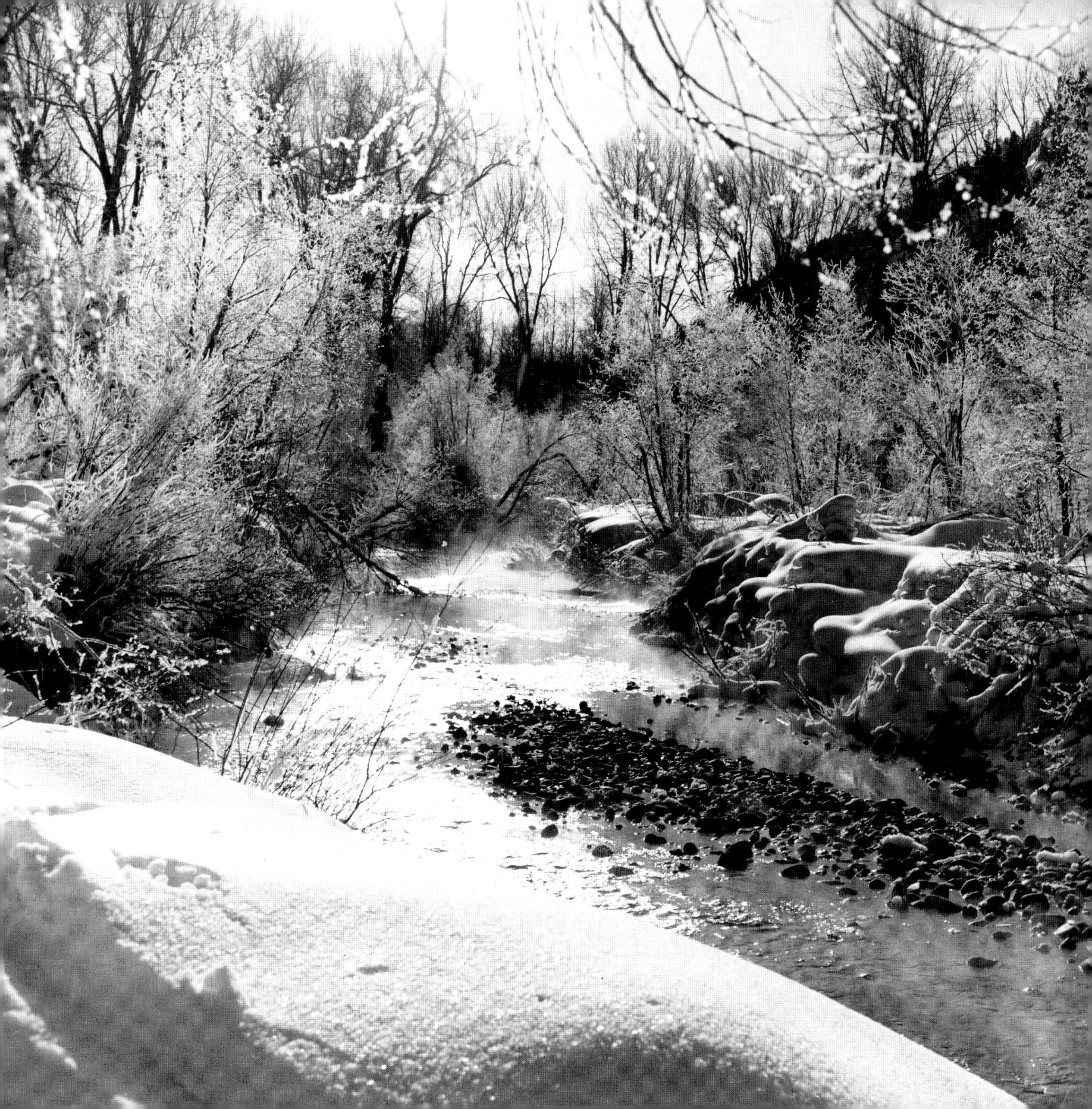

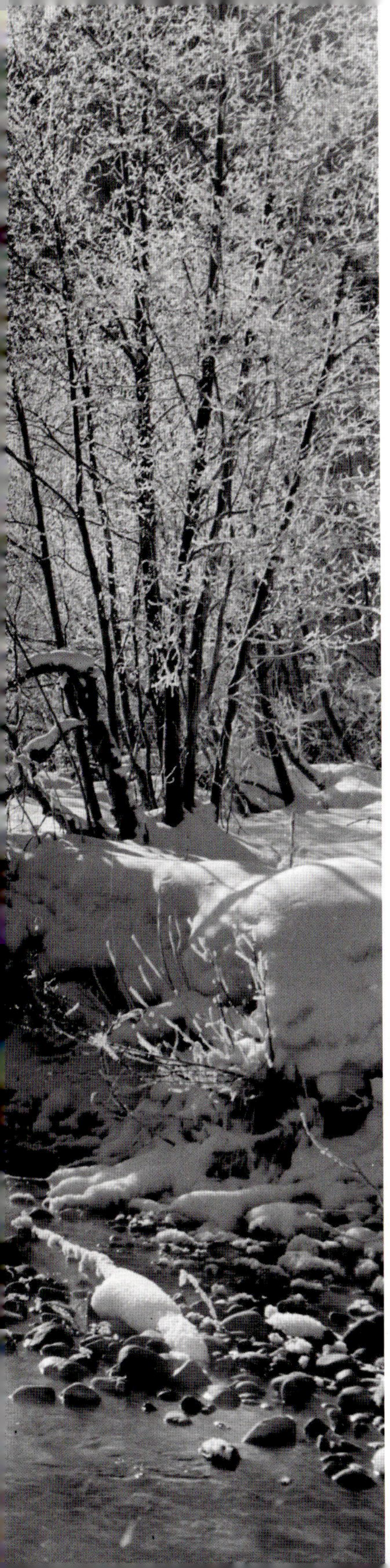

The mountains are calling and I must go.

JOHN MUIR

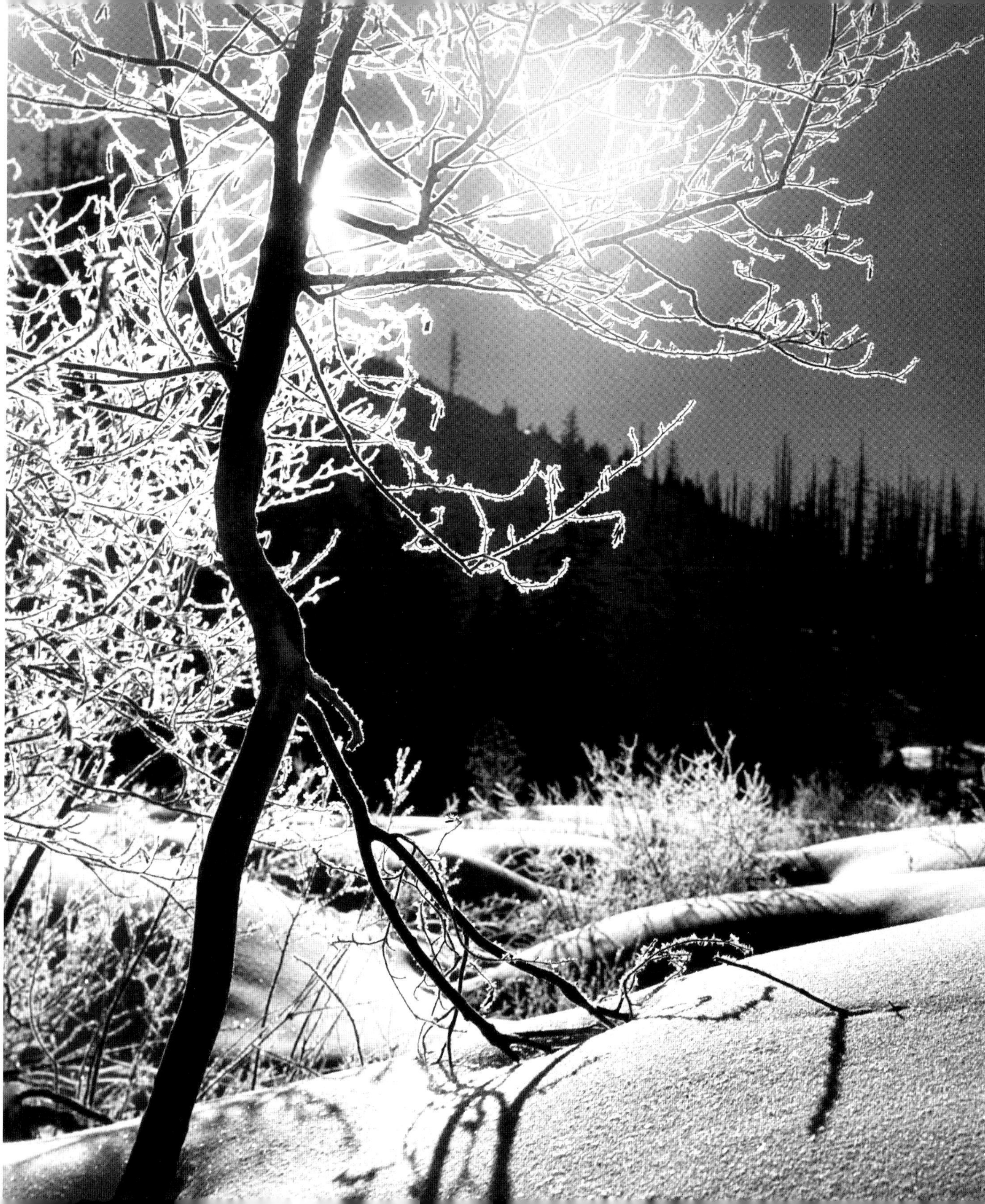

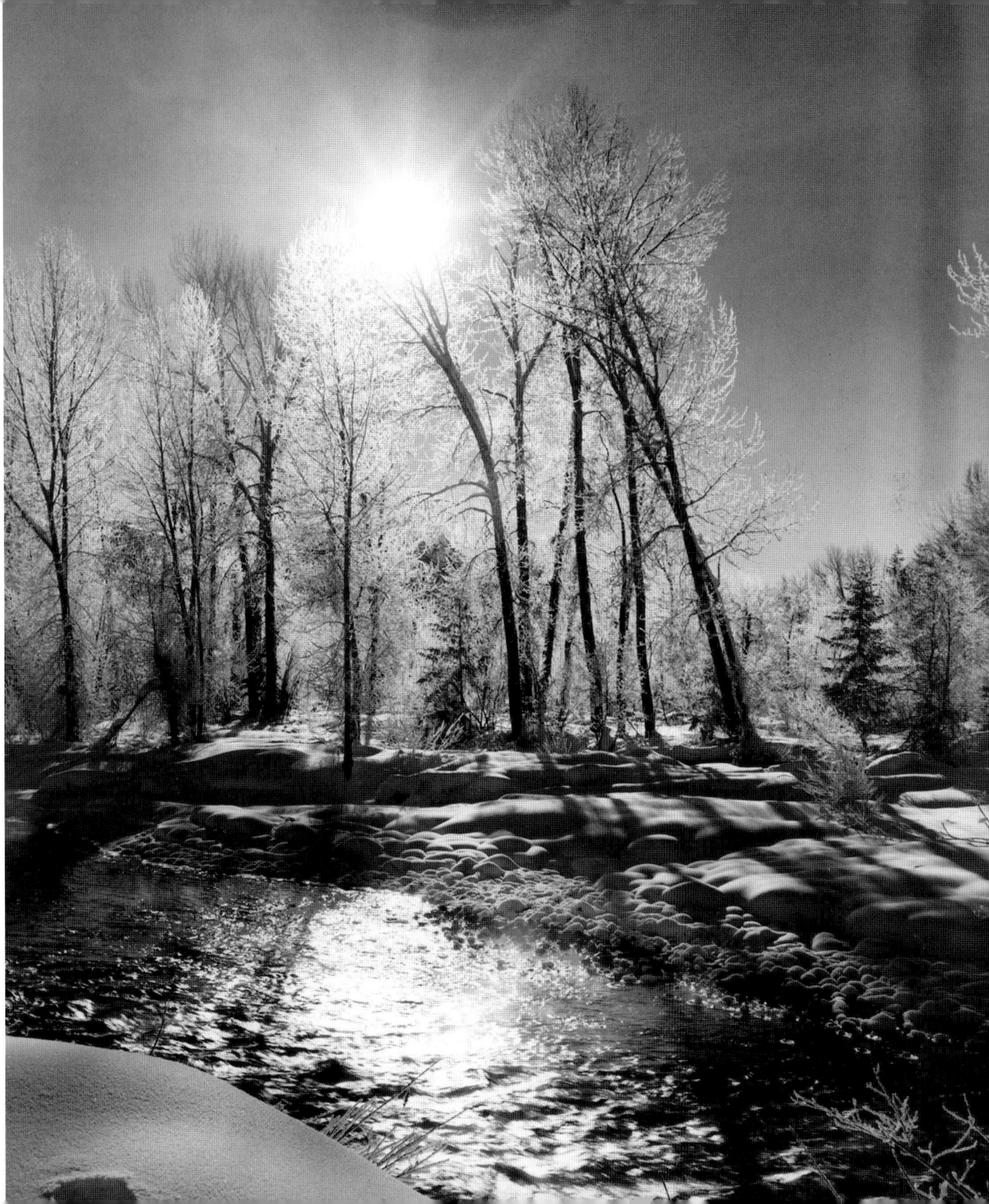

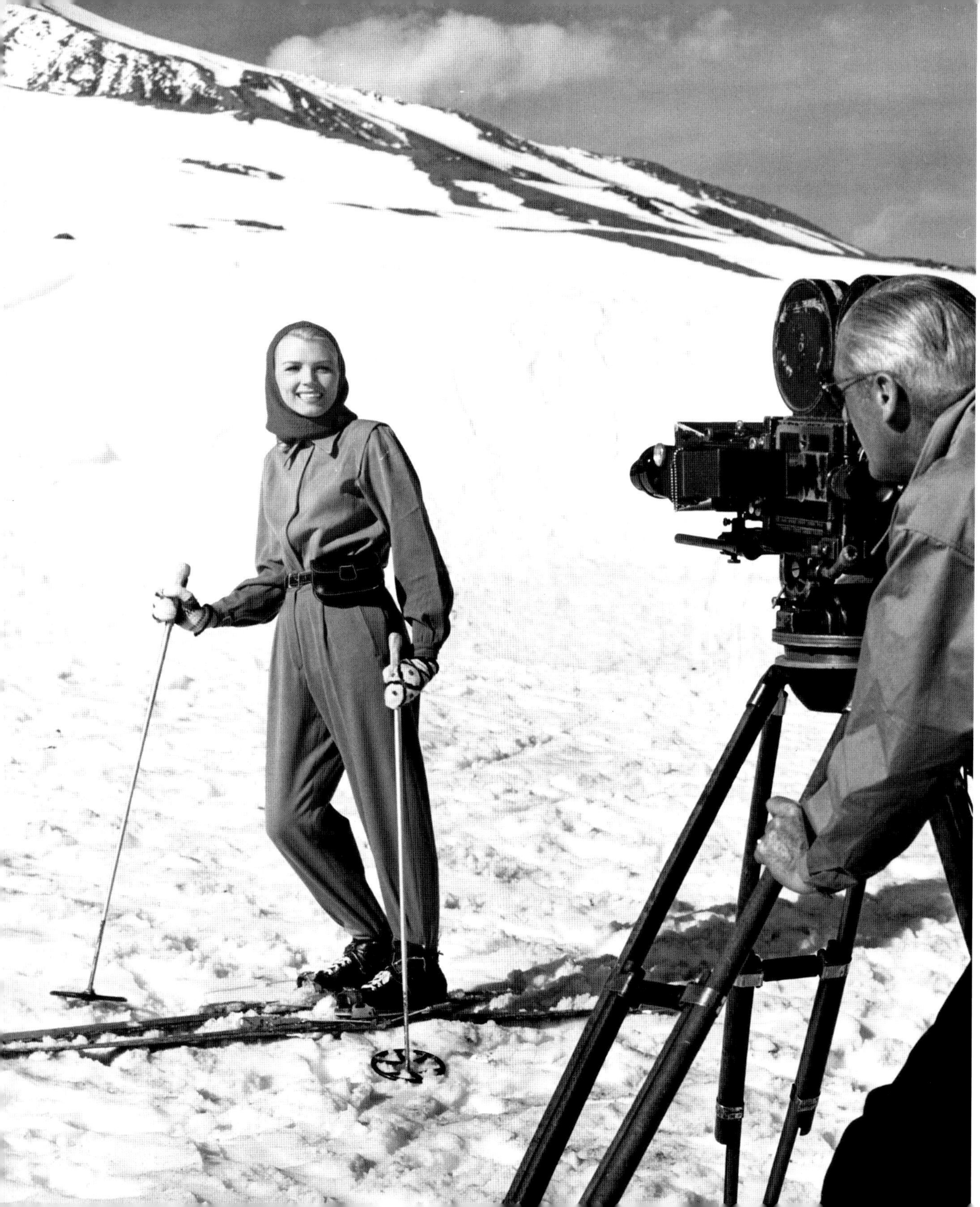

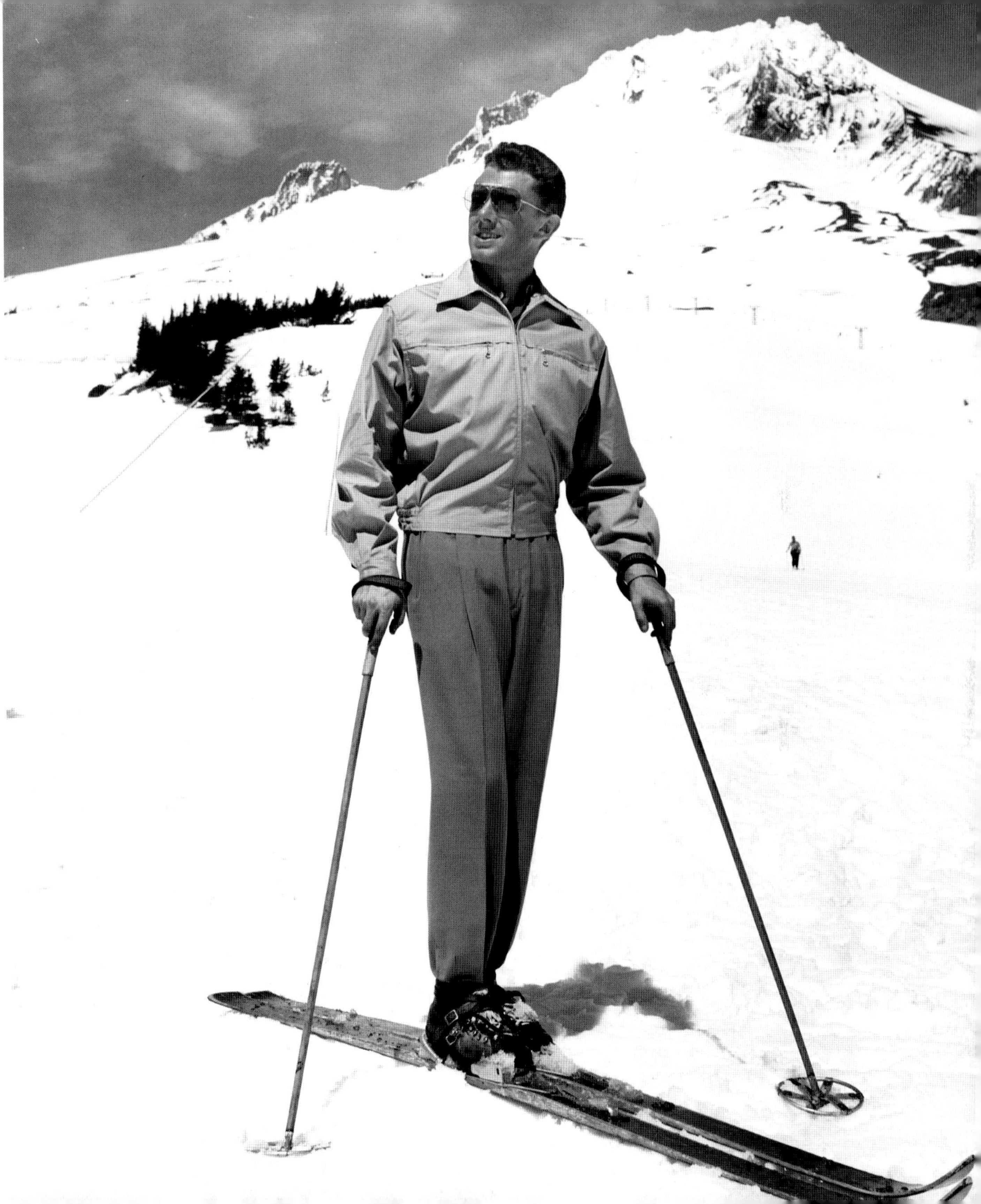

There's no such thing as
bad snow, just bad skiers.

AUTHOR UNKNOWN

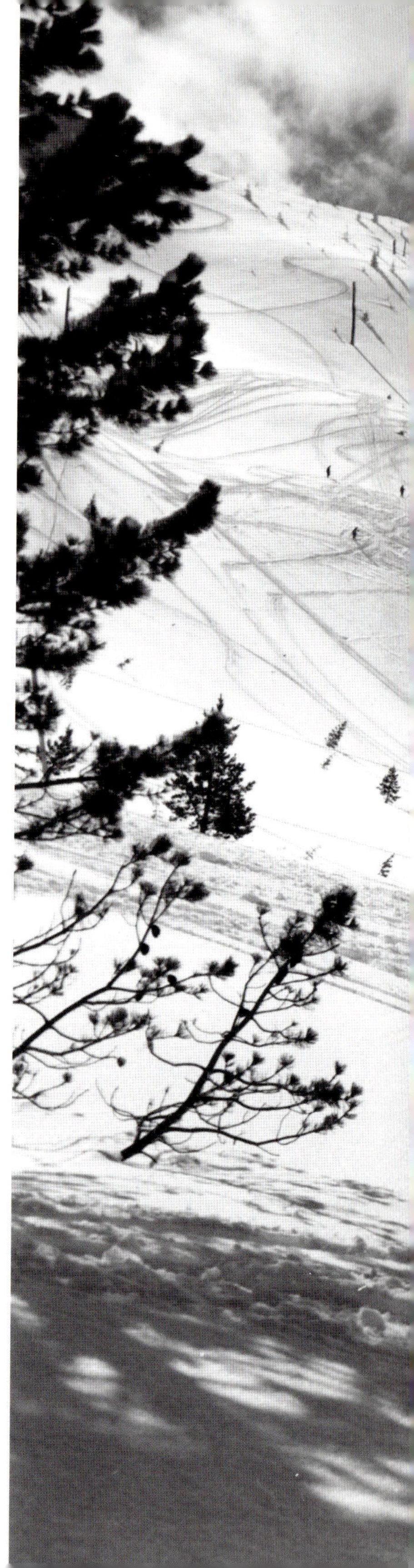

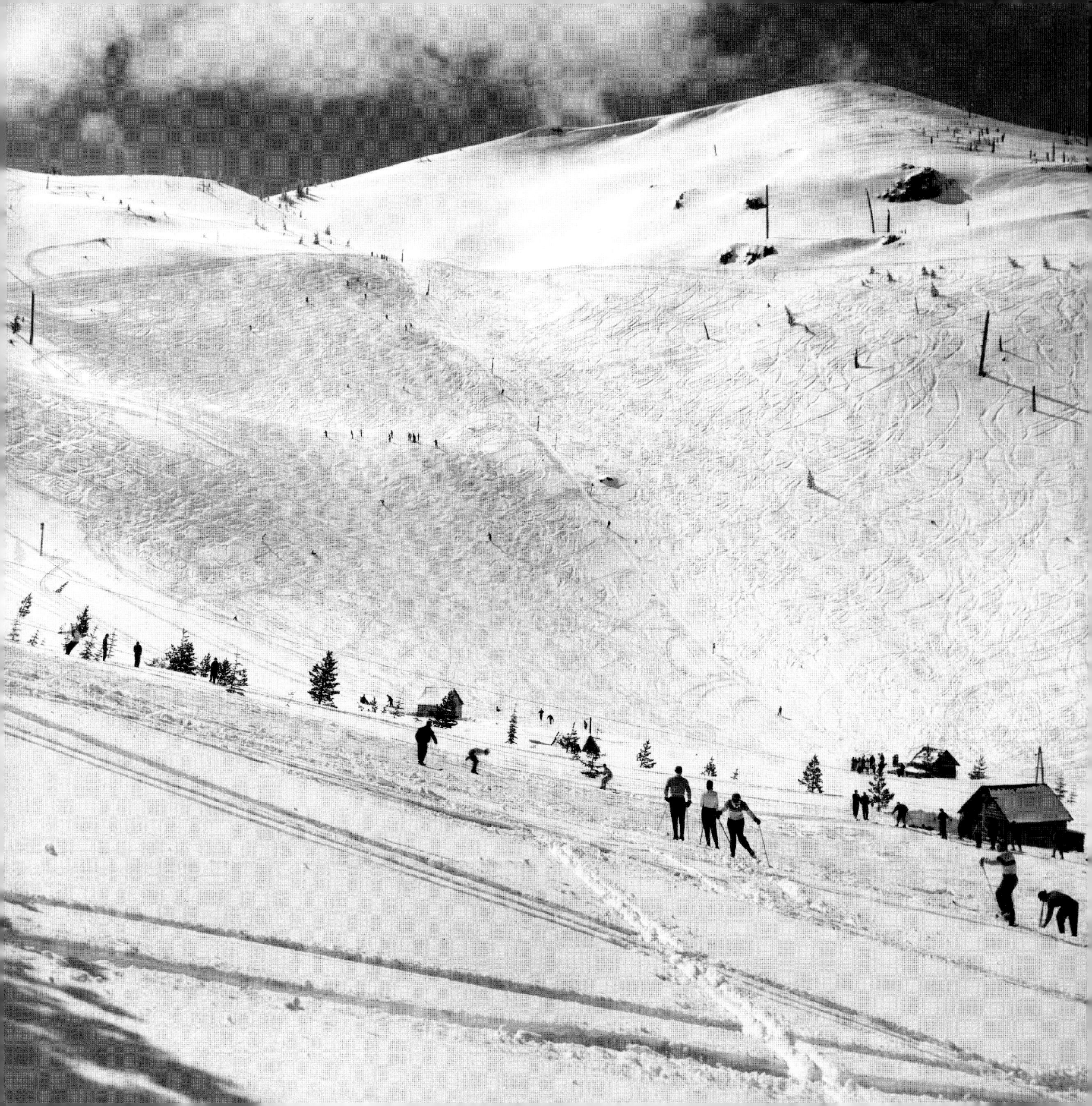

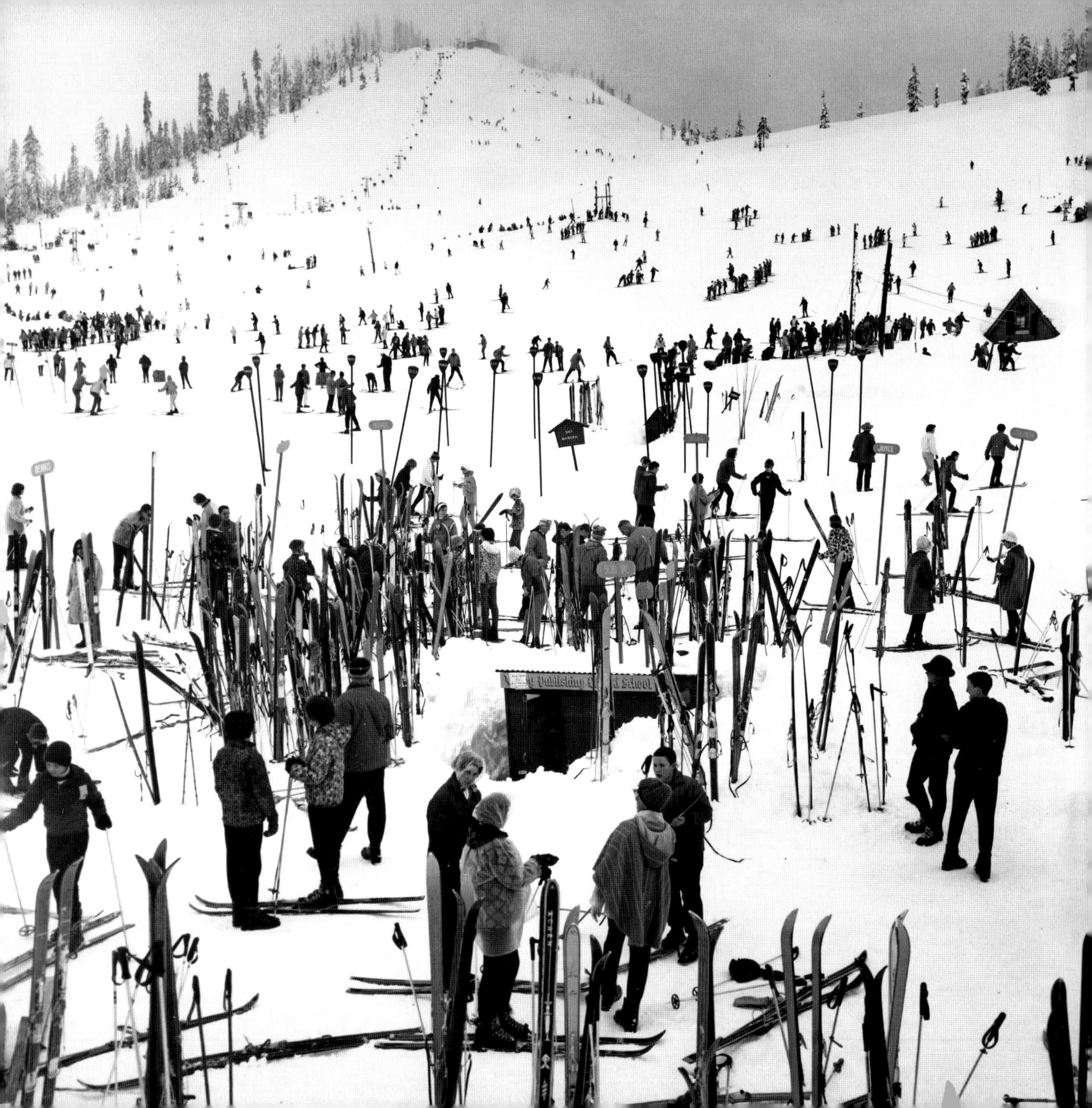
JOYCE

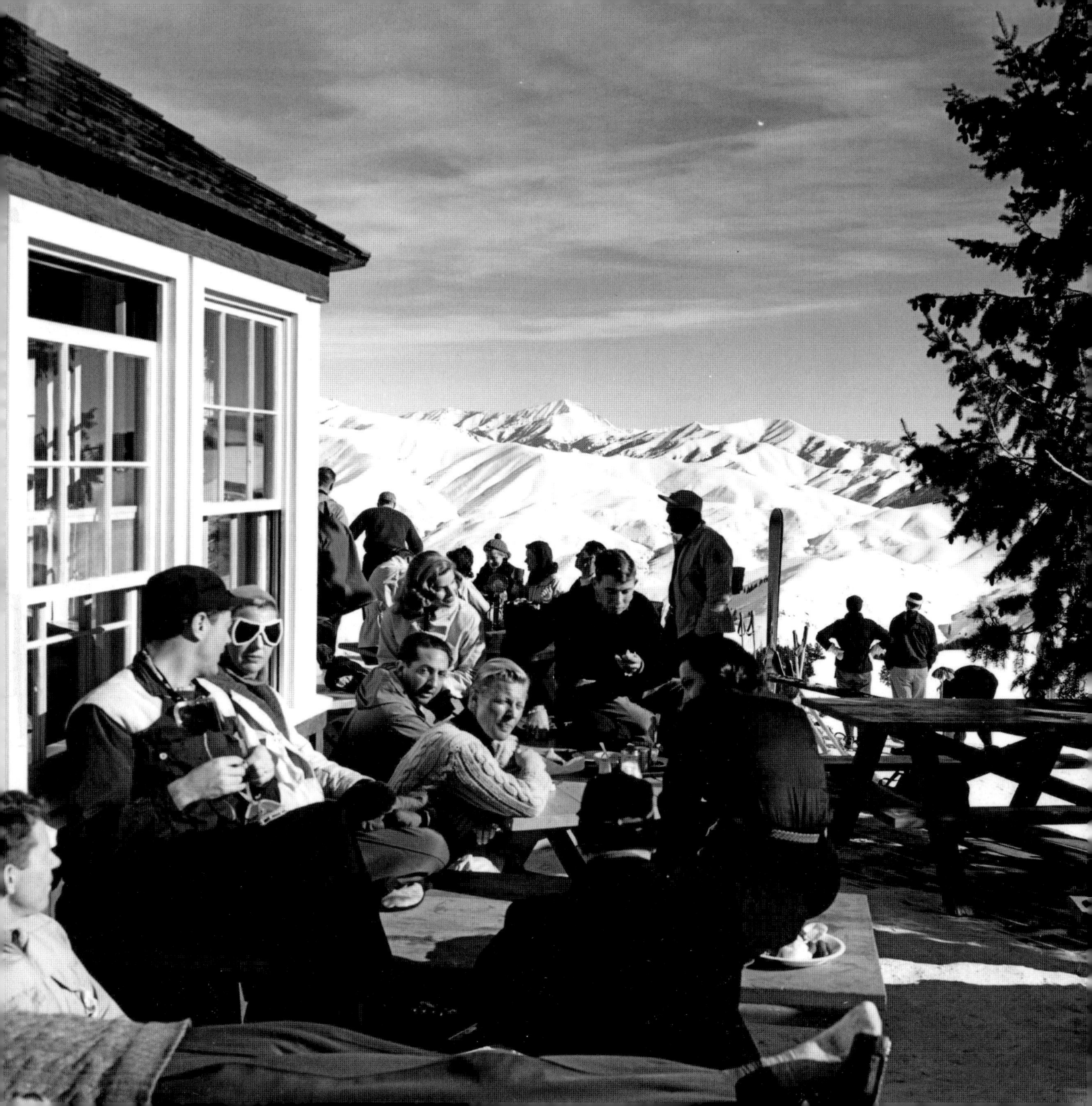

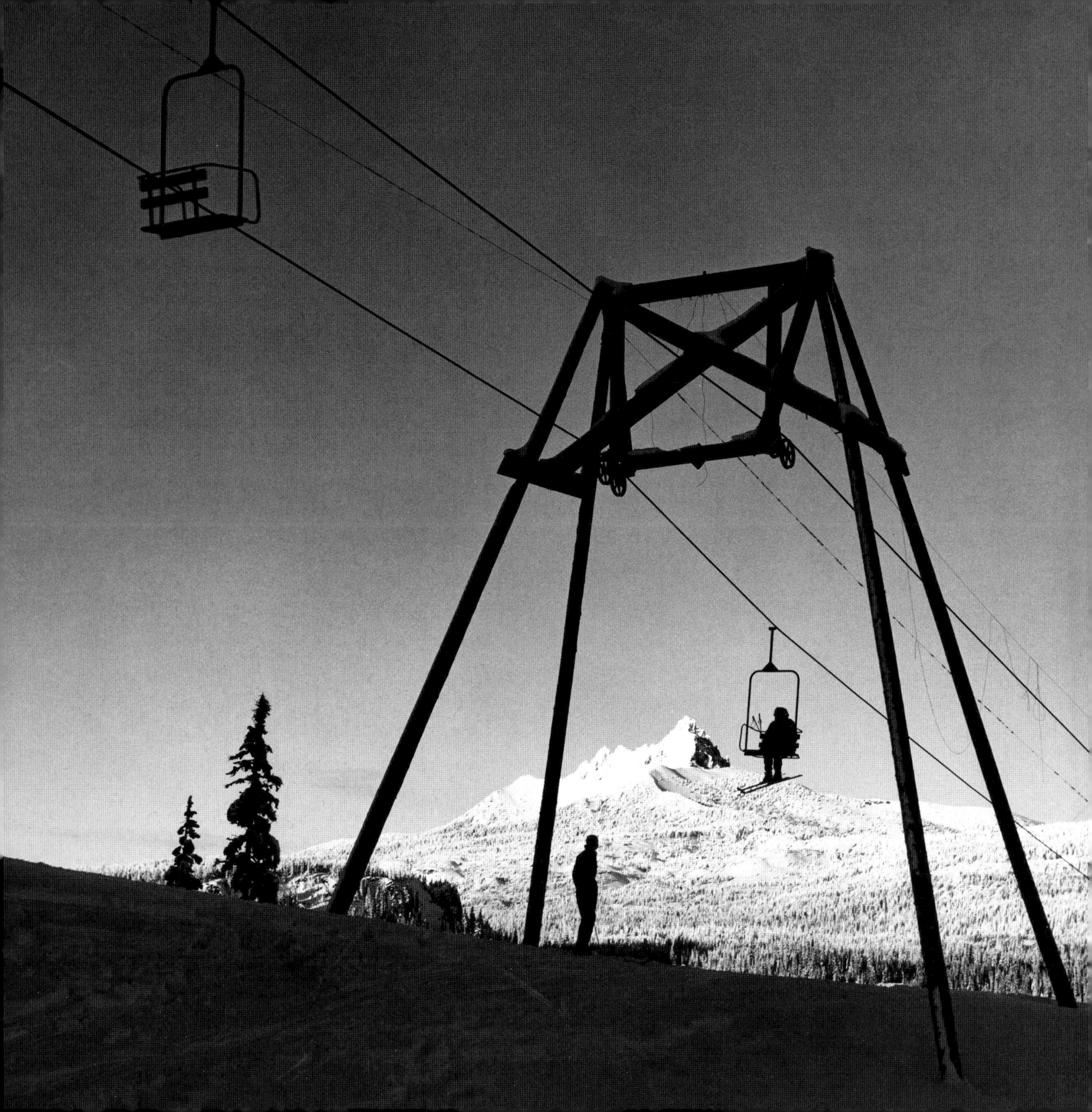

You can't buy happiness,
but you can buy a lift pass.

AUTHOR UNKNOWN

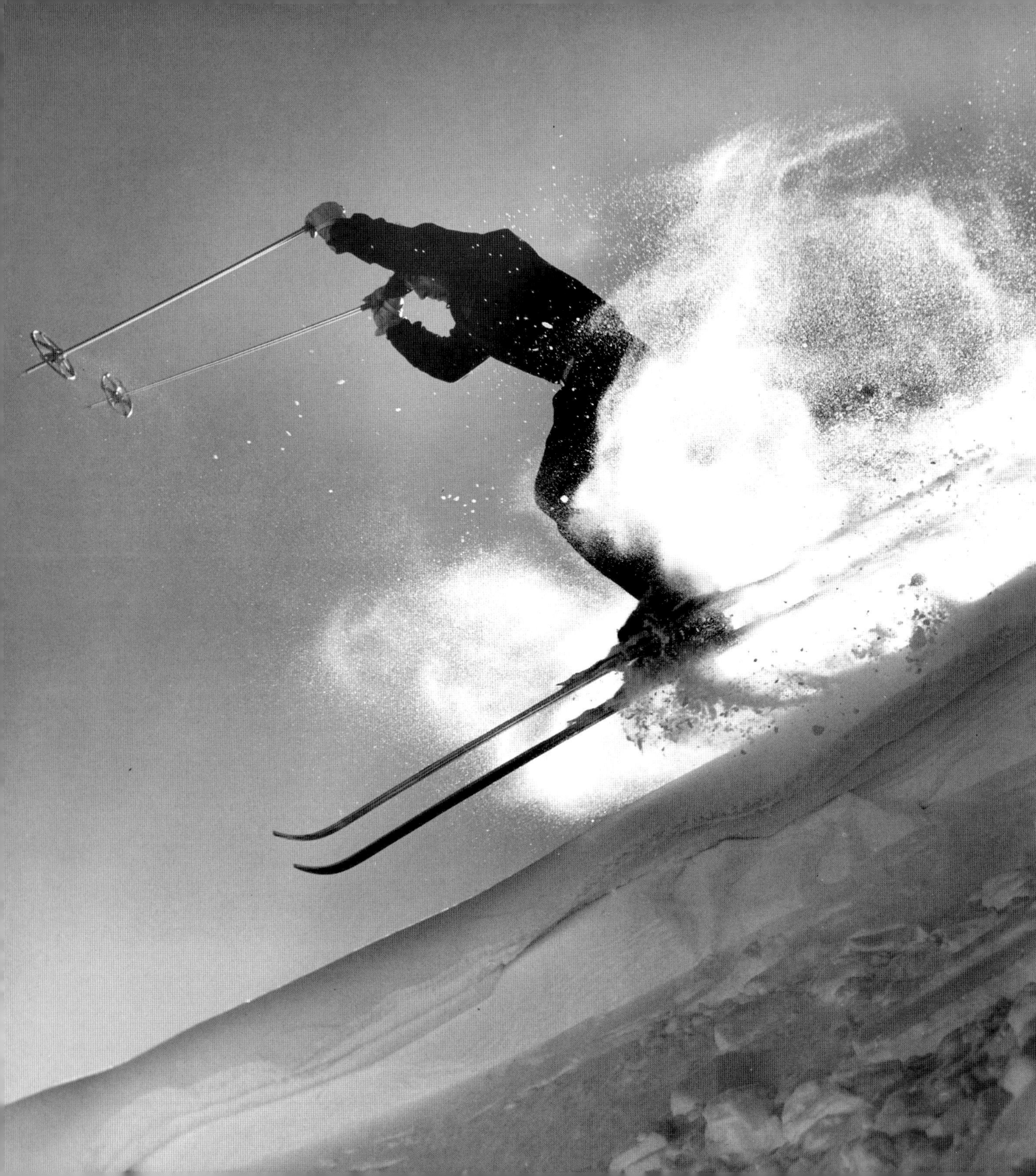

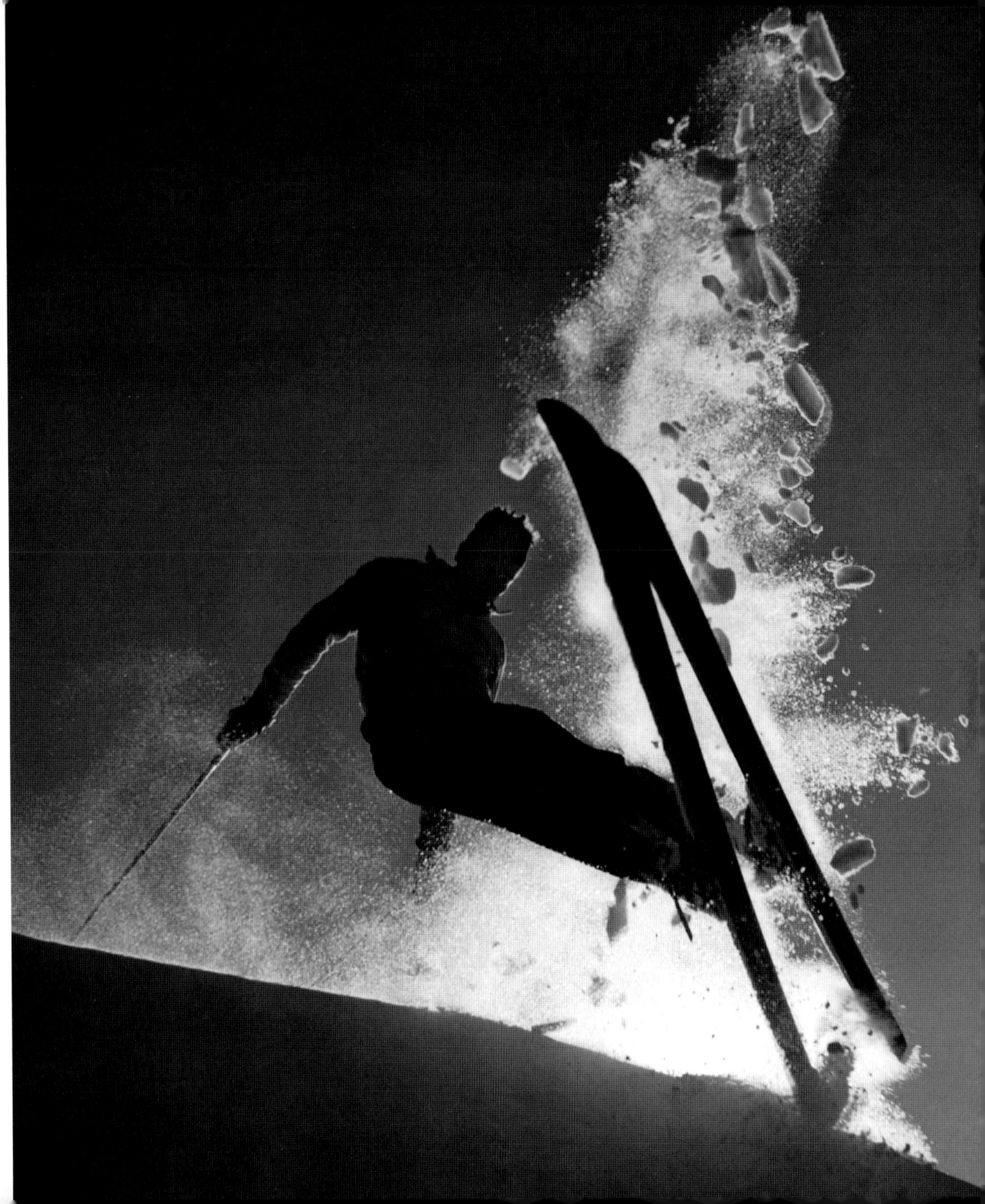

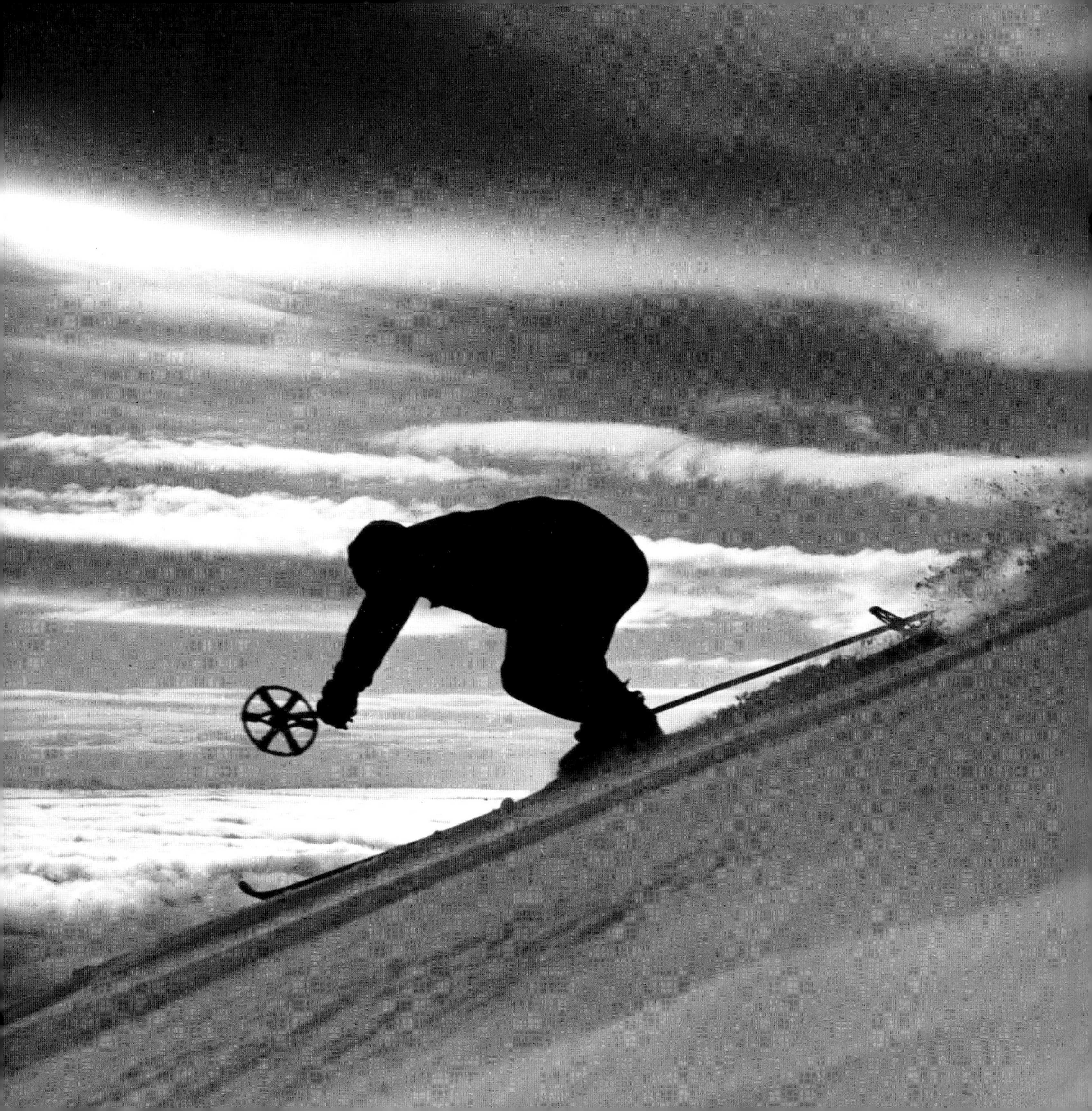

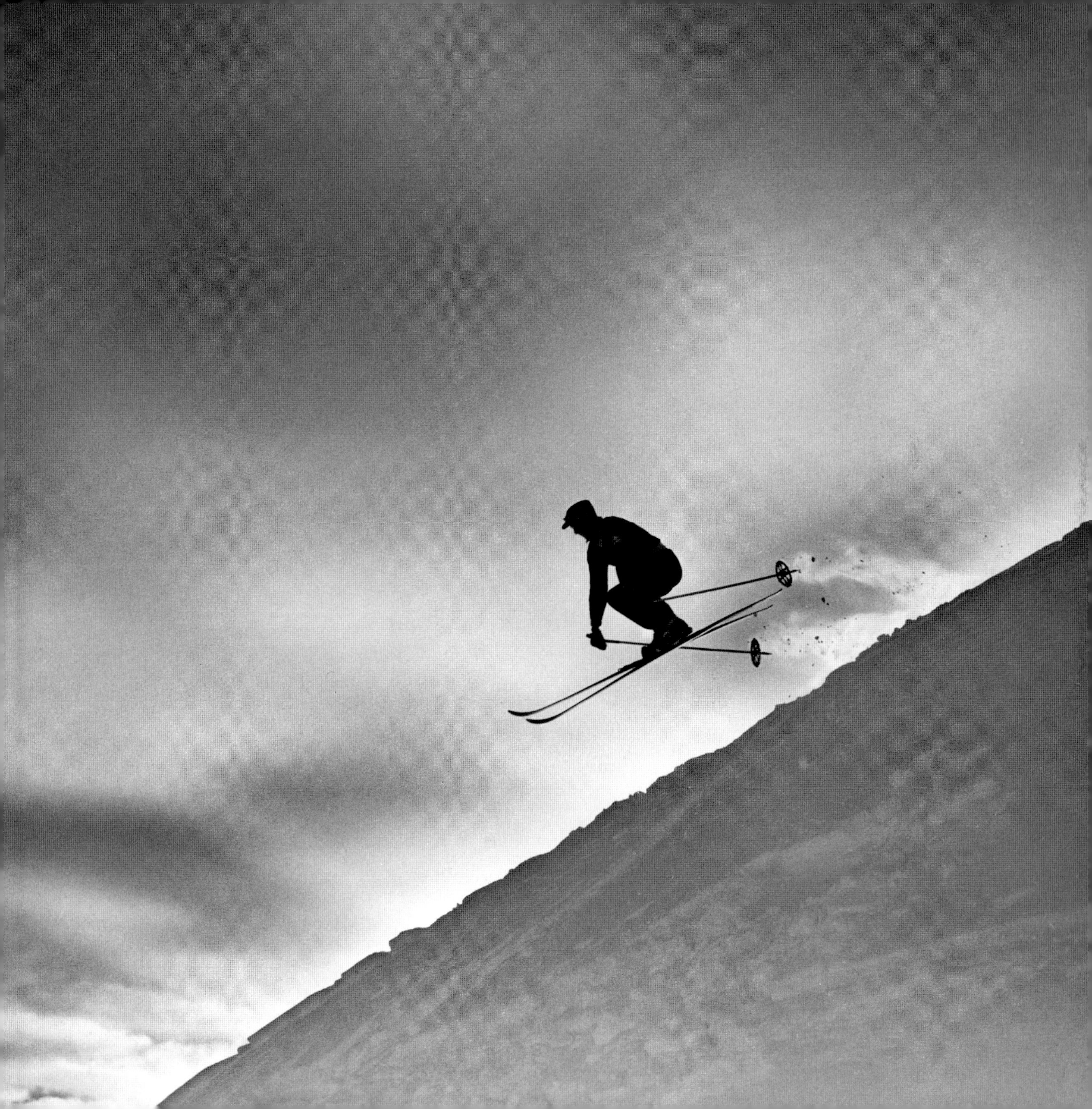

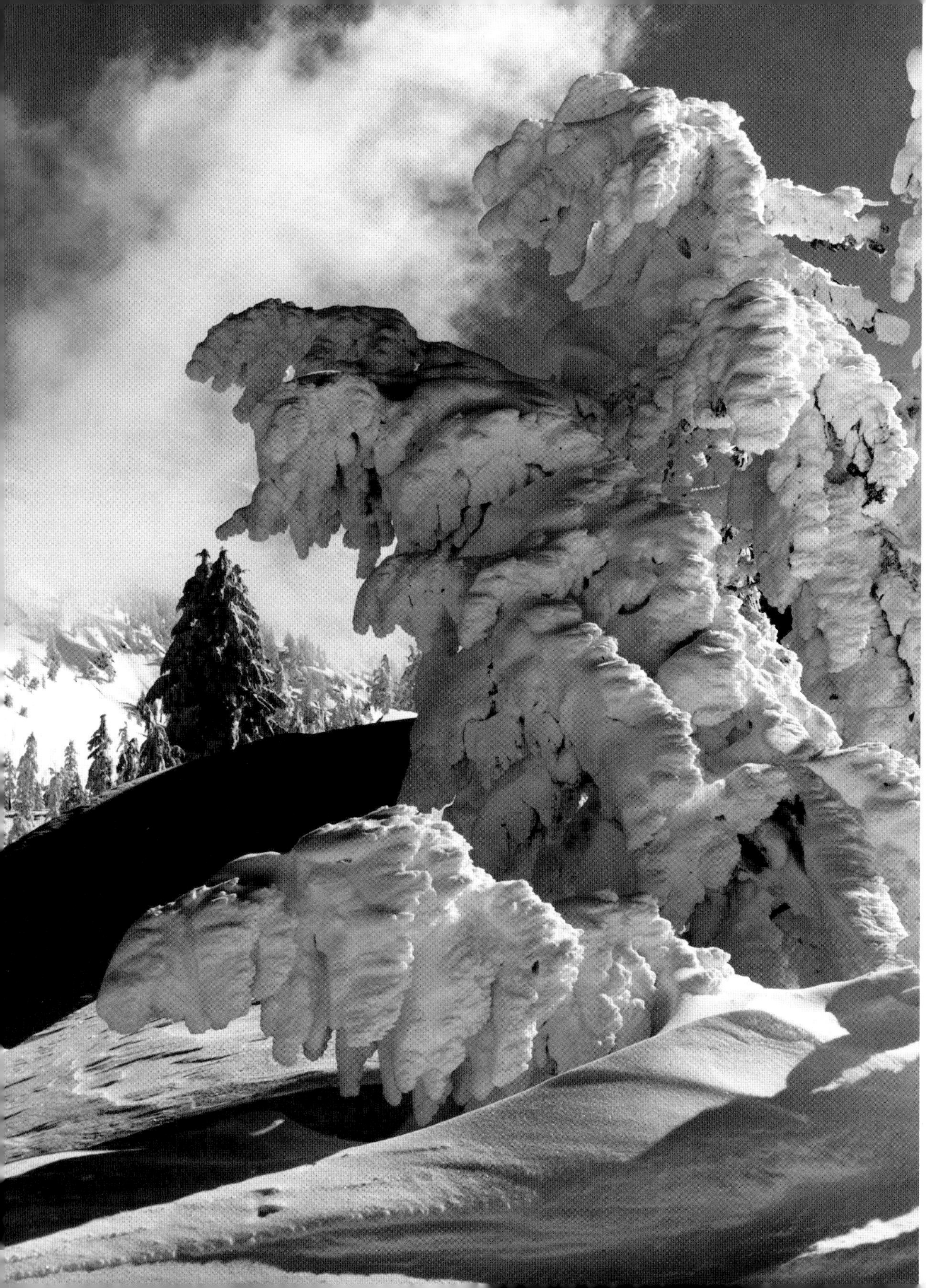
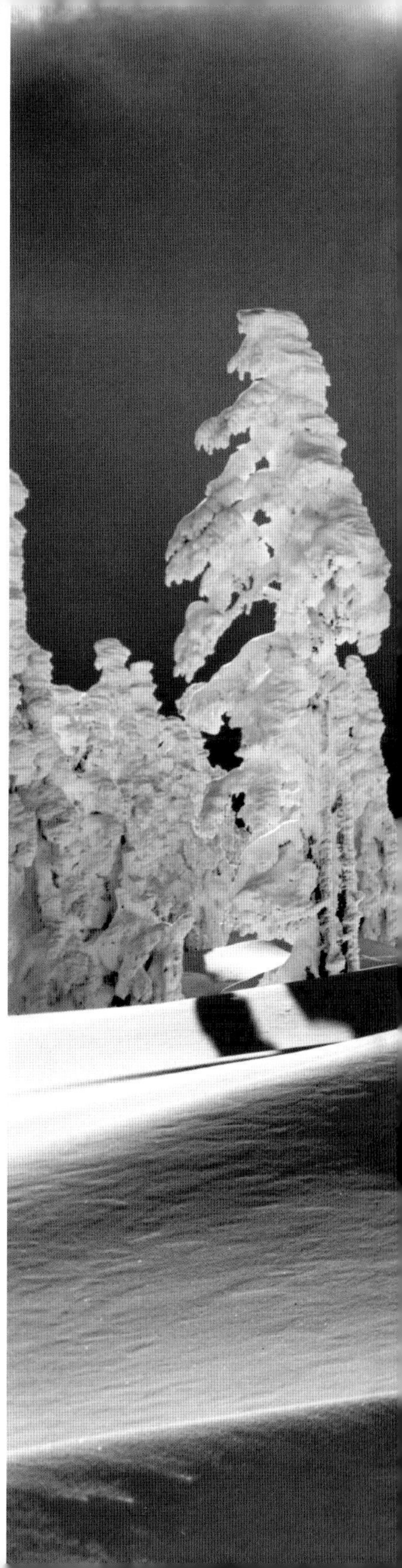

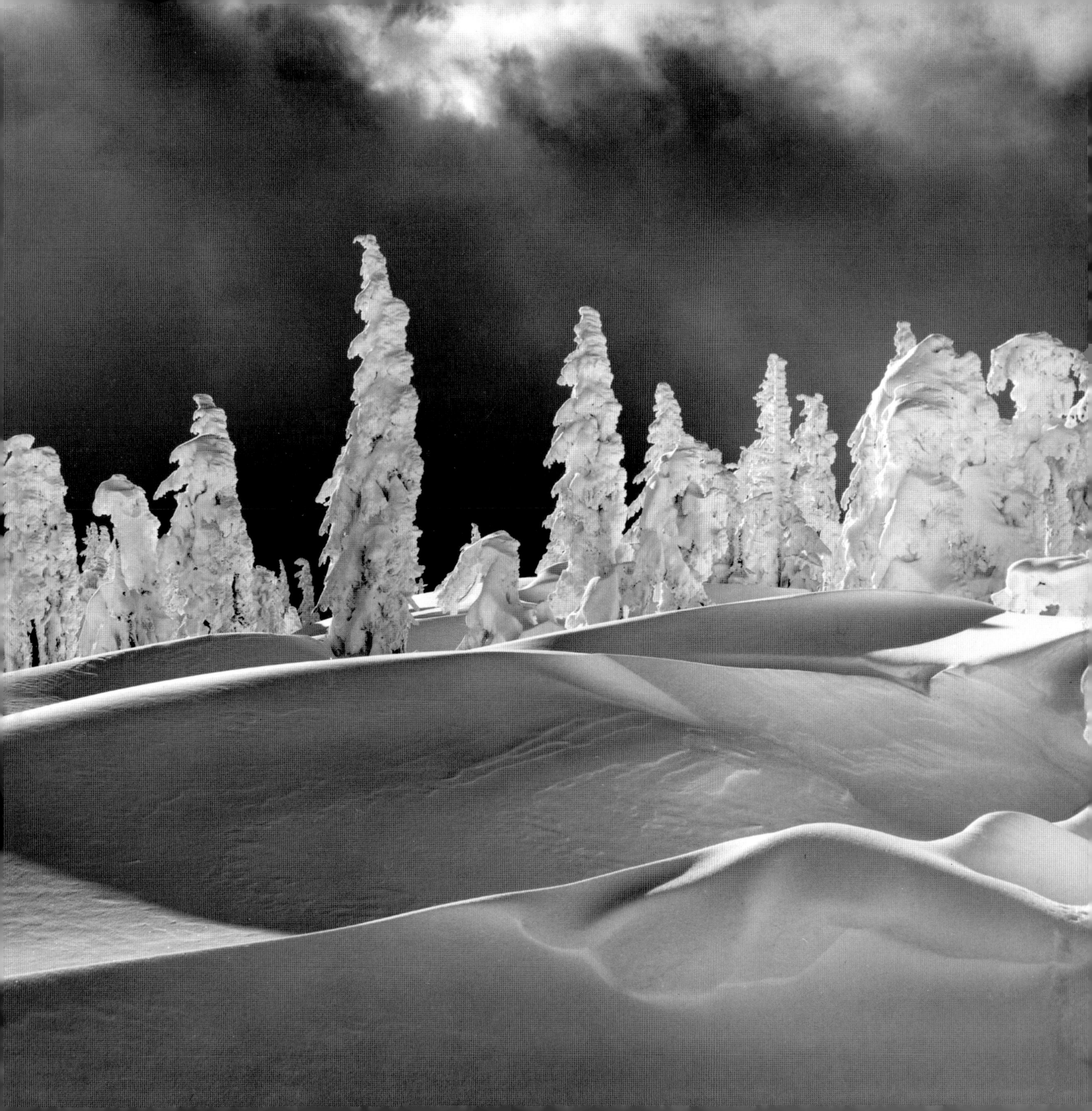

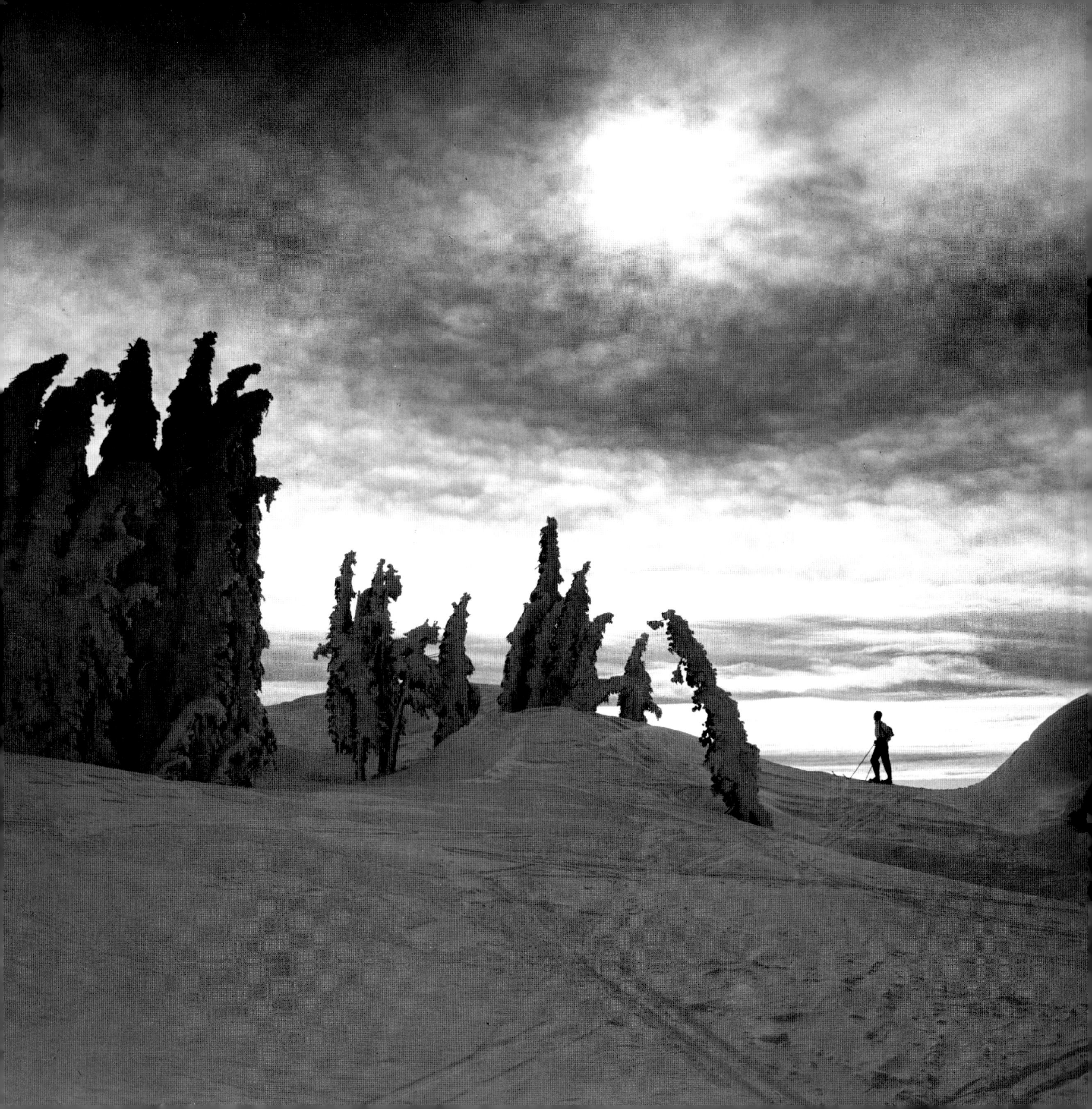

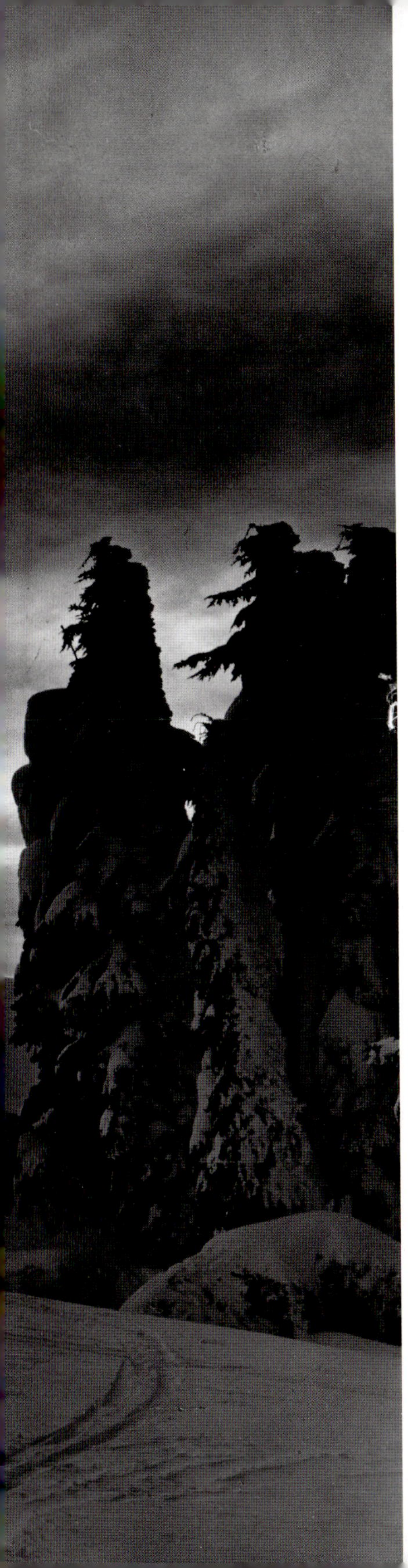

*The sensual caress of waist deep cold smoke—
glory in skiing virgin snow, in being the first to
mark the powder with the signature of their run.*

TIM CAHILL

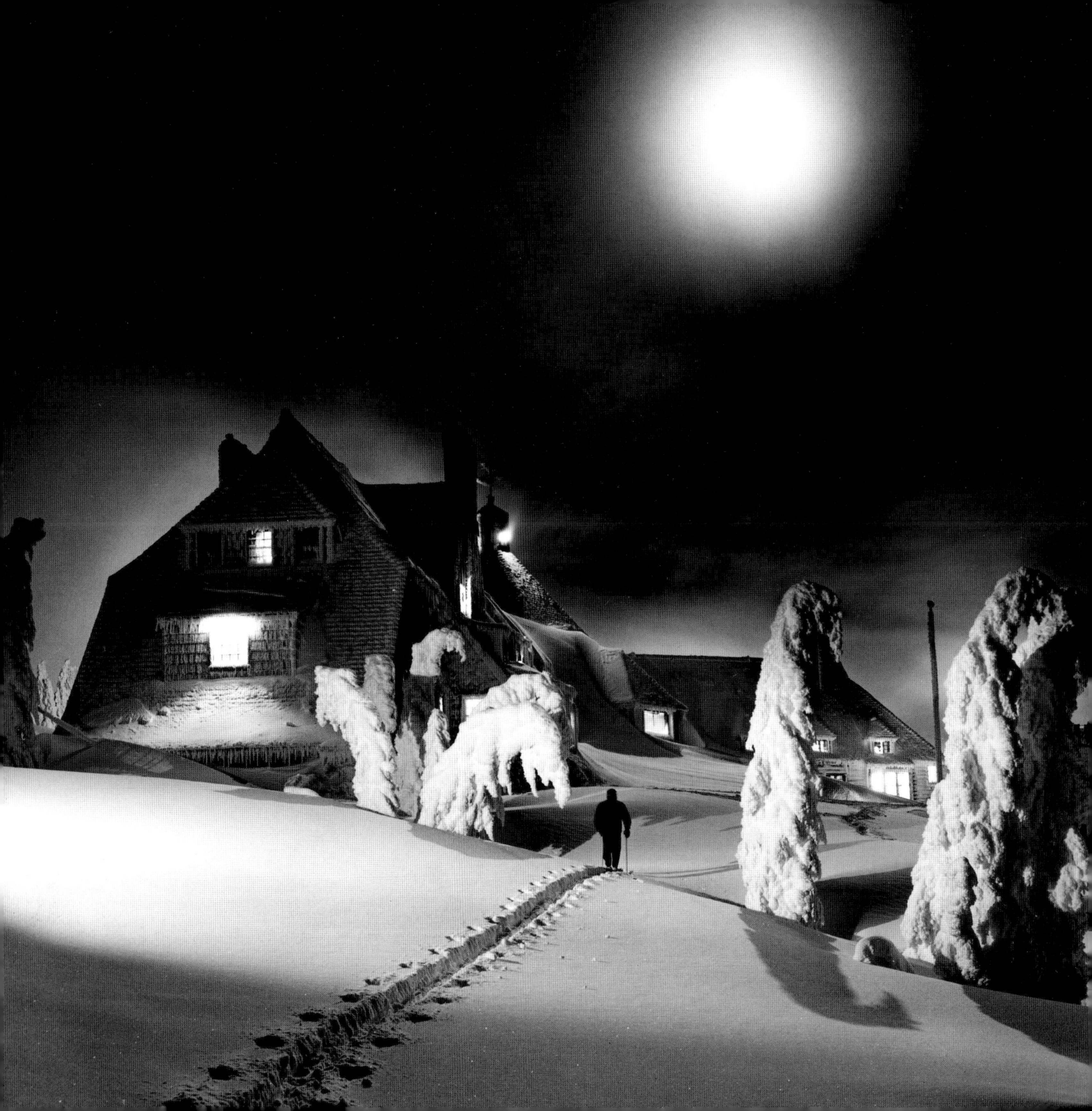

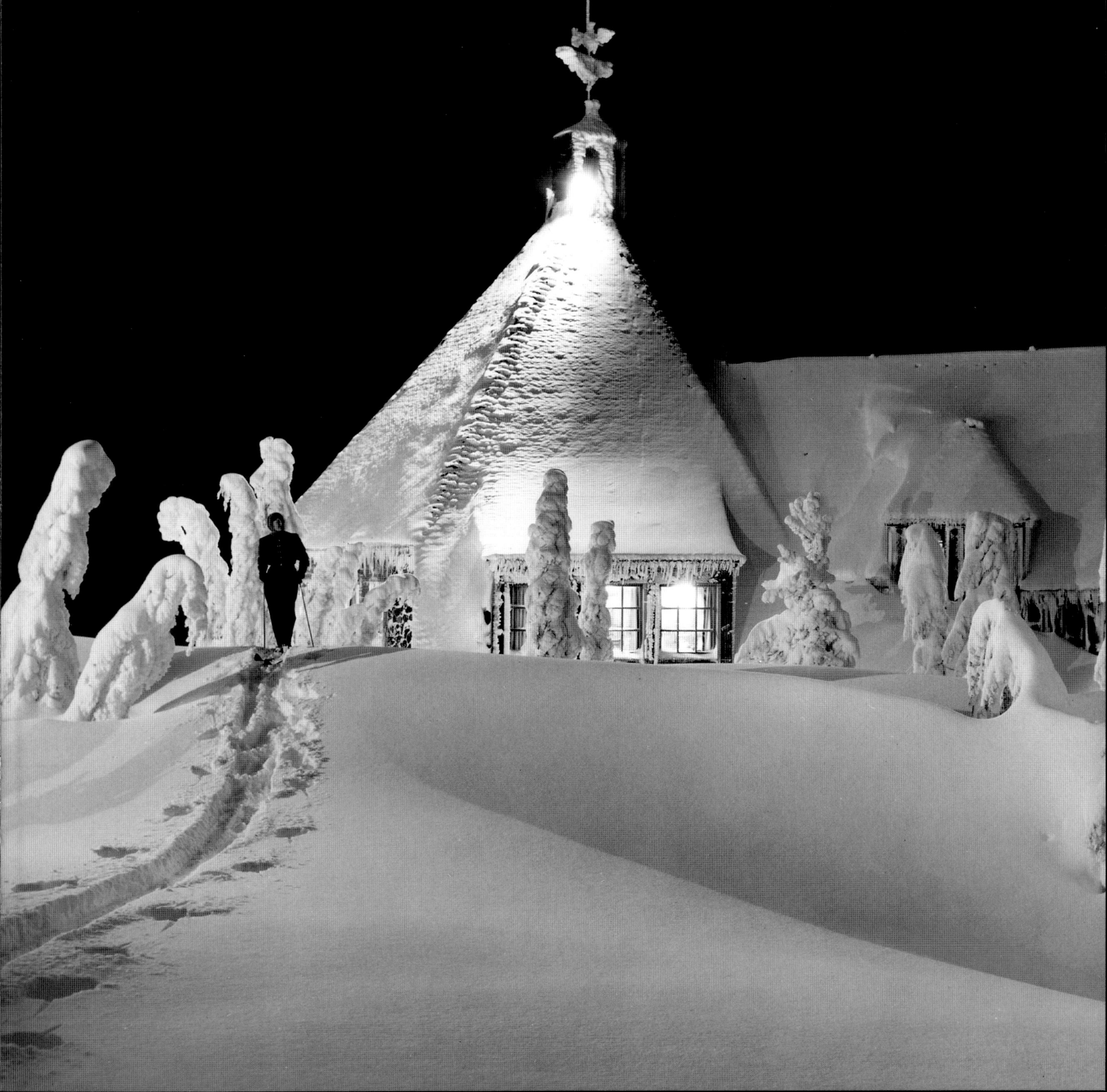

How could I live without powder?

DOLORES LACHAPELLE

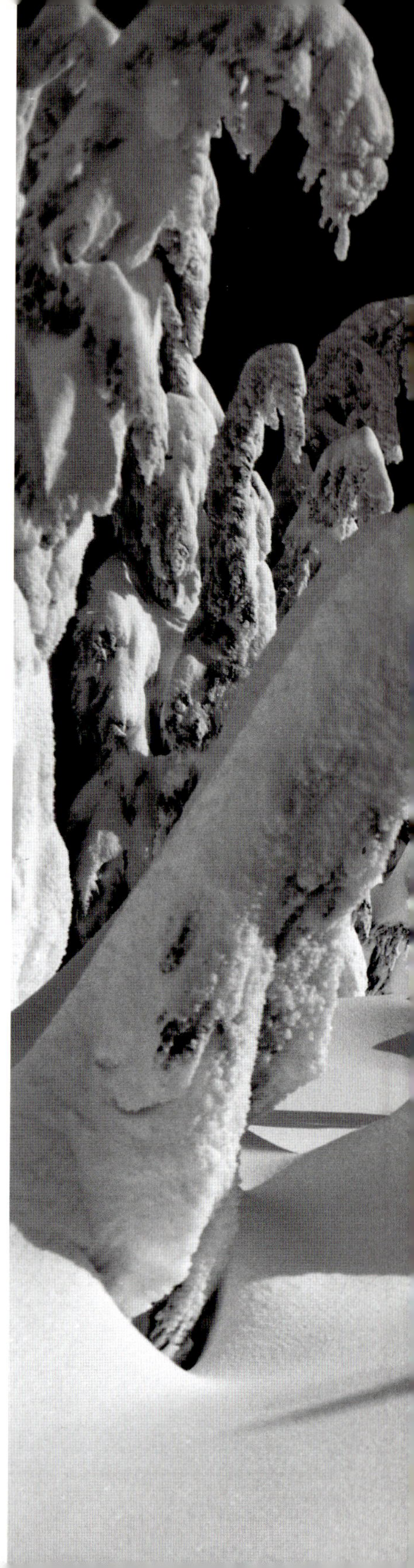

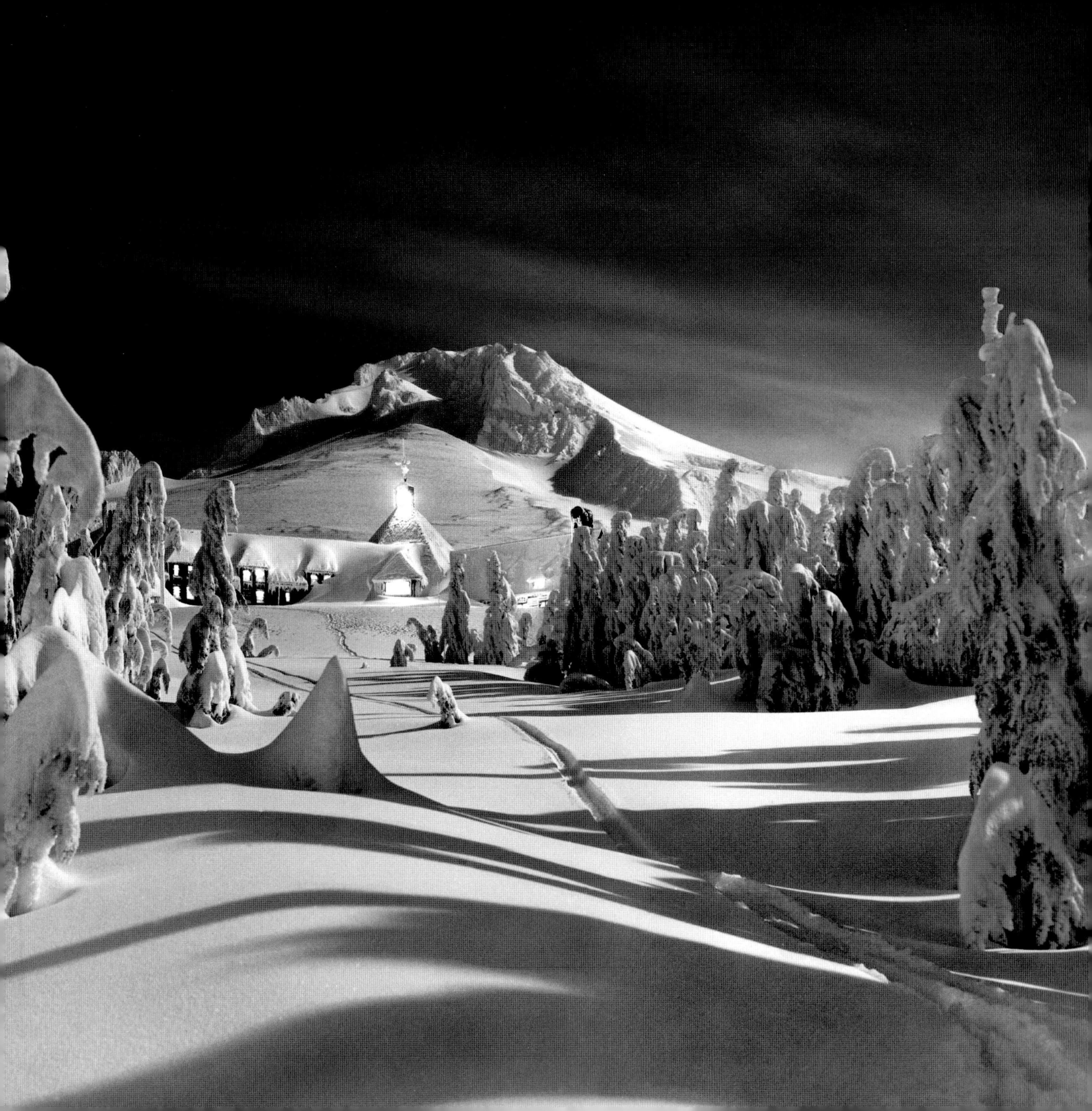

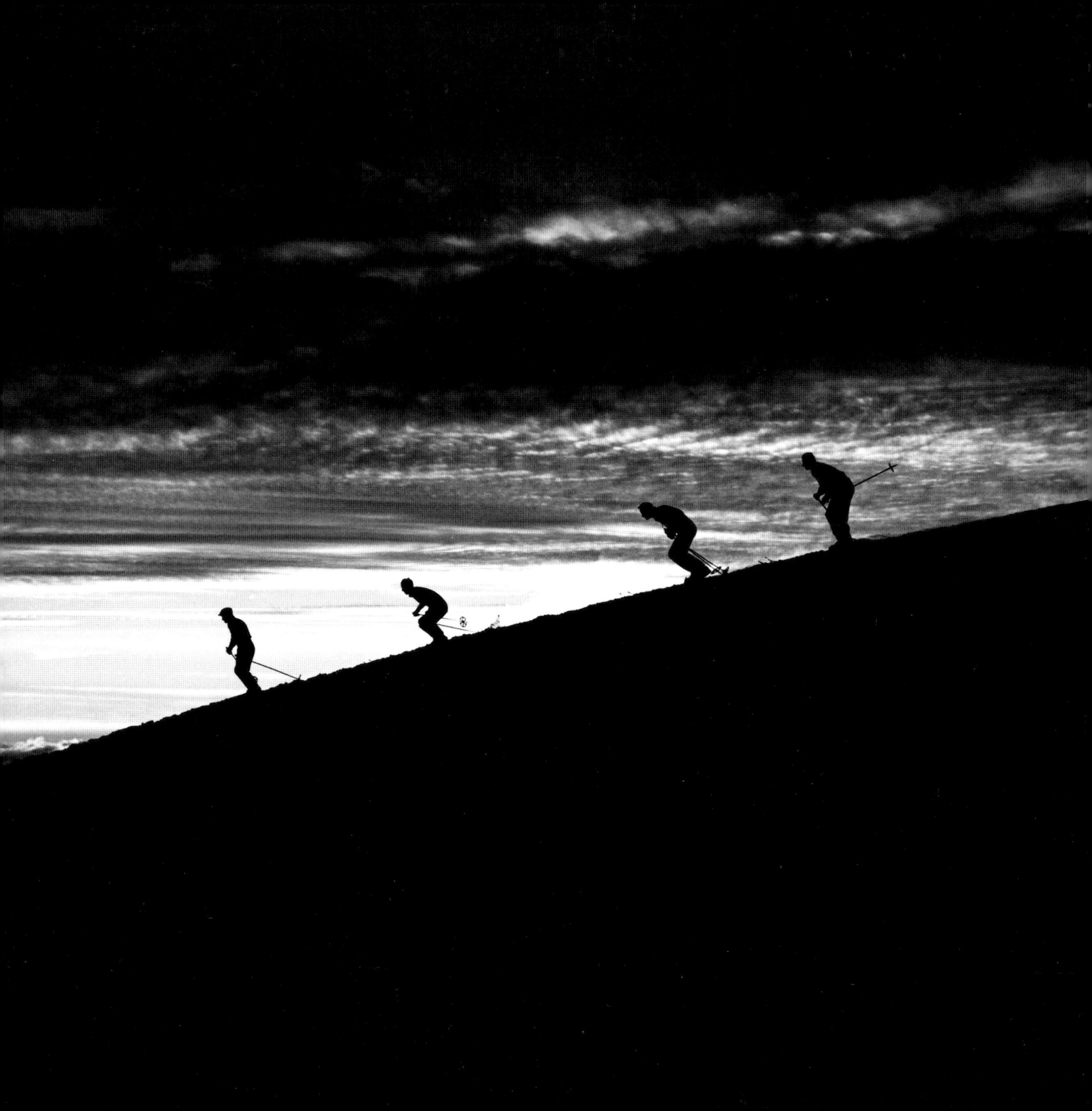

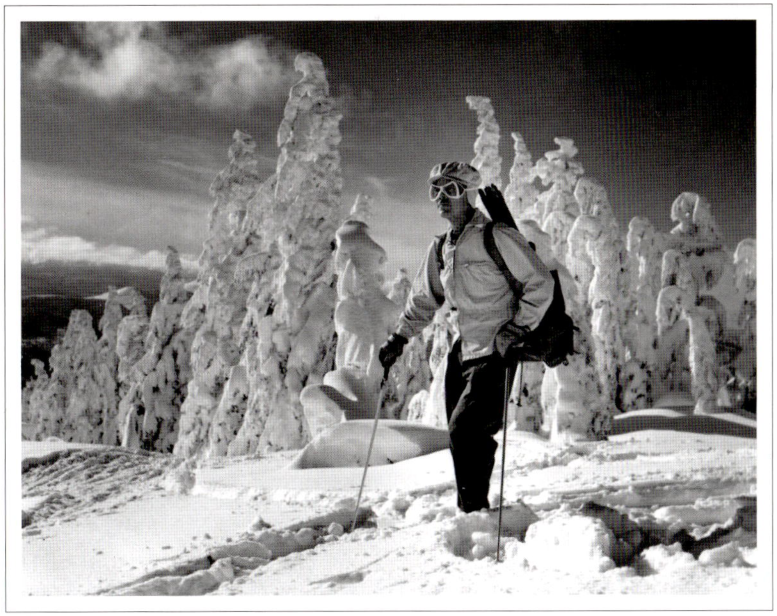

About the Author

RAY ATKESON, A PIONEER OF SKI PHOTOGRAPHY, WAS dubbed "the dean of Northwest nature photography" by the *New York Times*. Atkeson spent the majority of his life capturing majestic natural beauty and landscapes.

Atkeson was born in 1907 on a farm near Grafton, Illinois. He took his first impressionistic photograph by accident while working as a janitor, and the image, "Union Station at Night with Snow" was published in the *Kansas City Star* and the *Illustrated London News*. From there, his fame and acclaim grew as his photographs were featured in publications like *National Geographic* and the *Los Angeles Times*, used in numerous calendars, and collected in more than a dozen books, which sold over a half million copies.

His passion for mountain sports and the beauty of nature is evident in his photography. Atekson was an avid skier and mountain climber, scaling Mt. Hood sixteen times and Mt. St. Helens four times over the course of his life. He photographed a number ski resorts, including Sun Valley, Squaw Valley, and Sugar Bowl, making his name as a ski and snow photographer.

Among other awards, Atekson received the Portland Advertising Federation Award, the Western Oregon State College's Distinguished Service Award, an Honorary Doctorate of Fine Arts from Linfield College, and the Oregon Governor's Art Award. In 1987, Governor Neil Goldschmidt named Atkeson the Photographer Laureate of Oregon.

Ray Atkeson passed away in 1990 at the age of 83 after a six-month battle with colon cancer, but his artistic perspective lives on in collections of his timeless photographs.

About Familius

Familius is a global trade publishing company that publishes books and other content to help families be happy. We believe that happy families are key to a better society and the foundation of a happy life. The greatest work anyone will ever do will be within the walls of his or her own home. And we don't mean vacuuming! We recognize that every family looks different and passionately believe in helping all families find greater joy, whatever their situation. To that end, we publish beautiful books that help families live our 10 Habits of Happy Family Life: *love together, play together, learn together, work together, talk together, heal together, read together, eat together, give together*, and *laugh together*. Further, Familius does not discriminate on the basis of race, color, religion, gender, age, nationality, disability, caste, or sexual orientation in any of its activities or operations. Founded in 2012, Familius is located in Sanger, California:

- Love together
- Play together
- Learn together
- Work together
- Talk together
- Heal together
- Read together
- Eat together
- Laugh together
- Give together

FACEBOOK: WWW.FACEBOOK.COM/FAMILIUSBOOKS

PINTEREST: WWW.PINTEREST.COM/FAMILIUSBOOKS

INSTAGRAM: @FAMILIUSBOOKS

TIKTOK: @FAMILIUSBOOKS

FAMILIUS

The most important work you
ever do will be within the walls
of your own home.

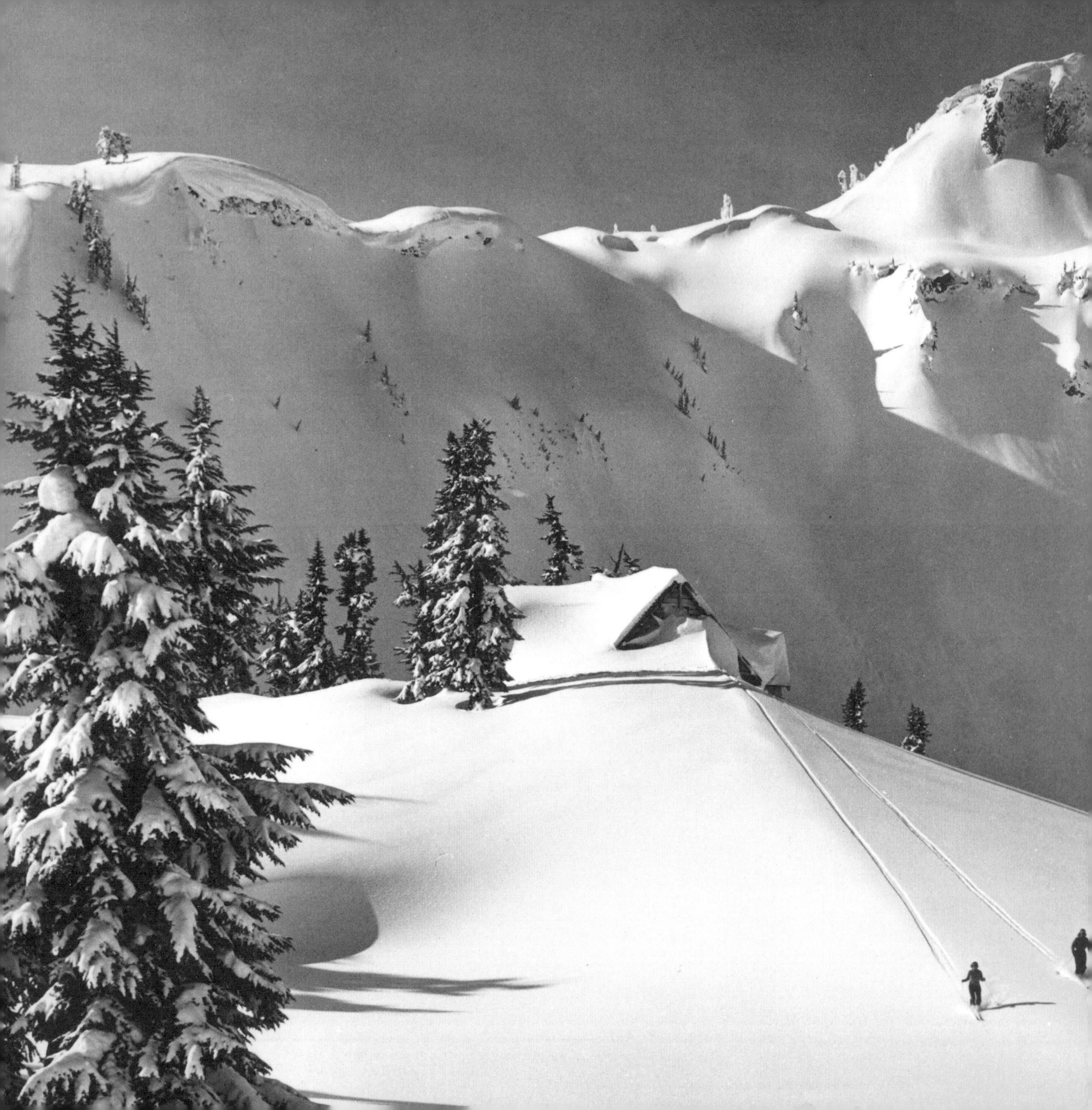